Why Switzerland?

Why Switzerland?

JONATHAN STEINBERG

*University Lecturer in History
and Fellow and Tutor, Trinity Hall, Cambridge*

CAMBRIDGE UNIVERSITY PRESS

Cambridge
London · New York · Melbourne

Published by the Syndics of the Cambridge University Press
The Pitt Building, Trumpington Street, Cambridge CB2 1RP
Bentley House, 200 Euston Road, London NW1 2DB
32 East 57th Street, New York, NY 10022, USA
296 Beaconsfield Parade, Middle Park, Melbourne 3206, Australia

Library of Congress catalogue card number: 75-36024

ISBN 0 521 21139 5

First published 1976

Photoset and printed in Malta by Interprint (Malta) Ltd

Contents

For
Matthew, Daniel and Peter

Preface

Switzerland is a hard country to get to know. Many tourists never see the 'real' Switzerland behind the neat façade of the tourist industry. I happened to be lucky. I married into a very large, very real, Swiss family. My father-in-law, Mr O. A. Meier, his nine brothers and sisters, and the horde of cousins in different parts of the country provided my introduction to Swiss life. I hope that they will forgive me for not mentioning each by name but I must make two exceptions. Seppi and Erna Seeberger-Krummenacher owned one of the last unspoilt Alpine hotels, Kurhaus Seewenalp. There was no electricity and no motor road to ruin the hiker's paradise until the army commandeered it for manoeuvre grounds. They, their friends and the lively assortment of hotel guests from all over Switzerland put up with a lot of questions. They know how much I owe them. The other exception is also a cousin; Dr Anton M. Meier, theologian and Director of the Kinder- und Erziehungsheim St Josef in Grenchen, has been the *spiritus rector* of this entire operation. He allowed me to use his flat in Grenchen during an extended visit in 1972, arranged many fascinating interviews for me and set exacting intellectual standards for the enterprise. I know that I have fallen short of them, but, rather like the Alps themselves, I have known that his standards were there as a permanent background and goal.

Professor J. H. Plumb of Christ's College first gave me the idea that there was a book in my fascination with the idiosyncrasies of Swiss life and has kept me cheerful during some bad moments. Dr John Barber of King's College noticed that I had left out the most important piece of the argument, the economic substructure of the special Swiss political and social framework. Dr J. A. Cremona of Trinity Hall served as my Virgil in the *selva oscura dei dialetti*. Professor Frederick P. Brooks Jr of the University of North Carolina let me have his only copy of his fascinating study of computer software at a crucial moment in the writing and reassured me that the historian can understand the world of high technology, if he has a good guide. Mr C. A. A. Rayner, formerly of CIBA—Geigy (UK) Ltd in Duxford, drew my attention to aspects of the chemical industry in Basel. Mrs Leonard Forster saved me from making a silly mistake about Gottfried Keller. Professor James Joll

vii

read the first draft of the manuscript and gave me a great deal of good advice about what was wrong with it. Miss Marjorie Shepherd helped me in preparing the manuscript and listened to my complaints when things were not going well. I owe them all my thanks.

Many people in Switzerland in every walk of life have been generous with their time and trouble. It would illustrate much of the variety of Swiss life if I paused by each to describe how he or she had opened new areas of Swiss reality to me. I hope that they will forgive me if I list them by name without further comment. My thanks and respect are theirs: Herr Dr Franz Birrer of the Swiss Embassy in Bonn, formerly cultural attaché in London; Herr Paul Adler of the Pro Helvetia Stiftung, Zürich; Dr Alfred Rötheli, Staatsschreiber of Canton Solothurn; Dr A. M. Schütz, President, Eterna Ltd; Professor Dr Adolf Gasser, Basel; Professor Dr Dietrich Schindler, Zürich; Dr R. J. Schneebeli, Director of the Volkshochschule, Zürich; Colonel Dr Walter Schaufelberger, editor of the *Allgemeine Schweizerische Militärzeitschrift*; Professor Dr Peter Stadler, Zürich; Professor Dr Arthur Rich, Zürich; Herr Ulrich Kägi of *Die Weltwoche*, Zürich; Dott. Flavio Zanetti, Corrispondenza Politica Svizzera, Lugano; Dott. Federico Spiess and Dott. Rosanna Zeli, Vocabolario dei dialetti della Svizzera italiana, Lugano; Professor Giuseppe Martinola, Lugano; Dr Alfred Peter, *National-Zeitung*, Basel; Herr Frank A. Meyer, Büro Cortesi, Neuchâtel; Mme Lise Girardin, Deputée du Conseil des Etats, Geneva; M. Claude Monnier, *Journal de Genève*; M. Ambassadeur Pierre Micheli, Geneva; Professor Dr Erich Gruner, Bern; Herr Rolf Siegrist, Schweizerische Politische Korrespondenz, Bern; Herr Benedikt von Tscharner formerly of Integration Section, Federal Political Department, Bern, and now Counsellor of Embassy (Economic and Labour) at the Swiss Embassy, London; Herr Peter Erni, Information and Press Officer, Federal Political Department, Bern; Sign. Piero Bianconi, Minusio; Sign. Enzio Canonica, Consigliere nazionale and president of the Federazione Svizzera dei Lavoratori edili e del legno, Zürich; Herr Otto Bättig, Kreisförster, Schüpfheim, Luzern.

I am grateful to the following publishers for permission to quote: *Die Weltwoche* for the table by Ulrich Kägi, copyright *Die Weltwoche*; *Schweizer Zeitschrift für Volkswirtschaft und Statistik* for the table by Peter Gilg; Francke Verlag, Bern, for the tables by E. Gruner; Huber & Co. AG for extracts from *Allgemeine Schweizerische Militärzeitschrift*.

J. S.

I pastori che passano l'estate sulle *alpi*, discendo di tanto in tanto nel villaggio a rinnovar le proviste, e le proviste sono: pane, vino, sale e giornali. E in alcuna di quelle alte capanne, simile a tante trogloditiche, in quell'odore acre di latte cagliato, di fumo, di sterco bovino, più d'una volta mi è accaduto di trovar chi sapeva fin 'ultime minuzie della politica cantonale e mondiale, chi, a me che parlavo dialetto, si studiava di rispondere in lingua letteraria.

— Francesco Chiesa

Überhaupt ist nicht gross oder klein, was auf der Landkarte so scheint: es kommt auf den Geist an.

— Johannes von Müller

Trois Suisses vont à la chasse aux escargots et ils comparent leurs prises en fin de journée. — 'Moi', dit le Genevois rapide, 'j'en ai cent.' — 'Moi', dit le Bernois, 'j'en ai attrapé quatre.' — 'Et moi', dit le Vaudois (imaginez l'accent), 'j'en ai bien vu un, mais il m'a échappé.'

— Denis de Rougemont

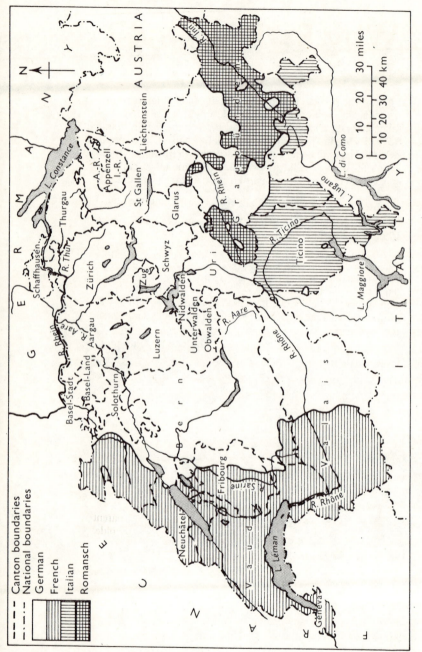

Map 1 Cantons and languages in contemporary Switzerland

1. Why Switzerland?

'Why Switzerland?' is really two questions not one. The first is the understandable question which any English-speaking reader who picks up a book on Switzerland must ask himself: 'Why should I read about Switzerland, when there are so many other things to read about?' The second, less obvious question is why there is a Switzerland at all. The present chapter will try to answer the former question; the whole book is devoted to the latter. What you have in your hands is not a guidebook. You will not find places to eat in Solothurn nor the height of the Matterhorn here. It is not a conventional history. The chapter called 'History' starts in the middle, goes backward in time and only after that does it proceed in the usual way. It is not journalism either, although most of the raw material which has been worked into the argument is drawn from our own day. If it has any clear claim to be any specific category of literature, I suppose that *Why Switzerland?* is a latter-day version of those eighteenth-century philosophical histories in which the men of the Enlightenment thought they discerned underlying laws. It is a history in the way that Dr Johnson thought of history, 'contrary to minute exactness, a history which ranges facts according to their dependence on each other, and postpones or anticipates according to the convenience of narration'.[1]

If the book is odd, so is its subject. There is no place like Switzerland and hence any attempt to catch its meaning must be pretty odd too. The sheer variety of Swiss life, what I think of as its 'cellular' character, makes it hard to write a coherent account of the place. Then there are the various institutions, habits and customs unique to Switzerland: its unbelievably complicated electoral procedures, its referenda and initiatives, its specialised economy with its banks and watches, its cheese and chocolates, its citizen-soldiers with their guns in the downstairs cupboards, its complicated federalism of central government, cantons and communes, its three official and four national languages, its neutral status, its astonishing wealth per head, its huge proportion of foreign workers, its efficient public services, its enormous number of very small newspapers, its religious divisions, and until recently, its exclusion of women from the vote. That is an impressive list of oddities for a country of only six million souls. But there is more.

In a world shaken by industrial unrest, Switzerland has been an island of labour peace. During 1974, there were six industrial disputes, three of which led to strikes of a day or more. The total number of days lost was 2,777. In Great Britain during the same year, the figure was 14.7 million. Nor was 1974 unusual in Swiss labour relations. The *Statistical Annual* reports that between 1962 and 1973 there was a grand total of thirty-five strikes and lockouts, just over three a year. In four of those years (1964, 1967, 1968 and 1969) there was only one. The worst year for disputes was 1971 in which there were eleven strikes, and it was also the only year in which more than 2,000 workers were involved.[2] A modern state which had done nothing else but achieve a truce in the battle between employer and employee would deserve close attention for that accomplishment alone.

Most people know that Switzerland is a country of many languages. There are in fact four national languages: German, French, Italian and Raeto—Romansch. The first three are official languages, which means that all official documents, railway time-tables or postal notices must be published in each. 65% of the population speak German, 18% French, 12% Italian and 1% Romansch. The operation of a country so con-stituted would be fascinating enough if that were the whole story. The reality is much more complicated, indeed, bewilderingly so. Here are some facts about language in Switzerland. The 50,000 people who speak Romansch as mother-tongue divide into those who speak the Ladino of the Upper Engadin and that of the Lower Engadin, each of which has its own written language, the Surselva of the Upper Rhine Valley also with a literary tradition, and the non-literary dialects of Surmeirisch and Sutselvisch. The 65% who speak 'German' are actually bilingual, for they speak a language they do not read or write, and read and write in a language which they sometimes speak but not as a mother-tongue. The language of the Swiss Germans, *Schwyzerdütsch*, divides itself into almost as many versions as there are valleys in the Alps, some of which, such as those of the Bernese Oberland and Ober-wallis, are incomprehensible to most *Schwyzerdütsch* speakers. There is one canton, Ticino, where Italian is the official language and another, Graubünden, in which three valleys and a few communes also use it as the official tongue. What sort of Italian? Let me cite a passage from Fritz Rene Allemann's *25 mal die Schweiz*, where he describes the village of Bivio in Canton Graubünden:

The census of 1960 recorded a total of 188 inhabitants for Bivio ... with an Italian majority (it is the only commune north of the main chain of the Alps which belongs to the Italian linguistic area), an old-established Raeto-Romansch minority and also some German enclaves, with a Catholic and a Protestant Church, which have co-existed in 'parity' for centuries. (Both pastors look at the congregation first before deciding which language to preach in.) But that is not all. If one listens closely, one can hear three different dialects of Italian: the native dialect which is closely related to the Raetolombardic used in the Bregaglia; the Bergamasco dialect spoken by shepherd families who during the centuries wandered over the Alps from Northern Italy; and written, 'High', Italian.[3]

Religious divisions cut deeply into Swiss life. As Urs Altermatt puts it, until recently Swiss Roman Catholics lived in a ghetto. There were Catholic bookshops, Catholic employment offices and Catholic old people's homes:

A Catholic might be born in a Catholic hospital, attend Catholic schools from kindergarten to university, read Catholic newspapers and magazines, vote for the Catholic party and take part in Catholic clubs or associations. It was not unusual for a Catholic to insure himself against sickness or accident with a Catholic company and put his savings in a Catholic savings bank.[4]

Even the Swiss constitution played a part in making Swiss Catholics feel themselves to be second-class citizens by forbidding the Jesuits to live and work in the country. The provision was altered by referendum in 1973.

Here then are three bits of Swiss reality, chosen more or less randomly from the thickets of Helvetic oddity. They seem to point in entirely different directions. There is evidently a national pattern in labour relations. All Swiss shun the strike, not just Swiss Germans or Swiss Catholics. Yet the other evidence illustrates the extreme particularism, the divisions within divisions or the 'cellular' quality of Swiss life. How can a place so varied have national behaviour patterns? How are the complex layers of identity (language, region, creed, party, class, occupation, age) reconciled in Swiss heads? These seem to me to be interesting questions which in a way hold up a mirror to our own less dramatic equivalents.

Switzerland is a useful place to look at some other European problems. It is small enough to be studied conveniently, odd enough to be an abbreviation for the whole of European life and advanced enough to be fully integrated into all the trends of the 1970s. In looking at the way the Swiss cope with mass culture, modern transportation, technological change, inflation, urbanisation, population growth, secularisation, environmental pollution and violence by extremist groups, we can see in a small arena what faces Europe in the large one. Can the 'Swissness' of Switzerland adapt to the great levelling trends of the time? If it can, there is reason to hope that the Europe of the year 2000 will not have doused national characteristics in bureaucratic grey. Particular identity will be still the essential feature of European identity, as the particularity of Switzerland is its most striking general characteristic.

The oddest thing about Switzerland is how little most foreigners know about it. No country is more frequently visited but less known. Switzerland has two faces, the smooth, expressionless, efficient surface which the tourist glides by without noticing and the turbulent, rich, inside surface which he never sees. The average English-speaking person, if asked to choose a few adjectives to describe Switzerland, would probably end up with a list containing the following: 'beautiful', 'efficient', 'expensive' and 'boring'. The last one crops up so frequently that I find myself shrieking 'Switzerland *is* interesting' over and over again, just to be heard. I know that Switzerland is in many ways a fascinating country but if I mention the word 'Swiss', eyes glaze and attention wanders. In a lecture course on European history of the nineteenth century, I once announced that I intended to devote the next lecture to the Swiss civil war, and halved my audience. Not only will a Swiss question never 'come up' in an examination but even a civil war, if it happened in Switzerland, cannot be interesting.

Part of this is sheer prejudice, and not new either. In 1797 the exiled French aristocrat Chateaubriand observed bitterly: 'Neutral in the grand revolutions of the states which surround them, they enrich themselves by the misfortunes of others and found a bank on human calamities.'[5] The following year French troops swept away the old Swiss Confederation and the Swiss revolution began. Chateaubriand should have waited a little. Like so many foreigners he was tempted to generalise because Switzerland sometimes seems changeless. How many of those who say flatly that nothing ever happens in Switzerland would recognise this picture of the country, taken from a letter of Prince Metternich, the Austrian Chancellor, in 1845?

Switzerland presents the most perfect image of a state in the process of social disintegration ... Switzerland stands alone today in Europe as a republic and serves troublemakers of every sort as a free haven. Instead of improving its situation by appropriate means, the Confederation staggers from evils into upheavals and represents for itself and for its neighbours an inexhaustible spring of unrest and disturbance.[6]

Another reason why Switzerland is unknown abroad is that it is hard to know. Eight centuries of tourism have left a mark. The Swiss simply do not reveal themselves easily to foreigners. An alien can live in some Swiss cities for years and never be invited to a Swiss home. Geneva is notorious for this but not unique. There are barriers everywhere to easy contact. It is also hard to know intellectually. There are so many puzzles and difficulties. Take the problem of frontiers. How does an artificial line drawn through a continuous stretch of countryside or marked on a bridge make everything change: table silver, currency, foods, smells, customs, appearance of the buildings and so on? For the frontier watcher, Switzerland is a paradise. Cross the language border in Canton Fribourg (this is one not even marked by an outward sign) on the road from Bern to the city of Fribourg, and the streets become dirtier, and the window boxes of flowers less frequent. It is Francophone territory. Why are French-speaking communities less neat than German-speaking ones? Travel the road from Biel—Bienne to Porrentruy (all French-speaking) and watch the 'Jura libre' slogans painted on walls appear and disappear as the car passes from Catholic to Protestant community and back again. How can one make sense of the invisible barriers which seem to divide otherwise identical settlements? The answers to such questions are extremely difficult to devise; it is not always clear what the question is. Understanding Switzerland is so hard that few ever try.

There are modest satisfactions for those who do, and I hope that you will end up sharing my delight in the variety and exuberance of Swiss life, as I try to sketch it for you. There are also some grander rewards for anybody who takes the case of Switzerland seriously, as Dr Johnson pointed out:

Let those who despise the capacity of the Swiss, tell us by what wonderful policy or by what happy conciliation of interests, it is brought to pass, that in a body made up of different communities and different religions, there should be no civil commotions, though the people are so warlike, that to nominate and raise an army is the same.[7]

2. History

Switzerland has no natural frontiers. The mountains and valleys of the Alps continue to the east and west into what is now Austria and France as they do on the southern slopes into what is now Italy. That the Bregaglia and the Valley of Poschiavo are Swiss, while the Valtellina or the county of Bormio are Italian can only be understood historically. Every Swiss frontier represents an historic act or set of events. Vorarlberg is Austrian because the great powers in 1919 refused to accept a plebiscite of its people for union with Switzerland. Geneva's borders on Lac Léman were settled by the Vienna Congress. Canton Ticino was conquered by Uri and later by other Swiss cantons. Constance, the 'natural' capital of the Thurgau, is German, partly because the Swiss Diet lacked the nerve in 1510 to accept another city-state into the Federation for fear of upsetting the urban—rural balance. Canton Schaffhausen contains one parcel of 41 hectares in its midst which is, in fact, German territory, and has three substantial enclaves, which cannot be reached without passing through German territory. Nor is the picture more coherent within Switzerland. Boundaries between cantons wander irregularly and unexpectedly over the landscape. Bits and pieces of Canton Solothurn lie embedded in Canton Bern, two of which, Kleinlützel and Mariastein, have borders with France as well. In Kleinlützel when people go shopping in one of the neighbouring larger towns, they tend to say 'we're going up to Switzerland'. Campione d'Italia on the eastern shore of Lake Lugano is a chip of Italy, precisely 2.1 kilometres long and just over 1 kilometre deep at its widest point. The territory, much of which is actually lake surface, is entirely surrounded by the Swiss Canton Ticino. The complex overlapping of political authority, the jagged nonsense of frontiers and boundaries, the bits and pieces of territory lying about the map, resemble a jigsaw puzzle constructed by a whimsical providence. Part of the key to the puzzle is what did not happen in Switzerland, rather than what did. The Swiss escaped the full consequences of three characteristic European trends: the trend toward rational centralisation, the growth of nationalism and the violence of religious conflict. Let us look at each in turn.

The French and their fellow travellers tried to make sense of

Switzerland in the period between 1798 and 1802. During those years in Switzerland and other parts of Europe, the French installed enlightened, rational, benevolent, centralised, puppet governments. The Helvetic Republic, as the Swiss version was called, introduced the latest achievements of the French Revolution: equality before the law, uniformity of weights and measures, and a uniform code of justice. It liberated large tracts of subject territory in Ticino, Vaud, Aargau and Thurgau and raised former subjects to the dignity of citizens. The French and their supporters intended to put an end to the fantastic array of tiny republics, prince–bishoprics, princely abbeys, counties, free cities, sovereign cloisters and monasteries, free valleys, overlapping jurisdictions, guilds, oligarchies and city aristocracies. On 12 April 1798, Switzerland received a new, modern constitution. Article 1 declared it to be 'a unitary and indivisible Republic. There are no longer any borders between cantons and formerly subject territories nor between cantons.'

The Swiss themselves had other ideas. At the time that unity was being proclaimed, the formerly subject communities of the old Confederation were asserting their diversity. In the area of the modern Canton St Gallen alone, eight independent republics had sprung up ranging in size from the Toggenburg Valley with 50,000 citizens to the tiny republic of Sax with 1,000.[1] The mountain cantons rejected the Helvetic Republic emphatically. Napoleon needed stability along the approaches to the great Alpine passes, and he saw the armed resistance of the Swiss as a military nuisance. The Helvetic Republic existed on paper; the reality was chaos. In 1802 he summoned the representatives of the cantons and the Helvetic Senate to Paris and, speaking to them as a man 'born in a land of mountains who understands how mountain people think', he charged them to work out a new constitution.

These deliberations resulted in what was called the Act of Mediation of 19 February 1803, which effectively restored political sovereignty to the old cantons under a loose, federal constitution. Napoleon, who had been much impressed by the *Landsgemeinden*, the popular assemblies of the mountain cantons, believed them to be the characteristic Swiss institution and insisted that they be restored. The *Landsgemeinden* were conservative but democratic, though not in the modern sense. Rousseau's 'general will' was not quite what emerged from the deliberations of the *Landsgemeinden* where *Praktizieren und Trölen* (electoral bribery and corruption) were the rule, and where the *Hintersässen* (copyholders) had no vote at all but, if that was the system the mountaineers wanted, Napoleon was prepared to return it to them, together with traditional Swiss federalism. The *Mediationsverfassung*, the constitution which he proposed, elevated many of the previously subject or allied (*zugewandte*) territories to full cantonal equality, and St Gallen, Graubünden, Aargau, Ticino and the Vaud took their places as full members of a federal union of nineteen cantons. Neuchâtel, which together with the prince–bishopric of Basel and the princely abbey of St Gallen had been one of the *zugewandte Monarchien* (allied monarchies) of the old Confederation, was not returned to it and, indeed, after the battle of Jena in 1806, Napoleon deposed the King of Prussia as Count of Neuchâtel–Valangin altogether. Geneva and the republic of Valais were annexed to France. Napoleon's intervention had paradoxical consequences. Elsewhere in Europe French armies swept aside petty sovereignties and abolished the lingering traces of 'feudalism'. In Switzerland they were preserved. Why were Swiss institutions tougher than those elsewhere in resisting French reforms?

Why was Switzerland not destroyed by another, more violent, child of the French Revolution, nationalism? Take the case of the Italian-speaking Canton Ticino, whose links to the Swiss began in 1478 when the German-speaking canton of Uri, the Gotthard Pass canton, annexed the Valle Leventina on the other side of the pass. The move brought both slopes approaching the Gotthard under one political authority and provided a base for further military expansion. Together with Schwyz and Nidwalden, the Urner extended their control during the following thirty years into the Riviera, Val Blenio and the city of Bellinzona, which remained under a tri-dominium of the three cantons until 1798. The rest of what is today Ticino, the cities of Lugano, Locarno, and the valleys around them, became joint property of twelve of the thirteen cantons of the old Confederation. (Appenzell got nothing because, by 1513 when it joined the Confederation, all these territories had been conquered.)

For more than 250 years these Italian-speaking communities were subject to alien rule by ignorant, corrupt, German-speaking bailiffs. Karl Viktor von Bonstetten, a Bern patrician, who made an official inspection of the areas of Ticino ruled by the twelve cantons in 1795– 6, was appalled by a regime which seemed to him to be 'organised ideally for evil, where the good is impossible. If a common meadow or a common field will be badly tended, how much more a commonly held, subject territory'.[2] It is hardly surprising that many Ticinese, organised into groups called *i Patriotti*, welcomed the French intervention which put an end to centuries of misrule. Liberty, the rights of man and the citizen, the liberation of their ethnic identity as Italian-speakers, all seemed to lie in union with the new Napoleonic Cisalpine Republic, an Italian-speaking sister of the Helvetic. On 15 February 1798, the Patriots attempted a *coup d'état* and proclaimed the union of Ticino and the Cisalpine Republic. A huge and surprisingly unfriendly crowd gathered in the Piazza Grande in Lugano. The insurgents who had seized the representatives of Unterwalden as hostages, in the face of the hostility of the crowd, were forced to release them. In exchange for a promise of free passage out of Lugano, the Patriots withdrew in confusion. That evening two lawyers from Ponte Tresa, Annibale Pellegrini and Angelo Maria Stoppani, led a group of armed men to the representatives from Unterwalden whose presence had forced the hands of the Patriots and demanded 'Swiss Liberty': 'We demand our sacred rights; we desire Swiss liberty; finally, after centuries of subjection, we are mature enough to govern ourselves.' The delegates from Unterwalden announced that they would support the request and left Lugano. In a delirium of popular celebration, the people planted a liberty tree with a William Tell hat on it and proclaimed themselves 'Liberi e Svizzeri'. During the next few days all the other subject territories in the area followed the Lugano example and declared themselves 'Free and Swiss'.[3]

Why were former subjects so loyal to former masters? Against the powerful trends toward unified national communities why was Switzerland able to remain a multilingual exception? Throughout the nineteenth century, as passions stirred during the heroic days of Italian nationalism, the Ticinese remained overwhelmingly loyal to the Confederation. How 'unnatural' this was may be seen in the evidence of two very different sorts of witnesses. The first of these, the greatest Swiss historian of his time, Jakob Burckhardt, offers us a vivid glimpse into the mind of a cultivated nineteenth-century observer. In a letter to a friend, written in 1845, Burckhardt argued:

Among better educated, thinking, German-speaking Swiss, if only quietly for the moment, the feeling of belonging to Germany, of our inner, original unity, is spreading as they are less and less able to convince themselves sincerely of the existence of Swiss nationality. They consider themselves lucky that no dialect raised to the dignity of a written language separates them from Germany as the Dutch are ... Are we really one nation with the Genevese or Ticinese as is repeatedly asserted?[4]

Very similar sentiments were expressed by Teresina Bontempi, the fiercely irredentist editor of *L'Àdula*, the leading Italianising journal in Ticino, on the eve of the First World War. In a leader entitled 'Una Sintesi' of 18 April 1914, Miss Bontempi wrote: 'We are Italians by soil and by soul, even if from the one we are divided by a customs barrier and from the other by the blindness which it creates.'[5]

Nationalism was not the only force which might have torn Switzerland apart. Religious conflict was another. The Confederation has often seemed a compact with the devil. Writing in 1525 Ulrich Zwingli, the great Protestant reformer, had no doubt of it: 'I prefer a league united by faith to one in which the members putrify. Alliances are more fruitful when faith makes them lasting than those into which treaties force us.'[6] Religious warfare divided the Swiss again and again between the sixteenth and the nineteenth centuries, and religious divisions inflame the Jura crisis today. It was only in 1973 that the paragraph of the Swiss constitution banning the Jesuits from the Confederation was finally annulled by the voters. To the political, ethnic and religious divisions of the past, the twentieth century has added class conflict, and there was a moment in 1918, during the General Strike, when that too threatened the unity of the state and of society.

Why has Switzerland survived these threats to the unity of the Confederation? Some observers, struck by all the exceptions to the rules, have been tempted to see Switzerland as simply *sui generis* as if the general trends of European development had no purchase there, but that is too easy. The Swiss have been affected by all the great events of history. Admittedly, for four hundred years they have been a neutral state in a continent more or less continuously at war, but that neutrality itself raises the problem of Swiss uniqueness in another form. The neutrality of the Swiss suited most of the European powers most of the time, but it has not always suited the Swiss. Zwingli's view is at least as common in Swiss history as the cautious circumspection of officials. Neutrality would have collapsed had there been no internal cohesion, no collective will to survive specifically as Swiss. The difficulty lies in defining what is specifically Swiss and in what belongs to more general European currents and movements. As Perry Anderson points out in his study of feudalism, the Swiss cantonal movement was 'in many respects a *sui generis* historical experience' — in many but not in all.[7] The struggle of peasantries against feudal magnates was general throughout Europe; the specifically Swiss question is how and why they won.

The first element of the answer is to be sought in the peculiar econo-mic organisation of the old Swiss mountain community. It used to be thought that Swiss communalism was a survival of primitive Germanic tribal custom. Hans Conrad Peyer argues instead that the settlement of the high Alpine valleys was part of the dynamic expansion of the feudal economy in the twelfth and thirteenth centuries, a 'movement almost never entirely spontaneous nor without specific leadership'.[8] Physical circumstances undoubtedly combined to promote the forma-tion of communal modes of enterprise. As Professor Adolf Gasser suggests, conditions in the Alpine valleys dictated a social organisation of a special kind.[9] The population organised itself naturally into extended valley communes and these rapidly turned into unified, en-closed cooperatives. Raising cattle implied the maintenance of com-mon pastures, the *Allmenden*, common marketing of animal and dairy products, common activity on the important passes and roads, the regulation of mercenary service and the purchase of weapons.

In the case of roads, this still goes on today; many extremely well travelled roads, such as that from Entlebuch in Canton Luzern over the Glaubenberg Pass to Sarnen in Canton Obwalden, are main-tained by compulsory payments to a road cooperative by all the property owners who benefit from it.

Alpine conditions preserved the non-hierarchical, undivided, that is, non-feudal valley communities, even where, as was frequently the case, the valley was subject to noble or clerical feudal lords. The case of the prince—abbot of St Gallen is characteristic of the kind of 'social contract' which powerful feudal princes observed in dealing with their subject territories. In his study of the legal codes of the abbey Walter Müller found that all of them, even those made during the height of absolutist practice in the eighteenth century, give some lip service to the 'fiction of a mutual agreement'.[10] The idea of a contract between free but not equal entities is, of course, a general characteristic of feudalism; the nature of the contracting parties is the peculiarly Swiss feature of it.

The establishment of valley communities, the *Talgenossenschaften*, was accelerated by rapid improvements in trade, commerce and economic specialisation during the twelfth and thirteenth centuries. Between 1100 and 1300 grain prices increased by 300% and trading communities sprang up to deal with the new traffic.[11] Switzerland became important for the first time as the number of people crossing the Alps increased sharply. Some time during the early years of the thirteenth century the way along the spectacular Schöllenen gorge, the key to the Gotthard Pass, was opened and the city of Luzern, established where the waters flow out of the Vierwaldstättersee into the River Reuss, grew astonishingly. Between its foundation in the late twelfth century and the middle of the next century, Luzern grew to very nearly its nineteenth-century size.[12] Since Switzerland has twenty-two major and thirty-one minor passes, the general movement of trade produced a wave of urban foundations, a struggle among the various existing cities, their feudal overlords and the valley communities for control of customs, tolls and carrying trade along the routes. As Anderson remarks, the 'penetration of the countryside by commodity exchange had weakened customary relationships'.[13] It had also produced economic specialisation. The Alpine communities concentrated increasingly on cattle and dairy products. Cereal production declined in the mountain cantons, except in bad years, to such an extent that by the early sixteenth century Canton Schwyz had to send to Zürich for help in a particularly bad year because they no longer had any corn seeds ('mit samen nit verfasst').[14] The process of economic differentiation had its counterpart in a political and social differentiation, very much accelerated by the great struggle between the Hohenstaufen Emperors and the Popes. Partisans of each protagonist often fought out local vendettas in the name of grander causes, and the fluctuating fortunes of the Emperors enabled agile families, especially in the valley communities, to bargain for 'freedoms' in exchange for allegiance. The interregnum caused by the death of the last Hohenstaufen in 1250, the 'schreckliche, kaiserlose Zeit', added to the political turbulence as the swarm of small lords, petty city-republics and valley communities scurried to find protectors among the remaining great lords. Even powerful, prosperous cities like Bern felt the winds of change and, together with the Free Hasli Valley and the imperial city of Murten, begged Peter of Savoy in 1255 to become their protector. Yet another element in the background was the extinction of so many of the important feudal families in the area in rapid succession, the Lenzburg in 1173, the Zähringer in 1218, and the Kyburg in 1264.

The emergence of Rudolf of Habsburg in 1273 as the new King of Germany changed the picture sharply. The Habsburgs were substantial local lords in their own right, and the combination of royal and local authority made Rudolf look dangerously strong. One of the most important of the Alpine valley communities, Uri, had taken advantage of its strategic position as the keeper of the keys to the Gotthard Pass and by exploiting the desperate financial circumstances of the last Hohenstaufen Emperor, Frederick II, managed to purchase back in 1231 the overlordship of their valley which had been pawned. The valley became *reichsfrei*, that is, subject to no lord save the Emperor. The neighbouring community, Schwyz, obtained a similar charter of freedom in 1240, but the legality of this, unlike that of Uri, was not unchallenged. Rudolf of Habsburg was apparently prepared to confirm the freedom of Uri but not that of Schwyz. The *Talgenossenschaften* had by now become well established communities of largely free-peasants under the direction of several powerful families (the Stauffacher and Ab Yberg in Schwyz, the Attinghusen, Meier von Silenen and von Moos in Uri, the Hunwil and Wattersburg in Obwalden and the Wolfenschiessen in Nidwalden).[15] The administration of justice under feudalism was their most important civic activity. As Perry Anderson points out, since feudalism had neither articulated legislative nor executive functions, justice came close to being 'the ordinary name of power'.[16] The *Ammann*, the valley head and generally one of the oligarchs, judged in the name of the Emperor, whose direct subject the community claimed to be. As the increasingly self-conscious valley communities extended their claims to feudal sovereignty over the ecclesiastical institutions within their territories, armed clashes oc-. curred (between Uri and the monastery at Engelberg in 1275 and a running feud between Schwyz and the Cistercian cloister at Steinen), conflicts which the Habsburg agents intervened to settle. To resist Habsburg claims and to prevent conflicts among themselves, the representatives of the three valley communities formed a league, swearing eternal fealty, in a famous oath taken on the Rütli meadow in 1291. A central feature of the treaty, the parchment of which still exists, was that the three *Waldstätte* or 'forest places' refused to accept any judge or law not of their own making. The actual text reads that

In view of the evil times the men of the valley of Uri, the *Landsgemeinde* of Schwyz and the community of the lower valley of Unterwalden, in order to preserve themselves and their possessions ... in common council have with one voice sworn, agreed and determined that in the above named valleys we shall accept no judge nor recognise him in any way if he exercise his office for any reward or for money or if he is not one of our own and an inhabitant of the valleys.[17]

This particular clause, which internal evidence (especially the use of the first person plural) suggests was probably added later, is the one feature which distinguishes the eternal alliance of 1291 from a variety of similar leagues and treaties (often very short-lived in spite of the use of the term 'eternal' or 'perpetual') which can be identified in the era. Unquestionably the idea of a union to which the individual members of a collective community adhered in their own persons reflected the special social context of the *Talgenossenschaft*. The valley dwellers, rugged, independent mountain peasants and shepherds, possessed vigorous and warlike customs. They were used to sharing in public discussions and they conferred a special force of will to the league of 1291, neatly, if untranslatably expressed in the name they gave themselves: *Eidgenossen,* 'comrades (with a strong communal overtone – a cooperative is a *Genossenschaft*) of the oath'. *Eidgenossenschaft* is still the Swiss German expression for the federal union and comes close to being a synonym for 'Swiss' in official usage.

The event which took place *incipiente mense augusto* 1291 on the Rütli meadow is hard to assess. As Walter Ullmann has recently pointed out, concepts of sovereignty were still fluid in the thirteenth century; the transition from personal to abstract sovereignty was not yet complete.[18] Hence, while the actual parchment of the 1291 document, the *Bundesbrief,* survives, its precise historical significance to contemporaries must remain uncertain. But we do know that the romantic vision of a free mountain peasantry rising as one man in defence of primeval German liberties is not quite the way it was. As Christopher Hughes has observed, 'the taste for mountains has followed the fortunes of the liberal ethic'[19] and the idea which many Swiss have of their virtuous ancestors has certainly been painted over by the enthusiasms of the liberal bourgeoisie. It is easy to see why the novelist Peter Bichsel rejects the mythology: 'I simply cannot imagine that the old *Eidgenossen* were more ideal types than my neighbour and I.'[20] The *Eidgenossen* of 1291 were not ideal types. They were something much more interesting – armed, free (or mostly so) peasants who had embarked on an alliance which they regarded as more than ordinarily solemn. Their own characteristics and the complex currents of historical development were to give that act permanent meaning. What they were doing was not uncommon; that it lasted was.

As so often in subsequent history, the key to the survival of the little league of mountain valleys has to be sought in general features of the era, and their interaction with Swiss realities. The first and most obvious point is the importance of geography, and its relationship to the general state of military technology. An example can be seen in the history of medieval Raetia, today's Canton Graubünden. Medieval

Raetia, the eastern neighbour of medieval Helvetia, was a loose association of three leagues of equally loosely allied sovereign valley communities. In his history of Raetia, Benjamin Barber notes that the canton contains 150 distinct valleys in an area of 7,000 square miles and that 188 of its 221 communes lie above the 700 metre line. In the conditions of medieval or early modern warfare, Raetia was simply impossible to control: 'To control Raetia would mean to control through military occupation every valley and village and village 'fraction' in the land. An army occupying Chur no more controls Graubünden than does one in Milan or Vienna.'[21]

A second and fascinating element is the physical prowess of the mountaineers. Evidence is hard to get, but it would appear that an unusually high protein diet, a well established system of warlike sports and games and the nature of his work made the Alpine peasant a formidable opponent in warfare.[22] Certainly the excellence of Swiss soldiery accounts for a great deal of the unique course of the subsequent events. The medieval Swiss soldiery used spears, axes, hammers and especially the halberd, a weapon consisting of an axe-blade balanced by a pick with an elongated pike-head fixed at the end of a five- or six-foot staff. This nasty object, which was the Swiss weapon *par excellence*, had the advantage that in skilled hands it could deal a mortal, cleaving blow on a mounted, armoured opponent. But if these weapons were not available, the Swiss soldiers would use stones, tree trunks and anything else which came to hand. Swiss cohorts won victory after victory on their own soil during the fourteenth century, especially at Morgarten in 1315 and in the Sempach War of 1386, the war in Oberwallis in the 1380s and the Appenzell War of the first decades of the fifteenth century.

The special significance of the military victories of the Swiss can be better appreciated if they are seen against the background of the economic and social crisis of the century. Almost at the same time as the Swiss *Eidgenossen* were winning their first victories, the supply of silver from Bohemian, German and French mines began to dry up as the technical difficulties of medieval mining made deeper shafts impossible. The shortage of currency led to frequent debasements and rapid price rises. The extension of area under cultivation to less good soils produced lower yields and in the middle of the century, to complete the calamity, the Black Death ravaged the European population.[23] Under these circumstances, it is not surprising that in the 1350s and 1360s waves of peasant revolt swept Europe of which the *grande*

Jacquerie of 1358 was the most dramatic. Switzerland did not escape the troubles, but in a paradoxical way they strengthened the tendency for Swiss development to deviate from the European norms. Revolts in the *Landsgemeinde* cantons attacked the powers of the prominent families and extended the communal features of the *Talgenossenschaft* at the expense of the oligarchical. In the lowlands, the wave of urban unrest of the 1330s strengthened the guild movement and widened the circle of those able to participate in civic affairs. In 1336 the assembly of Luzern was enlarged to become a 'Council of 300'. In 1353 the city of St Gallen introduced full guild participation in the Large and Small Councils. In the Small Council, the masters and vice-masters of the six guilds held twelve of the twenty-four seats, though, in practice, the guilds controlled all the seats, since nine of the remaining twelve were elected by the Large Council, whose complicated procedures ensured that some eighty of the ninety members belonged to one of the guilds.[24] The system eventually turned into a labyrinth of ever smaller oligarchical circles, but in the fourteenth century the victory of the guilds provided a strong democratic impetus, for within guild chapters themselves a communal expression of opinion could take place not unlike that of the *Landsgemeinde* in the countryside. The Swiss towns could meet the mountain communities on terms of political equality.

During the middle of the fourteenth century, leagues with overlapping membership gradually formed between the principal free mountain valleys and urban communities, so that by 1353 the three *Waldstätte* had been joined by Luzern (1332), Zürich (1351), Glarus (1352), Zug (1352) and Bern (1353) to form a union of 'eight places'. In neighbouring Raetia by a similar process during the 1370s the League of the House of God (*Gotteshausbund*) united the city of Chur, the surrounding villages, the Domschlag, Schams, Poschiavo and Mustair Valleys.[25] North of the Rhine similar leagues and alliances emerged, especially the League of the Swabian Cities of 1331; the only difference was that the Swiss and Raetian leagues survived and the German did not.

The spread of the Helvetic and Raetian leagues owed a lot to aristocratic bankruptcy. As the economic crisis deepened, small feudal lords collapsed under their debts and frequently pawned their feudal rights, dues or tolls. The still prosperous cities of the Swiss Confederation took the chance to buy up pawned territories, as in the case of Bern's purchase of a mortgage held by the impoverished lords of Weissenburg in 1334. This particular mortgage covered the Hasli Valley, an Imperial

Free Valley, in theory the equal of *reichsfrei* Uri or Schwyz. By buying the *Reichspfandschaft* over the Hasli, the city of Bern came into all the privileges formerly owed directly to the Emperor, as well as substantial feudal dues and payments. Characteristically, Bern confirmed the traditional 'freedoms' of the Hasli Valley dwellers, reserving for itself the right to name the *Ammann* and to demand a military levy.[26] These relationships remained unaltered until 1798. In 1393 the eight cantons and the city of Solothurn concluded a formal military alliance called the *Sempacherbrief*, and in the following year the second of the three leagues of Raetia, the so-called Grey League or *Grauer Bund* (from which modern Graubünden takes its name) was founded. What these leagues and associations have in common is not so much their origins as their success against foes more numerous and reputedly stronger. At the same time that the Swiss communal forces were defeating the feudal nobility at Sempach, Näfels and Visp, the nobility of South Germany and the Rhineland won decisive victories over the cities at Doffingen and Alzey in 1388. The hitherto seamless Upper German world began to divide. North of the Rhine the free city and free peasantry fell ever more firmly into the control of the larger princely and aristocratic authorities; south of the river a complicated network of autonomous, allied communities developed.

During the fifteenth century Switzerland began to swell to the proportions of a European great power. Her military superiority was so marked that the Confederation could afford to expand abroad and to carry on civil wars at home without fear of foreign intervention. In 1436 and again in 1450 the city-state of Zürich under the shifting influences of its commercial and artisan oligarchies fought bitter battles against its neighbours, mainly for control of valuable territories and trade. The economic foundations of Swiss power expanded very rapidly. Figures are difficult to come by for the Middle Ages, but in Fribourg surviving notarised contracts of sale show a sharp recovery of trade after the fourteenth-century depression. The growing point of the Swiss economy was cloth, wool and linen. By 1413 the average annual sale of Fribourg cloth pieces had reached 8,000; it exceeded 10,000 by the 1420s and achieved a level of 12,500 in the 1430s.[27] The causes of the growth of the cloth industry in Swiss cities are not simple to explain. Severe control of the quality would appear to have played a crucial part. The famous 'G' or *Mal* on every piece of St Gallen linen is the first example of the 'made in Switzerland' image. Another element must have been the high degree of urbanisation itself. The city of St

Gallen was a geographical oddity. In its centre, surrounded by a wall four feet thick and thirty feet high, stood the sovereign abbey of St Gallen, very like the modern Vatican City. Outside the walls of the city the prince—abbot ruled the traditional *Landschaft*, the hereditary lands of the abbey. The city, which was a separate republic entirely independent of the abbey, had a plot of land about two kilometres square as its entire territory outside the walls. Its seven or eight thousand inhabitants had no other occupations than commerce, artisan production and marketing.[28] This unusually marked disproportion between economic and political power (one of the striking features of Swiss economic life today, which I shall examine in a later chapter) would appear to have funnelled the entire civic energy into dominating markets not lands. By the end of the fifteenth century, an enormous trading network was carrying St Gallen linen to all parts of Europe. In Zürich it was silk which played the role of linen. In all the Swiss cities the merchants, organised in large, complex joint stock companies, became very rich, often at the expense of urban artisans and craftsmen and the peasants in the surrounding country districts who frequently did much of the actual spinning and weaving. Niklaus von Diesbach, who died in 1436, left 70,000 gulden and was known as the richest man in Bern. He had begun as an artisan, risen to power as a merchant and died a *Twingherr*, a quasi-feudal landowner.[29] Swiss wealth and commerce benefited from the great importance of through traffic, and not only north—south. The east—west route with its unusually favourable chain of easily navigable waterways, linked the Habsburg domains through the flourishing mercantile community of Geneva on Lac Léman to western Europe.

Inevitably social, communal and class conflict marked the underside of Swiss life. City fathers coped with the dangers by various devices. *Reislaufen*, mercenary service, was profitable to the authorities, attractive to turbulent young men and a means of keeping the peace. Games and sports were another. Organised competitions in *Schwingen* (a special form of Swiss wrestling) and in other sports were well established parts of urban and Alpine life in the fifteenth and sixteenth centuries. Zwingli reckoned that the Zürich city fathers ought to encourage sporting activities but only 'kunstliche Kurtzwylen und die zu Übung des Lybs dienend',[30] that is, only artificial or controlled sports which served to exercise the body. Finally, there is the emergence of what I can only call the ideology of democracy. The first full account of the story of William Tell in the famous *White Book of Sarnen* dates from 1474 and the first William Tell *Lieder* were composed during the last decades of the fifteenth century. It is not chance that 1470 is the date of an equally remarkable document, Thüring Frickart's *Twing-herrenstreit*, an eye-witness account of the social conflict between the *Twingherren*, those who held traditional, feudal rights in the country-side around Bern and the increasingly powerful and self-conscious urban authorities 'represented in the master butcher and Lord Mayor of Bern, Peter Kistler. The *Twingherren* demanded a return to the rights guaranteed in the 'alten Grechtigkeiten, Briefen und Siglen' (the old rights, letters and seals).[31] The language and tone of the Tell story, and that of Frickart's *Twingherrenstreit*, have a good deal in common. The image of Tell rapidly came to stand for the Swissness of things, for those 'old laws, rights and seals', which the new ruling classes of the fifteenth and sixteenth centuries threatened. Eventually, it came to define the official Swiss attitude to their own past. The hardy moun-taineer, who defies the Habsburgs and by his skill as a bowman thwarts their designs, who will not do obeisance to anybody, became for the Swiss and for others what the Confederation meant. The actual authenticity of the story is not the issue. The story of William Tell is not false, even if there never was a man of that name and he never shot an apple off his son's head. Its truth is the truth of a communal tradition by which the Swiss defined and made precise their public values. It was justification by history just as the protesting *Twingherren* of the 1470s, or the peasant revolutionaries of the 1650s and the citizens of Lugano of the 1790s justified themselves historically. Swiss liberty became associated with William Tell and the faded symbolism lingers on today. The cries of outrage which greeted Max Frisch's nasty but very funny version of the Tell saga for school children[32] were entirely under-standable. Frisch was more certainly undermining the public ideology by making fun of William Tell than any subversive agitator could ever do with radical pamphlets. For ultimately Switzerland is justified and sanctioned not by an 'ism' but by history alone. Hence the importance of the legend of William Tell.

Class conflict within Swiss communities had its roots in the sudden flood of new wealth. Much of it was simply booty seized from defeated enemies. The greatest haul was the huge collection of jewels, fine silks and money which the Swiss *soldateska* seized after they had defeated the Burgundians at the battles of Grandson and Morat in 1476. These victories, the most famous ever won by Swiss arms, were also histori-cally the most important. Since Charles the Bold, one of the greatest feudal princes of the age, died at Morat, his territories passed to various heirs and disintegrated. In a sense, the Swiss indirectly helped to found the sixteenth-century French monarchy by eliminating its most dangerous rival.

The official spoils were also huge and inflamed the raw feelings of the men of the mountains against the townsmen. In 1481, the peasants of the mountain cantons marched westward behind the banner of a fat sow to grab their share of the spoils from the urban cantons. The ultimate civil war, which would certainly have destroyed Switzerland, was avoided because an aristocratic hermit, Niklaus von Flüe, who had abandoned his great wealth and status in Zürich for the contemplative life, managed to stop the war simply by exercising his spiritual authority. We know little about Brother Klaus, as he was called, save that he succeeded in getting the urban and mountain cantons to sign a new covenant, the *Stanser Verkommnis*, which both regulated the matter of spoils and reasserted the Confederation's basic agreements. It is an extraordinary example of the power of the individual human spirit over masses of men.

Switzerland began the sixteenth century as one of the richest, most populous, and militarily most formidable of European states. The temporary balance of power among the Italian states after the Treaty of Lodi in 1451 created favourable conditions for Swiss expansion southward. Yet paradoxically, Swiss victories in the Burgundian Wars of the 1470s and the Swabian Wars of the 1490s undermined that late feudal Europe with its network of overlapping authority, which made Swiss greatness possible. The destruction of the great feudal house of Burgundy strengthened the French monarchy and it was that monarchy which invaded Italy in 1494. The decisive struggle for power in Italy began. As I said earlier in the chapter, the Swiss cantons had already become an Italian power by their conquests in the valley of the Ticino and on the shores of the lakes. Milan was a glittering prize only 60 kilometres away. The Swiss joined the Pope in coalitions against the French on the logical assumption that the weaker neighbour is always to be preferred to the stronger. They won spectacular victories. By 1512 Milan had become a Swiss protectorate and in June 1513 a Swiss army soundly defeated the French at Novara. This, the high point of Swiss power, proved also to be its end. Part of the subsequent collapse was military. In the 1490s, the *Landsknechtsorden* developed in Germany. *Landsknechte* were groups of foot-soldiers for hire, who used and mastered Swiss techniques. Unlike feudal knights, *Landsknechte* demanded to be paid in cash. The emergence of this new infantry and the expenses caused by innovations such as artillery priced the hire and fitting out of troops out of the small princely market. Only important princes with adequate sources of revenue could compete. The Swiss, whose strength had been diversity, now began to suffer from it. The thirteen cantons had different economic and international interests, and their only central institution was a Diet, the *Tagsatzung*, which was merely a formal assembly of ambassadors with no power to coerce its member states. Hence when the second round of the battle against the French began in 1515, the Swiss army fought without the support of the men of Bern, Fribourg, Solothurn and Biel. On 13 September 1515, Swiss troops suddenly burst from the gates of Milan to attack a surprised French army on the road to Marignano. A spectacular victory was just missed; the next day, the Swiss attack on prepared French positions was repulsed.

The defeat at the battle of Marignano was a startling event. The invincible Swiss had been defeated. The Diet, when the news reached it, immediately ordered the assembly of another army, but by now it could no longer command the support of the western cantons and especially of Bern, by far the most powerful, individual unit in the Confederation. Bern and the western cantons signed a separate treaty with France in November 1515, and in 1516 a Perpetual Peace was signed between France and the Swiss Confederation. The descent from great power to small neutral state after 1516 was sudden and is not easy to understand. Undoubtedly the scale of the defeat shocked the citizenry. Switzerland had been invincible and was now no longer. The cause of the defeat, internal disunity, was obvious; the remedy, to develop more powerful, central institutions, equally so, but none of the existing entities within the league, not even the powerful patrician republic of Bern, had the force to impose such a solution and none had the will. The internal equilibrium of the old Diet preserved the *status quo* but could not alter it. Moreover, from 1516 until 1792 the French were always ready with fat purses to persuade Swiss leaders of the wisdom of pursuing their wars under other people's banners. Solothurn became the residence of the French ambassadors and the strategic point from which French diplomacy operated to keep peace among the turbulent Swiss communities. The Protestant Reformation intruded only a few years after Marignano and divided the Swiss against each other in a new and more ominous way. Agreement between Catholic and Protestant cantons at the Diet was virtually impossible. If it had been hard to unite for gain, it was inconceivable for faith. Hence the Swiss Confederation sank into political torpor, gradually rotting away as an international force.

On 1 January 1519, Ulrich Zwingli, a thirty-five year old priest from the Toggenburg Valley in eastern Switzerland, mounted the pulpit at the Grossmünster in Zürich to preach on the Gospel of St Matthew. For Zwingli the Word of God, not ecclesiastical tradition, was the sole religious authority and with this revolutionary doctrine he attacked the entire apparatus of the medieval church and at the same time the degradation of standards in the Confederation. He condemned the sale of ecclesiastical office and also the sale of mercenary soldiers. Zwingli was an intensely political man. He rapidly gained a share of decision-making (never the control, as is sometimes argued)[33] in the city-state of Zürich. The reformed faith spread rapidly to towns like Basel, Schaffhausen and St Gallen but also into rural and mountainous areas like Glarus, Appenzell and Graubünden. The *Urschweiz*, the original Switzerland of the Forest Cantons, Luzern and Zug, remained Catholic, not least because they saw in the new faith merely a cloak for the old lust for expansion of Zürich, the cause of the fifteenth-century civil wars. As the Confederation began to disintegrate into religious camps, the old town—country fissure reopened, especially since after 1528 the Gracious Lords of Bern threw the patrician republic on to the Protestant side.

A new threat to the Confederation came from without. Not only did the two camps seek support among co-religionists outside the Confederation but both sides began to condemn as 'un-Christian' the policy of neutrality so painfully accepted after 1515. Zwingli urged the Confederation to grant asylum to the persecuted Protestants in 1524 and reacted furiously when the five central cantons not only refused but, in addition, banned the new faith in the *Gemeine Herrschaften*, the commonly administered territories. War broke out between Catholic and Protestant in 1529 and again in 1531. In the second of the two encounters, the Protestant forces were roundly defeated and Zwingli killed. In spite of the defeat the Reformation continued to make gains. In Geneva, independent but friendly to the Swiss Confederation, Calvin began his great work transforming the city into the capital of a worldwide movement and its city administration into the 'new Jerusalem'. Aristocratic Neuchâtel became Protestant under Guillaume Farel; the southern valleys of the Bernese Jura and the Vaud joined the Reformed ranks. So throughout the Confederation communities shifted, split, regrouped and fought. Canton Appenzell split into a Protestant and a Catholic part, forming the basis of today's half-cantons. Solothurn and Fribourg remained Catholic, and the situation in the subject territories remained complicated.

On a much grander scale Europe armed for ultimate conflict. The revived Catholic church of the counter-Reformation, the new militancy of Calvinism, the grand struggles for empire among the European powers, the Dutch revolt, massacres of Huguenots in France, the emergence of England, all represented explosive matter which eventually burst out in a period of very nearly continuous warfare from 1600 to the mid-century. Central Europe was consumed. Germany, not for the last time, became a pile of rubble. No one knows for certain how much of her population died as a direct and indirect result of the war, but it may have been as high as a third of the whole.

The Swiss cantons found the fighting swirling around them. When the great Gustavus Adolphus of Sweden led his all-victorious Protestant army to the very borders of the Confederation, many Protestants yearned to join him. J. J. Breitinger, the head of the pro-Swedish faction in Zürich, condemned his fellow Swiss bitterly:

So do I condemn utterly our harmful and ridiculous temporising and damn the ugly, shameful and loathsome Monster of neutrality. May God spit out the lukewarm, that is, the neutralists who are neither warm nor cold seeing that the Lord Christ holds such for his enemies in bright clear words when he says that he who is not for him is against him.[34]

The lukewarm neutral is easy to attack. Religious passions were violent but, undoubtedly, and not for the last time, passion was assuaged by prosperity. Switzerland was an island of peace and an important food supply to a starving Europe. Even before the outbreak of war, the Venetian diplomat, Giovanni Battista Padavino had observed: 'Travelling in Switzerland is very secure; one can travel the roads day or night without any danger and can halt in woods or mountains, and every class and family enjoys its own in profound peace and unbelievable security.'[35] Von Grimmelshausen described Switzerland in the war years as an earthly paradise which in comparison with other German lands seemed as strange as if he had been in China or Brazil. Three hundred years later William L. Shirer recorded in his *Berlin Diary* on 10 October 1940:

It was strange driving through Geneva town to see the blinding street-lights, the blazing store-windows, the full headlights on the cars — after six weeks in blacked-out Berlin. Strange and beautiful. In Basel this noon Demaree and I stuffed ourselves shamefully with food. We ordered a huge dish of butter just to look at it, and Russian eggs and an enormous steak and cheese and dessert and several litres of wine and then cognac and coffee — a feast! And no food cards to give in. All the way down in the train from Basel we felt good. The mountains, the chalets on the hillsides, even the sturdy Swiss looked like something out of paradise.[36]

That neutrality had its rewards was not lost on the Swiss either. Trade and living standards were never as good in the seventeenth century as they were during the Thirty Years War. The Swiss began to associate neutrality with profit, virtue and good sense. However they may have hated each other, they were better off living together as neutrals than dying apart as enemies. A natural feeling of superiority marked Swiss attitudes to the outside world. In a pious age it was easy to believe that God had willed them to prosper as a reward for their virtues. The attitude persisted and is not unknown today. In the midst of the First World War, the poet and novelist Carl Spitteler reminded his audience: 'Above all no superiority noises. No judgement!! That we as non-participants can see many things more clearly, weigh things more justly, than those caught in the passions of war is obvious. That is an advantage of our position, not an excellence of our souls.'[37] In 1647 the 'Defensionale of Wyl' created the first formal federal military command structure. In 1648 the mayor of Basel as Swiss delegate to the European peace negotiations managed to convince the powers that Switzerland was now independent, and no longer part of the German Empire, a view incorporated in the Peace of Westphalia. According to Edgar Bonjour, the leading authority on these matters, the Diet first formally announced its position as a neutral state in May 1674, but the practice had been increasingly accepted as the only way to hold the Confederation together.

The years immediately after 1648 brought trouble. As if the Swiss needed an external threat to remain one state, immediately it was removed they began to quarrel among themselves. An economic slump played a part. The artificial boom in agriculture sustained by the exhaustion of the countries around them came to an end. The peasantry faced disaster. Class hostilities long submerged burst out. During 1653 in the Entlebuch Valley in Canton Luzern a peasant protest against new taxation imposed by the canton turned into a full-scale rising, which eventually involved much of central Switzerland. Characteristically, the peasants organised themselves into *Landsgemeinden* and in the *Huttwiler Bund* repeated the entire ceremony of the Rütli Oath of 1291, complete with the costumes and symbols of the legendary first *Eidgenossen*. The victory of the cantonal armies led to a large number of summary executions and the end of the *Bund*. Yet it could neither wholly erase the traditional freedoms which the peasants claimed nor could the individual cantonal authorities exploit the civil war to enforce the sort of absolutist regimes which were emerging in Brandenburg, Saxony and, above all, in France.

In his stimulating study of absolutism, the companion to his work on feudalism, the marxist historian Perry Anderson argues that absolutism may be seen as a transformation of rule by the feudal aristocracy. Their traditional economic status was eroded by the spread of the money economy and the end of serfdom in western Europe. Absolutism, according to Anderson, is a dual process. It 'conferred new and extraordinary powers on the monarchy [and] at the same time it emancipated from traditional restraints the estates of the nobility . . . Individual members of the aristocratic class who steadily lost political rights of representation in the new epoch, registered economic gains in ownership as the obverse of the same historical process.'[38]

Another feature of the change is the replacement of 'conditional' categories of property, which Anderson regards as characteristic of feudalism, by the revived Roman Law category of 'absolute' property.[39] By these criteria, Switzerland remained medieval until the end of the eighteenth century. Conditional property relationship and medieval parcelised authority never disappeared. Elements of absolutism obviously entered Swiss life. The city of Bern exacted ever stricter subservience from its rural subjects, and the mini-absolutism of the prince—abbot of St Gallen, complete with a fashionable rage for grandiose buildings, has a certain distant similarity to the political edifice of Frederick the Great's Prussia. But ultimately, the prince—abbot or a city-republic are by definition those feudal, oligarchical, contractual authorities which proper absolutism of the enlightened type must destroy. Absolutism in the Swiss cantons resembled the process of sawing off the branch on which one sits. If the 'absolutist' abbot of St Gallen tried to destroy the traditional rights of the 'free' Toggenburg Valley, he would be destroying a part of his own rights, since both belonged to the same fabric of law and custom.

Religious wars continued in Switzerland later than elsewhere, which helped to make certain that no one absolute authority could emerge.

The first and second Villmergen Wars (1656 and 1712) strained the Confederation to the breaking point. The Catholic cantons began the dangerous game of alliance with foreign powers, a particularly perilous activity with Louis XIV on the throne of France. The Confederation became even more closely involved in French affairs when in 1685 Louis XIV revoked the Edict of Nantes, the religious compromise with his Protestant subjects which dated back to the previous century. Huguenot refugees poured into French-speaking Switzerland bringing their skills as goldsmiths, weavers and printers. It was a turbulent time in Swiss history, a time not unlike the present in its uncertainties. Europe was moving out of one age into another, and the Swiss were drawn out of the confessional conflict to face a new, secular international power system and a new intellectual climate of enlightened rationalism.

The Villmergen Wars were brought to an end in the Peace of Aarau of 1712. The Catholic party lost its commanding position in the Confederation and was forced to accept parity of faiths both in the commonly administered territories and in confederate tribunals. The French were furious, and the five original Swiss cantons, the Catholic Forest Cantons plus Luzern and Zug, made a secret treaty with France three years later in which the French promised armed support if the Confederation were again plunged into religious war. This treaty, the *Trucklibund* (from *Truckli*, the small box in which the treaty was concealed) would have meant the end of Switzerland, had it been carried out. Professor David Lasserre in his fascinating *Étapes du fédéralisme* points to the Peace of Aarau and the *Trucklibund* as one of the great crises of Swiss history along with the 'miracle of 1848' and the Labour Agreement of 1937. I would add the General Strike of 1918 to the list but his point is surely right. Here was a group of defeated states, profoundly convinced of the God-given rightness of their cause, accustomed to think of themselves, and rightly, as the founders of the Confederation, and absolutely sure that the heretical beliefs preached by Reformed pastors brought death and damnation. In the wings, a powerful Catholic ally with inexhaustible funds stood ready to finance their crusade. A war of revenge seemed natural, inevitable and right.

No war took place. The Confederation survived. Another turning point passed at which nothing turned. The reasons for this go to the heart of the mystery of Swiss survival. Undoubtedly the experience of two centuries of religious war had bent the awareness of the most fanatical *Urschweizer* in the direction of union. As Benjamin Franklin once said in an equally perilous moment in the history of a different federal union, 'we must indeed all hang together or, most assuredly, we shall all hang separately'. In spite of its baroque palaces and patrician style, and its pre-eminence in the Confederation, what was Luzern in a world of great European powers without the whole of the union? The particularism of the tiny Alpine democracies, too, needed the protection of the whole Federation, and to get it one had to give. This is not an obvious truth and never easy to accept. Democratic forms often conceal undemocratic sentiments. The man who is right and knows it never enjoys the prospect of triumphant error. It is always tempting to force men to be free or virtuous or class-conscious or whatever. The Catholic cantons had to swallow the pill that they could not force their fellow confederates to be godly nor, much harder and bitterer, ought they to do so, if they could.

In the crisis of 1712, which I might add the Swiss themselves have long since forgotten, we see in precisely what sense Switzerland can be said to be a European exception. Switzerland had not been exempt from the trends of the times. When Europe fought religious wars, the Swiss had them too. When Europe had revolutions in 1830, 1848 or 1918, the Swiss had them too. What differentiates Swiss history from the European pattern is the outcome. Swiss communities built from the bottom up, growing out of free peasant or urban associations, are in a curious sense bottom-heavy, rather like those dolls which spring up no matter how often the child pushes them over. The weight is at the base. The communities have a deep equilibrium to which, as the point of rest, the social and political order tends to return.

As always no one explanation is adequate. Clearly the mercenary service played an important part. A very shrewd Englishman travelling in Switzerland at just this period put it well: 'If they did not continually drain their Country, by keeping troops in foreign service, they would soon be so much overstocked in proportion to the extent and fertility of it that in all probability they would break in on their neighbours in swarms, or go further to seek out new seats.'[40] Obviously the service of the Bourbon King of Naples was a better place to see a turbulent young Obwaldner than at the gates of Basel, and no doubt the acceptance of compromise owes much to the export of the uncompromising. Yet compromise was in a way less galling because one tasted it rarely. Since the Confederation had long since abandoned collective enforcement of anything, Catholic Uri stayed as blackly orthodox as the dour temper of the mountain folk could wish. What the heretics and sinners did in Protestant Schaffhausen was as remote to the men of Uri as what the Protestants did in Scotland. Common affairs caused trouble, and any federal intervention might bring an explosion, but, in the daily round, the Peace of Aarau changed little save, perhaps, the subjects of conversation in the local tavern.

Because Swiss communities are bottom-heavy, they are stable and slow. Most general developments follow in the Helvetic Confederation after a discreet time-lag and no doubt when the end of the world comes it will be two days late in Altdorf and Schwyz. Hence the changing circumstances of European culture, its growing secularism and the emergence of new ideas about man and the community, began to affect public opinion in Switzerland in the decades after the Peace of Aarau for the first time. The unenfranchised citizenry, the peoples in the *Gemeine Herrschaften*, the non-voting burghers of old towns, the poorer peasants began to stir politically. In 1721 in Glarus, 1723 in Lausanne under the leadership of a Vaudois patriot Major Davel, in 1749 in Bern, in 1755 in Ticino and more or less continuously from the 1760s on in Geneva there were risings. These revolts under various banners and for various causes were accompanied by continuous struggle among the governing elites for control in places like Luzern, Zug and Schwyz. In other words, new issues diverted attention from the dangers of religious war. Ultimately, and very likely the most important element of all, there was economic prosperity. The whole of eastern Switzerland became a giant factory. By 1780, Georg Thürer reckons that there were 100,000 peasant weavers and spinners at work serving the specialised muslin, cotton and embroidery businesses of the towns, especially St Gallen.[41] A kind of micro-capitalism emerged, which I shall consider in the chapter on the economy. Here it is only necessary to note that the combination of peasant small-holding and organised production in individual, peasant dwellings made parts of Switzerland at once among the most densely populated rural areas in Europe but also among the most prosperous. The peasant way of life and the social structure survived the great economic changes of the eighteenth century better in Switzerland than elsewhere in central or western Europe.

The old Confederation in its last decades was a marvellous thing, a patchwork of overlapping jurisdictions, ancient customs, worm-eaten privileges and ceremonies, irregularities of custom, law, weights and measures. On the shores of Lake Luzern, the independent republic of

Gersau flourished with all of 2,000 inhabitants and enjoyed much prestige among political theorists of the time as the smallest free state in Europe. The famous Göttingen Professor Friedrich Christoph Schlosser seriously toyed with the idea of writing a multi-volume history of the Republic under 'universal-historical' aspect as a microcosm of all of European history. The pre-1798 Canton Zug was a kind of mini-confederation of a city-state (Zug itself with its subject territories) and three entirely 'free' peasant communes with equality of rights, Baar, Aegeri and Menzingen. Only if all four entities agreed could the canton act on anything. The government of Geneva depended on a quarter of the citizenry, themselves divided between Burgher and Citizen classes, and represented in a complex of large and small councils very like the flywheels of a gear box. The Act of 1738, guaranteed by the cantons of Zürich and Bern and the Kingdom of France, gave the Genevese a government of five orders': the four Syndics, the Small or Executive Council of Twenty-Five; the Council of Sixty; the Council of Two Hundred; and the General Council. Professor Robert Palmer explains its workings:

The General Council met once a year and elected the four Syndics from a list of candidates containing double the number of names, submitted to it by the Small Council. The Act of 1738 specified that all candidates for the office of Syndic must be members of the Small Council, whose members in turn had to belong to the Two Hundred. The Two Hundred, conversely, were named by the Small Council. In short, the Two Hundred (on which far fewer than two hundred families sat) were the ruling aristocracy at Geneva.[42]

Geneva was undoubtedly one of the most interesting and most turbulent representatives of this sort of oligarchy, but systems not unlike it existed elsewhere in the Confederation and, as always, elsewhere in Europe. The influence of Jean-Jacques Rousseau, the most brilliant Genevese of his age, and the constant attention of enlightened Frenchmen from across the frontiers, provided ideas and slogans for the Genevese revolutionaries. In Bern a splendid, slow-moving aristocracy of gentlemen ruled a peasant republic. In Zürich the city government was complicated by ancient guild survivals.

It was this set of rotting structures which the French pushed over in 1798 and which Napoleon reformed in 1803. When the Napoleonic Empire collapsed in 1814, the allied powers had the whole of Europe to put together, not just Switzerland. The old patricians and oligarchs demanded all their former rights and received some of them. Not all were lucky. The republic of Gersau, in spite of its illustrious history, was not revived, but it continues to exist as a separate administrative district within the modern Canton Schwyz. Similarly, the cloister-state of Engelberg disappeared for ever but remains a separate entity within the canton of Obwalden. The attentive traveller in Switzerland will notice everywhere the evidences of the survivals of the older political units as distinct presences within the structures of the new. The number of the cantons was enlarged by the inclusion of Valais, Neuchâtel (still a Prussian possession in spite of its new membership of the Confederation) and Geneva. The Confederation was given a much looser framework, closer to the old Diet than to Napoleon's version. Each canton now had equal voting rights regardless of size. War and peace and treaties required a three-quarter majority of the cantons, and the cantons were allowed some freedom to conduct foreign affairs individually. The one important restriction on cantonal sovereignty was the provision forbidding internal alliances between individual cantons. There was no central government but a sort of travelling secretariat which moved every two years to the *Vorort*, one of the three Director-cantons, Zürich, Bern and Luzern. The apparatus of government, including the two permanent officials, the Chancellor and Secretary, could travel in one coach, and there was a day when the whole Swiss central government was stuck in the snow by the Reuss bridge near Mellingen. The system had a pleasingly antique quality and was, of course, cheap.

Considering that they had been 'collaborators' with Napoleon, the Swiss could think themselves very fortunate in the treatment they received at Vienna. Their delegate, the deft Pictet de Rochemont of Geneva, proved to be fully the equal as a negotiator of the very distinguished members of the Swiss Committee of the Vienna Congress: Freiherr von Stein, Lord Stewart, Capo D'Istria and Stratford Canning. The biggest prize that he came home with was the agreement of the 'puissances à reconnaître et à faire reconnaître la neutralité perpetuelle du corps helvétique'. The external boundaries of Switzerland, under an international guaranty, were not seriously threatened until the 1930s.

If the international status of Switzerland now enjoyed wide acceptance, the domestic scene was unsettled. The attempt to turn the clock back proved unsuccessful and led to a series of revolutions. The oddest of these in my view was the attempt by French-speaking aristocrats in Canton Fribourg to restore German as the official language of the canton because in the period to 1798 it had always been so. In the wake of the revolution of 1830 in Paris, there were revolutions in Thurgau, St Gallen, Zürich, Luzern, Solothurn, Schaffhausen, Aargau and Vaud, all of which brought liberals to power and radical, democratic constitutions to the cantons. In 1831 the Bern aristocrats with becoming elegance surrendered their ancient powers to the massed peasantry of the country districts, and the less becoming patricians of Basel let the countryside split away to form a new canton rather than surrender one jot of theirs. The conservative European powers were not pleased to be so rewarded for their previous kindnesses, and watched with the irritation which can be found in the remarks of Metternich cited in Chapter 1. The new regimes tended to give asylum to outrageous persons such as Louis Napoleon or Mazzini. Above all, they were not pleased when enthusiastic liberals began to instal the free public school and attack the powers of the churches. Liberalism in nineteenth-century Europe was often no more than intense anti-clericalism. In 1841 there was a counter-*coup* in Luzern under the charismatic leadership of a popular churchman, Joseph Leu von Ebersol. In 1844 the liberal constitution was abrogated and the parliament, the Grand Council, against the advice of all sensible men (including Metternich), invited the Jesuit Order to take control of cantonal education. This provocative step happened while in neighbouring Aargau a Protestant, radical party had just gained control of the canton in the face of armed Catholic resistance and had dissolved the monasteries within its boundaries.

Gangs of radical volunteers attacked Luzern in 1841 and 1845. The conservative and Catholic cantons organised concerted resistance and formed the *Sonderbund*, composed of Luzern, Uri, Schwyz, Ob- and Nidwalden, Zug, Fribourg and Valais. The league was secret and had to be so, since it was illegal under the Federal Pact of 1815. The *Bürgermeister* of Luzern, Konstantin Siegwart, opened secret talks with Metternich and plans were worked out to reorganise the boundaries of the cantons and thus to drive a wedge between the radical cantons of eastern and western Switzerland. When the existence of the *Sonderbund* became known, the radical cantons pressed to have it abolished. During 1846 and 1847 more and more cantons fell into the hands of the radicals, and when in the spring of 1847 St Gallen elected a radical government in a hotly disputed election, there was an absolute majority of radical cantons in the federal Diet. The Diet declared the *Sonderbund* dissolved, demanded the expulsion of the Jesuits from all Swiss territory, and the promulgation of a new democratic federal constitution.

Switzerland stood on the brink of civil war and everybody knew it. The *Sonderbund* chose the Protestant aristocrat from Graubünden, Johann Ulrich von Salis-Soglio, as its military commander and appealed for help from abroad. In October 1847, the two sides met for the last time in Bern, the *Vorort* of that year. Passions were high. The issue of the Jesuits alone was almost a cause of war: here is Burckhardt writing in a relatively moderate vein by the standards of the time:

We have never deceived ourselves nor our readers about the true nature of the Order nor its character. For two decades they have insinuated themselves ever more deeply into the affairs of Switzerland. The Jesuits are a curse on all those lands and individuals who fall into their hands.[43]

The issues were equally clear on the other side. Here is Landammann Abyberg addressing the *Landsgemeinde* in Schwyz:

What is demanded of us is nothing less than the sacrifice of our freedom in church and state. We are not supposed to educate our children as we see fit, order our own house as we choose and — listen to this, you brave and solid men — if you try to save your own skins, then they say, you are breaking the law.[44]

The president of the Confederation, and hence presiding officer of the Diet, was Ulrich Ochsenbein, a leader of the Free Corps who had invaded Luzern, and a notorious radical. Under his direction the Diet voted to dissolve the *Sonderbund* by force. The representatives of the *Sonderbund* cantons rose and left the hall in absolute silence. The roll of the drums as the Guard of Honour saluted the departing deputies could be heard inside the hushed chamber.

The federal commander-in-chief, a shrewd, conservative Genevese, General Henri Dufour, saw that only a lightning strike at the heart of the *Sonderbund* could save the Confederation. If the war lasted for any length of time, the Austrians, the Prussians or the French might be tempted to intervene and the bitterness between the two sides would deepen beyond the point of reconciliation. Dufour saw too that the *Sonderbund* would have great geographical difficulties in concentrating its forces and by seizing Fribourg early on 14 November and then Zug, he drove a wedge between the western and central cantons. His next objective was the city of Luzern which he took nine days later. The brilliant twenty-six-day campaign cut the core out of the *Sonderbund* and the outlying cantons surrendered. The Federals had lost about 100 men and the *Sonderbund* rather less. Bismarck dismissed the affair contemptuously as a *Hasenschiessen* (a rabbit shoot).

The Swiss civil war may have been relatively bloodless, but, as in the case of the Peace of Aarau in 1712, the Confederation stood at a turning point. For twenty years unrest, guerrilla warfare, revolution and religious passion had turned Switzerland into one of the most turbulent countries in Europe. Yet within a matter of months a new federal constitution had been worked out which became the basis of modern Swiss government. An era of almost unbroken domestic tranquillity began which lasted until the 1914–18 war. Quick reconciliations are not common in human history. Most civil wars leave legacies of bitterness and recrimination which poison the reunited community for generations. Yet even more remarkable is the stability of the post-war arrangements. A quick glance at the other political settlements of the year 1848 is instructive. The second French republic lasted three years and gave way to a dictatorship and eventually to the Empire of Napoleon III. The united Germany of the Frankfurt Parliament lasted a few months. The Habsburg monarchy changed its constitution several times between 1848 and 1851 without arriving at a permanent equilibrium. There were three Austrian constitutions during 1860–1 alone. Yet the Swiss Confederation or, more accurately, some twenty-three leading figures in it, drafted a document so suited to the conditions that the Switzerland of 1849 and that of 1847 seem to belong to different eras. J. H. Plumb has written about stability:

There is a general folk-belief, derived largely from Burke and the nineteenth century historians, that political stability is of slow coral-like growth: the result of time, circumstances, prudence, experience, wisdom, slowly building up over the centuries. Nothing is, I think, further from the truth. True, there are, of course, deep social causes of which contemporaries are usually unaware making for the *possibility* of political stability. But stability becomes actual through the actions and decisions of men, as does revolution. Political stability, when it comes, often happens to a society quite quickly, as suddenly as water becomes ice.[45]

The Swiss example fits Professor Plumb's hypothesis very neatly. Stability was achieved by political decisions; in this case decisions taken initially by the twenty-three delegates of the Diet who drafted the new federal constitution but ultimately by the entire people. The basic issue, and the one which had caused the war, lay between two different visions of the Swiss Confederation. A Luzern politician put one side well: 'For me Switzerland is only of interest because Canton Luzern — which is my fatherland — lies within it. If Canton Luzern no longer existed as a free sovereign member of the Confederation, I should be as unconcerned about the Confederation as I am about Greater or Lesser Tartary.'[46] This stubborn parochialism expressed in the Swiss phrase *Kantönligeist* ('little cantonal spirit') or the Italian *campanilismo* is the heritage of centuries of narrow, often petty sovereignty. The other side, the protagonists of a 'new' Switzerland, wanted a more centralised, parliamentary, progressive or even radical union.

The conflict between the two views met in the basic dilemma of all federalism: how to divide sovereignty between the centre and the autonomous or independent units which created the union in the first place. One historic answer has been to divide it by assigning parts of the system to each side and so to balance the two structures. In the Swiss case, as in the United States of America, state or cantonal equality expresses itself in an upper house (the US Senate; the Swiss *Ständerat, Conseil des Etats, Consiglio degli Stati*) in which the states or cantons have equal representation regardless of size, while popular sovereignty rests in a parliament based on population (the US House of Representatives; the Swiss *Nationalrat, Conseil national, Consiglio nazionale*). The two views of federalism, the centralist versus the federalist, are then built into the actual structure of representation, but neither is superior to the other. In the constitution of Switzerland of 1848, Article 89 read: 'Federal law and federal decrees require the consent of both houses.' The constitution is silent on what would happen if that consent were refused and, as in most federal systems, there is a grey area of uncertainty where federal and state powers overlap. The solution of the civil war rested in part on this compromise between centralism and particularism, a compromise which in retrospect looks natural and almost inevitable. There were precedents in the successful union of states in the United States constitution, although the auspices there, a successful collective war against Britain, had been more favourable than the aftermath of a civil war in the Swiss case. There was the long historical experience of consultation among cantons on matters of joint concern. During the bitterest religious divisions of the Reformation, neither Catholic nor Protestant cantons had seriously interrupted or denied the rights of their religious opponents to cooperate in running the *Gemeine Herrschaften*. The new constitution merely put into modern form what had always been an established grey area of Swiss practice, an area in which negotiation had to occur. Having said all that, I am still impressed by the willingness of passionately committed, nineteenth-century liberals, who had just won a short, glorious war, to share the victory with what they must have seen as bigoted, backward

Catholic communities. As in the Peace of Aarau the drafters of the new constitution returned to an essential feature of all Swiss life — that the identity and survival of the one is a function of cooperation with the many. While they were at work in the early months of 1848, revolutions broke out all over Europe, and the frightening news of rebellious masses surging through German, French and Austrian towns must have concentrated their attention on the task at hand. If the civil war were not tidied up, much nastier difficulties might arise.

The constitution was ratified by popular vote, and here too the continued existence of an ancient form of popular voting known as the referendum played an important part. Since the old Confederation had no powers of its own, the delegates to it were said to be *ad audiendeum et referendum*, to listen and to report back. In the mountain cantons with *Landsgemeinden*, the sovereign body of citizens had the ultimate right to accept or reject confederal decisions. In Graubünden before the French revolution the government had been of 'the most marvellous complexity', as A. L. Lowell put it. Here were leagues of sovereign communes or districts united in a central diet which, in turn, referred back to the over two hundred 'sovereign villages' almost everything of substance. The village community remained the repository of legal sovereignty.[47] The Valais had a similar 'microscopic' organisation. Consulting the people had traditional roots and, covered with modern representative theory, the drafters of 1848 and the Diet adopted the new constitution as the basic law of the new Swiss Confederation.[48]

In the years between 1848 and 1914 the issues in the domestic politics of Switzerland differed little from those of other central European states. The Vatican Council in 1870 and the *Kulturkampf* in Bismarck's Germany had strong reverberations in Switzerland, where the Catholic church split on the issue of papal infallibility. The new constitution of 1874 contained two articles banning the Jesuits and their establishments from the Confederation. As in Germany, so in Switzerland and Austria, the 1880s saw an unwinding of the church–state issue, marked in the Swiss case by the election in 1891 of the conservative, Josef Zemp of Entlebuch in Luzern, to the Federal Council. The other issues of the period in domestic affairs reflected the rapid industrialisation of the country and the improvements in transport. The special variant of capitalism which began to develop in the eighteenth century continued to evolve. This 'micro-capitalism' with its decentralisation and specialisation brought great prosperity to some areas of the country in ways which did remarkably little to alter the pattern of settlement or the class structures of the countryside. Chapter 5 deals with the Swiss version of the modern economy. Here I only want to point out that economic growth acted to stabilise social relations in Switzerland.

The restored conservative Europe of the 1850s found the new stable Switzerland more to its taste than the old Confederation. Swiss neutrality became entrenched, although not without moments of excitement. There was a point in the autumn and winter of 1856–7, when Switzerland nearly went to war with Prussia. This extraordinary state of affairs arose because the allies of 1814 had restored the King of Prussia as rightful heir to the counts of Neuchâtel. Between 1815 and 1848 the canton had been both a monarchical enclave within a republican Confederation and the personal territory of a foreign prince. The city of Neuchâtel's picturesque medieval streets and the walls of its fairy-tale fortress were not safe from the troubles of the times. When the reactionary royal authorities refused to answer the Confederation's call in 1847 for a levy of troops to fight the *Sonderbund*, republican sympathisers began to plot the overthrow of the Hohenzollerns. 1848 was a good year for such schemes and, a week after the French revolution had broken out, the republicans seized power in a quick *coup* on 1 March 1848. In the aftermath of the revolutions of 1848 and as part of the settlement of the Schleswig–Holstein succession question (which Palmerston claimed later that only three men had ever understood; two were now dead, and he had forgotten) the King of Prussia was restored as 'Prince of Neuchâtel'. The Swiss refused to accept the London Protocol of 1852 and went on recognising the republican constitution of 1848. Count Frédéric Pourtalès led a royalist *coup* on 2 September 1856, and for two glorious days, while the local bourgeoisie recovered from the shock, the flag of the *ancien régime* fluttered from the ramparts of the castle. The counter-*coup* of 4 September rapidly put an end to the restoration, and a hundred or so of the royalists were taken prisoner. When the Swiss refused to release the aristocratic revolutionaries, Frederick William IV of Prussia, furious at this 'slap in the face for all the monarchs of Europe', mobilised his army. The Swiss responded with enthusiasm. Henri Dufour was elected 'general' (very Swiss is the fact that the commander-in-chief in war-time, *the* 'general', is elected by the *Bundesversammlung*, that is the two houses of parliament meeting in joint session) and raised a force of 30,000 to defend the Fatherland. Patriotic enthusiasm reached as far as the Swiss guard in the Vatican. The Prussian envoy reported to Frederick William IV that the Vatican authorities had intercepted one of 'those curious pieces, edited in three languages, which breathe the spirit of 1848 in their snorting style. William Tell and the battles of Sempach and Morat are naturally represented in it.'[49] Napoleon III intervened at this point to prevent trouble on his frontiers and after protracted negotiations the Swiss agreed to release the prisoners, and Frederick William IV declared himself satisfied by the agreement that he had the right in perpetuity to style himself 'Prince of Neuchâtel'.

The Neuchâtel crisis was the last of the old struggles between Swiss and foreign authority. The eviction of Frederick William IV from his historic rights as hereditary prince of a Swiss canton ended a process which had begun in the early Middle Ages with the Habsburgs. It gave to modern Switzerland its final territorial integrity. Swiss borders were permanently engraved on the map of Europe, but if territorial integrity was now secure, national identity faced serious challenges. 1848 was a year of national as well as liberal ferment. For conservatives Switzerland had become too radical; for radicals it had become contemptible and conservative. The Milanese revolutionary leader, Carlo Cattaneo, wrote furiously to the Ticinese newspaper *il Repubblicano* in June 1849 suggesting a new note to be added to the Swiss dictionary of national biography: 'They thought they were carrying on as Tells and Winkelrieds by chasing Mazzini and Garibaldi from Swiss territory; for the identity of the latter, cf. the history of France, anno domini 1849.'[50] Nationalism threatened Swiss stability overtly by compromising Switzerland's status as an internationally recognised, neutral state. From 1848 to 1945 successive Swiss governments had to balance the claims of free speech and free press against the demands of powerful nations across the frontiers. They had to defend the traditional practice of asylum granted to fighters for liberty against massive threats from neighbouring states if 'criminals' were not delivered up to rightful authority. But the real threat of nationalism was covert and insidious. The doctrines of race, of nationality, of social darwinism, of biologistic popular science eroded the historical category 'Swiss' by elevating the 'organic' ideas of nation, *Volk* and blood. To be Swiss was by definition to assert a political, historically determined notion of citizenship against the seductive, 'modern', 'scientific' conceptions of national self-determination. It was also to choose dull reality and not romance. The fading image of William Tell could not compare with the heroic reality of Garibaldi and his thousand red-shirted young poets, scientists, artists and professional men. Even Cavour with some distaste had to admit that the unification of Italy was being widely regarded as 'the most poetic fact of the century'.[51] The brilliant revival of French culture and art under the Third Republic and the achievements of the new German Empire with its scientific prowess, its immense military prestige, its flourishing economy, its advanced social welfare systems (Germany introduced the first compulsory insurance schemes against accident, old age and sickness in the 1880s) and its cultural landmarks, exerted a powerful attraction in advanced circles in both French- and German-speaking Switzerland.

Intelligent Swiss Germans warmed themselves vicariously in the glow from the Reich. German triumphs were their triumphs, German literature and language theirs too. In French Switzerland the movement called *helvétisme* attracted the interest of young Swiss intellectuals like Gonzague de Reynold, Robert de Traz and J.-B. Bouvier. They drew inspiration from the elitist ideas of the Frenchmen Maurras and Barrès. As one critic saw it at the time,

If one takes the trouble to dissect a little bit of this *helvétisme*, one realises quickly that it is simply vulgar plagiarism, covered in Swiss sauces, of the ideas of *L'Action française*. We find there, in fact, the same haughty disdain for democracy and parliamentary government, the same aspirations to become a separate, privileged caste, destined to govern.[52]

Foreign cultural influences spread. That there was no 'Swiss' culture to resist it reflected the extreme particularism of Swiss life. The poet Carl Spitteler suffered from it:

The direct literary commerce from city to city and canton to canton is virtually nil . . . Under such circumstances the main stream of literary life flows from one of these small places into the far distance, here toward Germany and there toward France and only then does it find its way back to the other Swiss towns.[53]

What was Swiss anyway? In the overheated, fetid climate of extreme nationalism, the crablike defensiveness of Swiss authorities toward foreign influences seemed absurd. The Swiss Italian philologist Carlo Salvioni mocked them in 1914: 'Every schoolboy becomes used to saying "we" for the Helvetiae but not Julius Caesar, to call "his" writers whose language he cannot understand, to claim Rousseau, Bodmer and Keller but to consider as foreign Dante and Manzoni.'[54] Yet if the cultural boundaries disappeared completely, the language groups would be sucked into the larger cultural worlds of their neighbours, and Swiss identity would disappear. The intoxicating ideas of race and nationality were sliding the Confederation toward a crisis as real (if less apparent) as the religious divisions had been.

The central institutions of the state, especially the higher commands of the army, had been thoroughly Prussianised. The chief of the General Staff, Colonel-Corps Commander Theophil Sprecher von Bernegg, had agreed with the German General Staff in 1910 that his staff would provide the Germans with secret military information. Many Swiss officers, blinded by their Prussian sympathies, expected gross violations of their neutrality to come from the French side only. When the war broke out, the exchange of intelligence began, as the German minister in Bern reported on 29 September 1914:

From the very first day since the outbreak of war Switzerland has discreetly placed at our disposal her entire secret military intelligence service. They give us information about intercepted cables, which might be useful and important news from their overseas representatives.[55]

For leading German Swiss, it was obvious which side to support, as the head of the Military Department of Canton Bern, Karl Scheurer, wrote in his diary in August 1914: 'On general cultural grounds as well as political I believe that a German victory is desirable.'[56] A deep fissure, which came to be known as the trench or the *Graben*, opened between French and German Switzerland. Scheurer noticed how meetings of the federal parliament were poisoned by the division. The long period of general mobilisation began to take its toll. To maintain an army of 250,000 in varying degrees of readiness out of a total population of about 3 million required immense effort. The economic situation was parlous; surrounded by belligerents, Switzerland had to depend on the goodwill of neighbouring countries. Writing in his diary on 15 June 1915 Scheurer expressed his despair:

Our situation is getting worse. Externally things are not too bad, and even the entry of Italy does not seem to threaten us too much. At home, on the other hand, things are nasty. The conflict between German and French gets worse rather than better as does the struggle between town and country over food prices.[57]

As the war dragged on, relations between French and German Switzerland became entangled with the issue of neutrality. The General Ulrich Wille came under increasing criticism for his pro-German bias, and when two of his staff officers were caught and tried for passing secrets to the Germans and Austrians, the demand for his resignation grew. The most spectacular violation of neutrality, however, occurred at the very top of the political hierarchy. Federal Councillor Arthur Hoffmann, head of the Political Department (the Swiss foreign office), had to resign in 1917, a very rare event in Swiss politics, when his secret attempt to bring about a separate peace between Germany and the new revolutionary regime in Russia became known. He had used the Swiss socialist Robert Grimm, who knew all the leading Bolshevik and Menshevik leaders, to act as his agent in the promotion of a peace without annexations. Hoffmann had to submit to a formal inquiry during which he defended himself by arguing that 'it was definitely in the interests of Switzerland that peace be concluded before either France or Germany had been definitively beaten'.[58] This proposition was based on a reading of Swiss history which had a lot to be said for it. Swiss neutrality had always been safest when Europe was in an international equilibrium and most threatened when one European great power achieved a position of hegemony. This was clearly true during the Napoleonic era and was to be demonstrated again under Hitler in the Second World War. Hoffmann was not wrong about ends but about means. Swiss neutrality forbids the conduct of an active foreign policy of any sort. By trying to serve Swiss neutrality, Hoffmann had dangerously compromised it. The line between what a Swiss foreign minister may or may not do is unusually delicate.

A different crisis began to erupt during 1918. During the war the conditions of Swiss working men deteriorated. Long, poorly paid periods of military service left many of them destitute at the very moment that the peasants seemed to be squeezing the last centime out of the town dweller. The traditional Swiss custom of asylum had opened the doors to a distinguished collection of dangerous men, including Lenin, Trotsky, Zinoviev, Axelrod and Martov among the leading Russian revolutionaries as well as exiles from Germany and France. Between 5 and 8 September 1915 at Zimmerwald in Canton Bern, and from 20 to 24 April 1916 at Kiental, two conferences were held which made Switzerland the revolutionary capital of the world. The influence of these powerful presences on Swiss socialists was great. Swiss social democracy began to develop an extreme revolutionary wing.

The progress of the war made a revolutionary socialist interpretation of events very plausible. Lenin believed that the First World War represented a final stage, a kind of Armageddon of capitalism. What else could account for the prolonged slaughter? The bourgeois governments of all European societies were financing the war at the expense of the poor, and Switzerland was no exception. Between 1914 and 1918, the cost of living index had gone up from 100 to 229, while mobilisation and the resulting short-time working had reduced wages by an average of 6%.[59] The Swiss government had, in addition, reneged on a long-standing promise to permit a referendum on proportional representation. The Socialist Party of Switzerland knew well what the reasons were. In the elections of 1914 based on a single member and majority vote system, the ruling Radical Party, the party of bourgeois liberalism and capitalism, had 111 of the 189 seats, while the Socialists had 19. For every 34,000 votes in the elections of 1908 the Radicals had picked up eight seats in the federal parliament, while the Socialists required the same number to win two. In fact, when proportional representation finally began in 1919 in national elections, the Socialist Party jumped from 19 to 41 and the Radicals fell to 60.[60] Hence the sense of being disenfranchised added to the grievances of daily life and the demands of ideology.

The leaders of the radical wing of the Swiss Socialist Party and trade union movement began to look to the general strike as the weapon to use. The notion of the political mass strike had a distinguished, if untested, pedigree in socialist theory and seemed to offer a compromise between the armed seizure of power, Bolshevik style, and ordinary 'reformist' political tactics. Robert Grimm, the most influential left-wing socialist, had seen the Russian Revolution at first hand on his secret mission for Federal Councillor Hoffmann and had worked closely with Lenin earlier in the war. After the Bolshevik seizure of power, he decided to act. He first formed an action committee of party and union leaders, the Olten Action Committee, which met for the first time in February 1918. It served as the revolutionary equivalent of the federal executive during the preparation and conduct of the General Strike of 1918.

Swiss realities and revolutionary illusions met head-on during that year. Among the realities were the characteristics of industrial history in Switzerland which I shall discuss in Chapter 5. The growth of industry had mainly taken the form of small-scale, high quality production (watches and precision machinery in the Jura and the textile industry of central and eastern Switzerland). There were no natural resources, but there was water power. The free, relatively well educated population and highly developed mercantile communities were an additional strength of the Swiss economy. As a result, industry fanned out in small producing units along the rushing streams. 'White coal' left none of the filthy marks of black coal on the environment so the Swiss escaped the most degrading stages of the industrial revolution. Textile units flourished in the deepest rural peace. The workers were part-timers who never lost contact with the soil, the harvest and the peasant communalism of their village. A self-conscious working class emerged slowly where it appeared at all. Cities developed less violently and slums less gruesomely than in Britain or Germany. In 1910, of the total Swiss population of 3,750,000 only 25% lived in towns of over 10,000. England and Wales by comparison had reached that level of urbanisation by the late 1840s. Moreover the union movement was small compared to other advanced countries. In 1914 the nineteen unions in the *Schweizerischer Gewerkschaftsbund* counted 65,177 members, and even today the SGB can only claim 445,235 members out of a total of 2,934,000 employed persons. The total number of union members in Switzerland (there are other unions not part of the SGB), equals 28.4% of all employed persons. The equivalent figure for the UK is 48%.

The peasantry remained a powerful economic and political force in Swiss life. The bottom-heavy features of Swiss society and politics, the existence of an upper parliamentary chamber based on cantons rather than population, and a certain amount of gerrymandering assured the peasantry a disproportionate role in politics. Ernst Laur, the 'king of the peasants', was a leader who knew how to exploit it. Laur used his close friendship with the director of the Economic Department, the powerful Federal Councillor Schulthess, to solve many a small problem. While the war accelerated industrialisation and union membership tripled, it also gave the peasants unusual economic leverage. Cut off from the outside world, Switzerland might starve unless the peasantry cooperated. Many socialist leaders such as Otto Lang saw these realities and in the Central Committee of the Socialist Party he pleaded against the call for a general strike: 'Look at the facts. We have worked ourselves into deep hostility to the peasants. Look at our import and export figures, our 8000 factories and 25 cantons. No Russian illusions can help that . . . Radicalism is no temperature measure of the rightness of a principle.'[61] In spite of such warnings the General Strike went ahead in November 1918 and for three days the country was paralysed. The Federal Council, having first negotiated in a manner not unknown today to university administrators, hesitated and then turned hard. The army was called out. By November troops had begun to take controlling positions in Bern and Zürich, the main centres of radicalism. By the 14th the army controlled the country and had even begun to make use of the railway rolling stock. The strike collapsed. The Olten Action Committee capitulated and ordered a general return to work.

The General Strike of 1918 was no joke. A little more heat here, a little more intransigence there, and a bloody civil war would have occurred. Again the Swiss managed to escape the worst. The wounds healed, not so quickly as in the case of 1848, but in good time. The citizenry showed its remarkable political canniness by voting for the referendum on proportional representation by $19\frac{1}{2}$ to $2\frac{1}{2}$ cantons and by 198,550 to 149,035, even though they were, in effect, rewarding the Socialists for having brought the country to the edge of civil war. The Federal Council for its part, having finally settled on a firm line, met the Olten Action Committee face-to-face for concrete negotiations. The fact that Grimm and eight other Olten Committee members were also parliamentarians helped to save face on both sides, but the Federal Council deserves credit for recognising the need. The civil prosecutor and army leaders were shrewd enough not to press home their triumph. General Wille forbade any sort of parading in Zürich or Bern to celebrate the collapse of the strike, and the treatment of the accused at the trial of the members of the Action Committee was matter-of-fact and sensible. As the right to strike existed, the accused were only charged with having undermined military and civil authority by urging soldiers and civil servants to refuse to obey. The penalties inflicted on the four found guilty were as near the minimum as the court could give: six months imprisonment and an eighth of the cost in three cases and four weeks plus 50 francs for another.

In the subsequent years both sides gradually moved toward a reconciliation. The Federal Council took up many of the Olten Committee's demands and by 1 January 1920 had introduced the forty-eight hour week as law. In 1919 work began on the extension of the social security system and the introduction of laws on worker participation, still an issue today in Swiss industrial life. The trade union and socialist movements gradually abandoned class war and intransigence, not least because of the split between the communist and socialist parties which took place everywhere in the Western world in these years. The participants in the Olten Action Committee returned to public life and many, such as Grimm, served for years in parliament.

Two further developments hastened the move from class war to reformism: the impact of the depression and the rise of fascism. For reasons which I shall discuss in Chapter 5, the depression hit the specialised Swiss manufacturing industries (watches and embroidered textiles) with unusual severity. The collapse of whole industries and regions occurred. One St Gallen manufacturer offered to sell his entire textile company for one franc to anyone who could keep his employees in work for one year. There were no takers. The capitulation of the marxist parties before triumphant fascism in Italy in the 1920s and Germany after 1933 had a sobering effect on the Swiss left. It became clear that the Swiss proletariat had a homeland after all, one very much worth fighting for. The transition was aided by the remarkable openness of Swiss democracy, which enabled both Swiss socialism and communism to find expression in the prevailing order, no matter how bloodthirsty their rhetoric. Between 1925 and 1939 there was always at least one Communist representing Basel-Stadt in the national parliament. Zürich's Communists were represented in the 1920s and 1930s on local, cantonal and national level. Walther Bringolf led a Popular Front government in Schaffhausen as an ex-Communist and Léon Nicole led one in Geneva, gaining over 40% of the votes in the 1935 elections. By 1935 with fifty seats the Socialist Party was the largest party in the *Nationalrat*. In 1943 the Radicals gave up one of their 'reserved' seats on the Federal Council to the Socialists. It was a considerable sacrifice. For the first time in the 100 years of the modern federation the Radicals did not have an absolute majority of the seven seats on the Federal Council. Here too one of those curiously Swiss arrangements had been made by which those with power surrender it not always cheerfully, but usually smoothly, to those who might otherwise claim it by force.

In 1937 Konrad Ilg, president of the Swiss Metalworkers and Watchmakers Union, signed an agreement with Ernst Dübi, the president of the Federation of Metal and Machine Industry Employers, which effectively ruled out the strike as a weapon of collective bargaining. The so-called *Arbeitsfrieden* of 1937 is an astonishing achievement. It was initially accepted for two years but has been renewed at five-year intervals ever since. Other industries followed the engineering and metalworking branches and have made their own agreements. In 1956 the *Nationalrat* passed a law making such agreements 'generally binding' (*allgemeinverbindlich*) across an entire industry whenever the parties who have signed the agreement constitute more than half of the employers and employees of a given branch (Article 2, Section 3). Hence a labour peace treaty can be made to extend to firms and workers not party to the original agreement. Built into the new law is the principle of arbitration from without (Article 6) in the case of disagreement, but in the new law as in the original 'Pact' the basic principle is of self-regulation within an industry by its own members. The employers and unions accepted each other's claims to recognition 'in loyalty and good faith' and shortly thereafter the strike virtually disappeared from the Swiss industrial scene.

It is tempting to see in this uniquely Swiss institution another of those special turning points which I have underlined so heavily. The parallel with, say, 1481 or the Peace of Aarau is real. If 1481 marked the acceptance of a political compromise between urban and rural states, 1712 peace between the confessions, then 19 July 1937 can be called 'peace between the classes'. Giuseppe Motta, perhaps the most distinguished of the inter-war members of the Federal Council, called it just that, 'the *Stanser Verkommnis* of the machine industry', an obvious play on the intervention of Brother Klaus between the feuding cantons in 1481. Konrad Ilg, the union boss who signed for the workers, had, after all, been an active figure in the Olten Action Committee, and remained both a militant trade unionist and committed socialist. He saw perfectly well that the *Arbeitsfrieden* supported the *status quo* and put off the advent of socialism. Ernst Dübi for the employers had to surrender the entire arsenal of lockout, 'black leg' labour, non-recognition and so on, which a very conservative group of employers were loath to drop. Yet they did it, and the example spread. Characteristically all such agreements follow the original model and have a prologue. The law now requires (Article 357 OR) that when such agreements are 'unlimited', a prologue is obligatory. The prologue has the features of a state treaty and very much reflects the traditional Swiss desire to keep the control of internal affairs in the hands of those inside. Sometimes, as in the original case, caution money must be laid down by both parties as a pledge of good behaviour. Is it far-fetched to see this treaty of arbitration in the same context as the Treaty of Alliance of 1291 or the other compromises of Swiss history?

It was also helpful, and very characteristic of Swiss politics, that Konrad Ilg not only led the Swiss Metalworkers but was also a member of the Bern City Council, of the cantonal parliament, the *Grosser Rat*, and a socialist deputy in the federal parliament. The present head of the Swiss Trade Union Federation and president of the Swiss Building and Wood Workers Union, Signor Ezio Canonica, represents a Zürich constituency as a socialist in the national parliament. The overlapping of political, economic and social functions in modern Switzerland makes what has been called 'bargaining democracy' much easier. There are circles within and across circles, and many points of contact exist on many levels. As Professor Gruner remarked, 'In Switzerland one is always in a minority by comparison with somebody.'

The world scene in the 1930s undoubtedly fostered the tendency to reach across the class lines. By 1933 Switzerland saw powerful, anti-democratic states on its northern and southern frontiers. The unusual experiment of membership in the League of Nations had been disappointing and merely increased friction with Fascist Italy and Nazi Germany. In 1934, Mussolini, addressing factory workers in Milan, made threatening noises about the *Italianità* of Canton Ticino. An active Nazi network had begun to work in Switzerland, and a native Swiss 'National Front' movement was stirring. Its membership was small but Nazi Germany knew how to use such tiny cells of sympathisers as pretexts for invading peaceful small countries. Relations with the Soviet Union were dreadful. Motta, a deeply conservative Catholic politician, wielded his prestige at the League of Nations to delay Soviet membership and personally prevented any improvement in relations between Bern and Moscow. After Munich and especially after the Nazi invasion of Czechoslovakia in March 1939, the Swiss realised that they were diplomatically isolated, and, when war broke out in September, they were in fact physically isolated from the outside world.

War meant mobilisation of the entire Swiss army, as it had in 1914. On 30 August 1939, Colonel Henri Guisan was elected general by 202 of the 229 votes of upper and lower houses of the parliament. Guisan made a marked contrast to the Prussian ponderousness of General Wille, the general during the First World War. Guisan, a Vaudois, had the right democratic image. Edgar Bonjour describes him approvingly as an 'affable, open, hearty, natural man from the countryside'.[62] His superior at the Military Department, Rudolf Minger, represented the Peasants Party in the Federal Council and rural doggedness in his person. These men embodied the values which the Swiss demanded and still expect of their politicians. The ideal is simplicity of manner and a direct humanity of heart. In the darkest days of early 1940, Giuseppe Motta died after more than twenty years as a Federal Councillor. The eulogy read over Radio della Svizzera italiana sums up perfectly the portrait of the ideal Swiss statesman:

He was a man of exemplary simplicity. For nearly thirty years the citizens of Bern saw him leave for his office on foot, wait for the bus to go home for lunch and back to the office, and then return home on foot in the evening after a day of work guiding the destiny of our country . . . Patiently, serenely, cordially, he replied to everyone; he answered, he wrote letters, sometimes only a single line but always in his own hand, sometimes only a single word added to an official letter above his signature but in his own hand. It was enough. People said, 'he answered me, he remembered me, he understood me'.[63]

The tone may be a little cloying for our tastes, but against the background of Hitler's 'new order' the democratic virtues of a Minger or a Motta were more precious than they seem today.

The country mobilised rapidly. With pride Guisan reported to the Federal Council on 7 September: 'On Sunday, 3 September, 1939, when at 12.10 Central European time, Great Britain declared war on Germany, our entire army had been in its operational positions for 10 minutes.'[64] The American journalist William Shirer, travelling through Switzerland in October 1939, was very impressed:

Swiss train full of soldiers. The country has one tenth of its population under arms; more than any other country in the world. It's not their war. But they're ready to fight to defend their way of life. I asked a fat businessman in my compartment whether he wouldn't prefer peace at any price (business is ruined in a Switzerland completely surrounded by belligerents and with every able-bodied man in the army) so that he could make money again. 'Not the kind of peace that Hitler offers', he said. 'Or the kind of peace we've been having the last five years.'[65]

It would be pleasing to be able to say that this Churchillian doggedness was universal and permanent. Certainly the first months of the war showed the Swiss united and resolute, more so than at any time in the twentieth century, but conditions in 1940 began to erode that cohesion.

On 9 April 1940 German armies invaded Denmark and Norway and on 10 May they marched into Holland, Belgium and Luxemburg. By 15 May the Dutch had capitulated and by 28 May the Belgians. General mobilisation was again declared in Switzerland; the entire army manned the frontiers. By the end of May, the defeat of France was certain and on 14 June 1940 a German army entered Paris. By this time no British troops were left on the continent of Europe and Hitler stood where only Napoleon once had, but more powerful and threatening.

The conduct of foreign policy lay in the hands of Federal Councillor Marcel Pilet-Golaz, a French Swiss who lacked the democratic virtues, as Professor Bonjour describes him: 'With his overly sharp expressions, his snobbish elegance and glittering personality, he got nowhere with the ordinary citizen. His often thoughtless jokes were taken too heavily and too seriously . . .'[66] It is not clear which of these grave defects most harmed Pilet. I suspect that making jokes may have been the worst of his sins; the Swiss demand high seriousness of their leaders. In any case, he lacked the common touch and the collegial habits of a good Swiss politician. On 25 June 1940, after a brief consultation with some of the other members of the Federal Council, he made a famous radio speech in which he announced partial demobilisation and in extremely obscure phrases warned the Swiss that they must be prepared to play a part in a Europe 'très different de l'ancien ... et qui se fondera sur d'autres bases'. Ominous references to 'redressement', to 'décisions majeures' and to the breaking of 'd'habitudes anciennes' dotted the misty prose. One such habit was shooting down German planes violating Swiss air space. Swiss fighter pilots had begun to run up a respectable score on that front, and Pilet-Golaz wanted them to stop. He knew, which the public did not, that Germans had uncovered compromising documents in French headquarters at la Charité-sur-Loire. The German advance had been so spectacular that French intelligence officers had not had time to destroy their papers, among which were the terms of a secret agreement on the exchange of military information between the Swiss and French intelligence staffs. The Nazi regime had used much flimsier pretexts than that in their other aggressions.

Pilet's speech had a mixed reception. Several leading parliamentarians noted with dismay that he had not said a word about democracy. His choice of words had a sinister similarity to the language of the new Vichy regime in France. A group of young army officers was so alarmed that they began to make preparations for a possible putsch if the Federal Council showed any further signs of weakness. The commander-in-chief then took a dramatic step, one so risky that only a grave crisis could have justified it. On the morning of 25 July 1940 the entire senior officer corps, over five hundred men, boarded a steamer in Luzern to cross the lake to the famous meadow of Rütli, the birth-place of the Confederation. General Guisan described it:

Toward noon of a very fine day I had nearly all my senior officers before me. On the Rütli meadow, where the flag of the Uri Battalion 87 fluttered, the officers formed a large semi-circle looking out over the lake. The Army corps commanders in the first row, behind them in rows the divisional commanders, the brigadiers, regimental officers, battalion and section chiefs.[67]

The general took a few notes from his pocket and spoke, in German, for half an hour. According to the official communiqué the general issued an order of the day: 'The will to resist any attack from without and all dangers on the home front, such as sloth or defeatism; Faith in the value of resistance.' It was a grand and significant moment in Swiss history. Guisan saw that the symbolic renewal of the Rütli Oath a mere month after the questionable radio talk of Pilet would be a pledge of good faith. The risk in putting the entire army command in one lake steamer was the token of his seriousness. The staging was perfect, and the gesture worked. The radical young officers were calmed. Guisan was then able to make precisely the same compromises, including extremely questionable dealings with SS General Walter Schellenberg, that Pilet knew had to be accepted.

Guisan also altered the defensive posture of the Swiss army. He saw that the German victory in France had created an extraordinary situation. From Geneva to Sargans there was one enemy who might attack at any point. The army's mobilisation, hitherto based on the defence of the frontier against any aggressor, could hardly be sustained against Hitler's Germany. In July 1940 the army was withdrawn from the frontiers and took up positions in the massive chain of the Alps. By the spring of 1941 all the field divisions had taken up Alpine positions, in some cases as in that of Division 4 on the Pilatus mountain near Luzern, in almost impassable terrain. Over 900 million francs were spent on fortifications, and the Swiss army settled into its *réduit*. It was an uncomfortable nest for modern officers schooled in the tactics of Guderian and Rommel, but it had, as had the Rütli Order of the Day, the highest possible symbolic significance. General Guisan declared openly by this strategy that the Swiss army would fight to the end. It would watch Zürich, Basel, Bern, Lausanne, Geneva, Biel, the entire lowlands, fall to the Germans but it would not surrender. As the chief of the General Staff, Jakob Huber, put it in reply to attacks on the idea of the *réduit national*: 'In our situation there can only be one aim, to resist as long as possible . . . We want to go down fighting, leaving the aggressor only a totally devastated country without material or personal resources of any kind.'[68]

There is now a good deal of evidence to support the view that the Germans seriously considered dealing with Switzerland, once and for all, in the summer of 1940. The chief of the German General Staff, Franz Halder, said: 'I was constantly hearing of outbursts of Hitler's fury against Switzerland, which, given his mentality, might have led at any minute to military activities for the army.' 'Operation Tannenbaum', the German code name for the invasion of Switzerland, was prepared for just the sort of eventuality that Halder feared.[69] We shall never know how far Hitler was deterred by the spectacle of hardy mountaineers defending their crags and how much dissuaded by other considerations. In the German Foreign Office, Secretary von Weizsäcker thought Switzerland 'an indigestible lump' and not worth swallowing. After all neutral (on the whole, cooperative) Switzerland had its uses in Hitler's plans. It is probable that the obvious determination of the Swiss to defend the Alpine passes, even at the sacrifice of the lowlands, had some effect, but, even if it did not, it is certainly no hyperbole to call 1940—5 one of Switzerland's 'finest hours'.

The trouble with 'finest hours' is that less fine ones follow them. The heroic years in the *réduit national* not only left a legacy of patriotic rhetoric (N.B.: the Swiss did not actually win the war; they just stayed out of it) but also some unfortunate illusions about the real degree of unity. The cohesiveness of the years between the 1930s and the late 1950s had been artificial. For roughly thirty years, international fascism and the ensuing cold war threatened the Confederation externally. As in the years 1618 to 1648, an entire Swiss generation had been hermetically sealed off from the general trends of European development, and in both post-war periods, the sudden reappearance of strife, rapid change and innovation was a shock. The emergence from the *réduit national* has not been easy. The generation who went through the annealing of 'active service' finds it hard to accept dissent, student unrest, Jura separatism, criticism of the army and all the other manifestations of what is now in many ways an entirely normal western European society. In some quarters, it is shameful even to discuss the future of the army; to question the army is to question Swiss honour. If the young 'won't go', it must mean that they no longer think Switzerland worth defending.[70]

Another important legacy of the war years was the special position of the Swiss economy, which I shall discuss more fully in Chapter 5. In a Europe covered in rubble, the Swiss offered an island of fiscal stability and industrial capacity. For nearly twenty years, artificial boom followed artificial boom. Hundreds of small and not wildly efficient firms made money. Rationalisation was put off as hordes of foreign workers flooded the labour market. Huge reserves of capital, much of it foreign, stood behind the economic activity. This too came to seem normal, inevitable, right. The Swiss government looked with benevolent disinterest on the early stirrings of European unity. It postponed its infrastructure investments and public works for the rainy day which it gloomily expected to occur at any moment. The late 1960s brought a rude awakening. Growth had outstripped the powers of federal, cantonal or communal government. The precious Swiss environment was threatened in all sorts of ways: pollution, the sale of land to foreigners, the destruction of unspoilt nature for roads, hotels, ski lifts or army manoeuvres.

A final consequence of the *réduit* era is that, as so often in the past, Switzerland managed to carry into a new age the structures and habits of the old. Everywhere else in continental Europe, the Nazi occupation, the disruption of battle and the flow of refugees provoked vast up-heavals. The old order was frequently swept away or much transformed. In Switzerland things stayed put. The cramped defensive posture of the *réduit* made change very difficult.

During the 1950s Switzerland began to be 'quaint'. There, in comfort, and for a fee, the modern German or Italian could enjoy a bit of the 'old' Europe, with its pretty dresses and antique folkways. Swiss habits changed slowly. The generation who had known privation in the 1930s and isolation in the 1940s saved their new money, and went on living as they had before. During the 1960s spending and consumption habits changed sharply. Not only had a younger generation reached the age at which pop culture and its tastes made an impact on spending habits, but the older groups began to consume as well. Washing machines appeared in peasant houses which had always washed by hand, and in the evening the family gathered before the television, which by the 1970s had been exchanged for a colour set. The once frugal govern-ments at federal, cantonal and local level also began to spend lavishly. Switzerland had a backlog of autobahns, old age and pension systems, schools, new jet fighters, sewage plants and atomic power generating equipment, which suddenly seemed urgently necessary. Total spending by all three levels of Swiss government tripled in money terms between 1959 and the middle of the 1970s.

Changes of every kind seemed to cascade onto the country like one of its disastrous spring avalanches, and as the unity and sim-plicities of the *réduit* era receded into the distance, many Swiss grew very nervous. Reactionary movements to preserve the Fatherland sprang up. The political peace was broken by protest from right and left, and the 'Helvetic *malaise*' spread.

The return to the mainstream of European development has strained the traditional Swiss political machinery. It is possible that the histori-cal inheritance of Switzerland has finally been spent. The next three chapters will attempt to assess the cohesive elements in the political, linguistic and economic structures of past and present Switzerland. In Chapter 6, I take up the question of the survival of a distinctive Swiss identity under the pressures of the 1970s. It is one thing to show why there was a Switzerland in the past, a very different one to answer 'Why Switzerland?' now.

3. Politics

The Swiss are justly famous for their political institutions and practices: the ancient assembly of free citizens in the *Landsgemeinde*, the elaborate devices for direct participation by the citizen in the process of decision through referenda and initiatives, the variety and precision of the federal system, the refinements of voting practice and proportional representation, the thriving local and cantonal governments, the evolution of the uniquely Swiss collective executive bodies on local, cantonal and federal level, the overlapping office-holding which enables a man to be simultaneously an elected officer of his township, canton and federal parliaments, the instrumental attitude to constitutions which enables easy revision and extension to what elsewhere would be legislative activity, the astonishing stability of Swiss voting habits which have held the four main parties in very nearly perfect equilibrium since 1919 and the exclusion, until recently, of women from politics. The simple enumeration of Switzerland's 'peculiar institutions' adds up to an impressive statement of the uniqueness of Switzerland in the western European context. Other societies have some but none has all these channels of direct and semi-direct democracy. The net of politics seems to stretch farther in Switzerland than elsewhere. Activities thought of as technical or administrative in other countries tend to be made elective and political in Switzerland. The ground rules of politics, that unspoken agreement about what is or is not 'done', and the unwritten provisions of Swiss constitutionalism make up a further middle area of values and habits which profoundly affect the workings of the machinery. For example, the Swiss prefer to see the executive at federal, cantonal and local level vested in a committee rather than a president and that committee must be elected. Yet candidates are rarely defeated and thrown from office; it is simply not 'done'.

Describing how all these things work is hard enough, and most of this chapter will do little else. Understanding their significance is much more difficult. How do all these elaborate bits and pieces of machinery fit the economic, social, linguistic, historical and legal aspects of Swiss life? The 'national character' is frequently deployed to help in this difficulty. The Swiss are famous for their *Feinmechanik* and they themselves often mock their own perfectionism, so it is not too far-fetched to compare the delicate machinery of a watch with the intricacies of Swiss proportional representation. In a general, very general, sense, these comparisons are legitimate. A society in which the work ethos is so highly developed and in which precision is valued will certainly seek the same attributes in politics. But why have these attitudes and values established themselves across linguistic and historical boundaries? Why is a Swiss French as likely to rise at dawn as a Swiss German or Swiss Italian? 'National character' ends up in circularity: the Swiss behave like Swiss because they are Swiss. Another objection is that looking at the machinery of politics distracts one from the 'real' sources of power, which are economic. It is certainly true that today tiny cantonal sovereignties are dwarfed by the international corporations whose headquarters they are. Giant firms have turnover figures many times larger than cantonal or even federal budgets, and the three biggest banks have balance sheets whose collective totals almost add up to the amount of the Swiss gross national product. The disparity between corporate and conventional political power is wider in Switzerland than in any other European country, but this does not make the political machinery and its functioning irrelevant. Big Swiss firms depend on the government to manage currency, to pass laws, to administer taxes and to cope with social conflict as do any other groups in society. Yes, corporate enterprise is very powerful in Switzerland, no doubt unduly so, but what makes Swiss companies behave in certain ways and not others is a function of the characteristics of political life. It is an illusion to suppose that political structures and institutions are simply passive filters through which 'real' forces pass unaltered. They affect events, making some outcomes possible and others not. Jeremy Thorpe's Liberals achieved a higher percentage of the vote in February 1974 than Adolf Hitler's Nazis achieved in their 'sensational' breakthrough in September 1930, but the differences between the single member constituency system and pure proportional representation reduced in one case, and magnified in the other, the 'underlying' realities. The machinery of politics acts on and is in turn acted upon by the other elements in a given community and, as the marxist historian, Perry Anderson, emphasises, 'history from below' is only part of the story:

struggle between classes is ultimately resolved at the *political* — not at the economic or cultural — level of society. In other words, it is the construction and destruction of states which seal the basic shifts in the relations of production, so long as classes subsist. A 'history from above' — of the intricate machinery of class domination — is thus no less essential than a 'history from below'.[1]

One does not have to be a marxist to accept Mr Anderson's good advice. The difficulty, as Chesterton said of Christianity, is not that it has been tried and found wanting but that it has been found hard and not tried. It is much easier to preach the unity of political and other 'factors' than to apply it in the midst of the real world. I am sure that links of every sort ought to be established between each piece of political apparatus discussed in this chapter and the historical, legal, economic, social, cultural, religious and geographical contexts in which it was devised — if only I knew how. The description of Swiss politics which follows offers no solution to this difficulty; it merely evades it.

The most striking single aspect of Swiss politics is the intricacy of the parts. The Swiss have developed instruments for measuring the popular will of such delicacy that, as Christopher Hughes shows, sometimes even official publications get things wrong. Take one case which Professor Hughes cites: the workings of the d'Hondt system of proportional representation. He quotes an official handout at the Swiss Embassy: 'If ten National Councillors are to be elected in a canton, and of the 60 000 voters, 36 000 vote for List A, 12 000 for List B, 6000 for List C, 5000 for List D, and 1000 for List E, the distribution of seats will be $6:2:1:1:0$.' As he points out, this seems common sense. 'The interesting point about it is that it is wrong. List A, surprisingly, would elect 7 members and List D none.' The reason is that under the d'Hondt system the seats are based on a 'Final Quotient', that is, the number which can be divided into each party's total of votes to give the right number of seats. In the particular example, it would work as follows:

Divide the total vote (60 000) by the number of seats *plus* one (11). The result is called the Provisional Quotient (5424). In our example, it gives the provisional result of $6:2:1:0:0$. But this only adds up to 9, and there are ten seats to be allocated. The second sum seeks the Final Quotient. This is obtained by dividing each party's votes by the provisional number of seats it obtains, *plus* one. Thus List A (36 000) is divided by 7 (6 plus 1) and gives the result 5142. This sum is repeated for each seat in turn, and the highest of the results is the Final Quotient; in our example, 5142 is the highest. It is the number which when divided among each result in turn gives the right number of seats.[2]

Those of you who have just put aside your pencils will know that it works. The rest will have to take it on faith. In both groups sympathy must be growing with the ordinary Swiss citizen in the face of such intricacy. The system is also opaque. It is impossible to tell without pencil and paper what difference to the final outcome a shift of, say, 1,000 votes from List B to List C might have. Swiss politicians call the curious permutations and combinations which occur *Proporzpech* and *Proporzglück,* 'proportional bad luck' and 'proportional good luck'. Since the citizen has the right to alter the party lists by voting twice for the same candidate (*cumulation*) or by striking a name on, say, List A and replacing it with a name from another list (*panachage*), devices which are frequently used both by the party in preparing its official list and by the citizen in editing the list sent to him, the game of voting becomes more and more complicated and hard to see through. In the Appendix there are some concrete examples taken from the official guide to these procedures prepared by the Federal Chancellery.

To make matters worse, the complicated electoral system tends to reproduce itself not only on the national but also on the cantonal and local level. A resident of the city of Zürich, for example, has the privilege (or burden) of electing the *Nationalräte* (deputies to the national parliament) from Canton Zürich, two members to represent the canton in the *Ständerat* (the upper house of the national parliament), the members of the cantonal parliament, the members of the city parliament of Zürich city, the members of the city executive council, district councillors, district magistrates, district prosecutors, members of the district school board, members of the area school board, arbitration magistrates, a notary public, who is both agent in bankruptcy and keeper of the property records, secondary and primary school teachers and so on. He may also have to vote on matters of substance, for in Switzerland the citizen has powers which are known as 'semi-direct democracy' and which take the form of votes on referenda and initiatives at all three levels of government. Jean Meynaud in his study of semi-direct democracy calculates that there were eighty-one such referenda and initiatives on the national level between 1945 and 1969, or about three a year. To these must be added cantonal and communal referenda of various kinds. In 1972 there were four major national referenda, still far short of the maximum of nine reached in 1952.[3]

Each canton has a somewhat different political system, and there are twenty-two cantons or, more accurately, since three of the cantons are divided into half cantons (Basel into city and country; Appenzell into Inner and Outer Rhodes; Unterwalden into Nidwalden and Obwalden) there are really twenty-five cantons. Each has a constitution and a characteristic set of political institutions, a separate history, religious and economic peculiarities, a party system with special features unique to that canton, and sometimes a language problem as well. In the face of this bewildering variety in so small a compass it is not surprising that the foreigner ignores Swiss politics, assuming that he is aware that they are going on around him, for the Swiss are more discreet about offending the eye and ear with political slogans than any other European people. The basic unit of Swiss politics, and the key to understanding them, is the *Gemeinde* or commune. There is no suitable English translation of *Gemeinde* because there was no parallel development in the English-speaking world. The nearest equivalent is, perhaps, the self-governing New England town, where the citizenry assembled in the town meeting constitute the ultimate legislative authority. In certain parts of Switzerland from earliest times, as I tried to show in the previous chapter, the community of free citizens has always been understood as the lawful 'sovereign', and in Swiss political parlance today, the citizenry as a whole is still the 'sovereign'. Politicians 'consult the sovereign' or they 'fear the sovereign' as the case may be. Nowhere is the basic sovereignty of the people more obvious and direct than in the *Gemeinde*, the basic unit of the Swiss political community. Typically there is no 'Swiss citizenship' as such. A Swiss person is in the first place a citizen of his *Gemeinde* and as such a citizen of his canton and hence automatically a Swiss citizen. In theory each of the 3,072 *Gemeinden* in Switzerland could draw up its own regulations for conferring citizenship. In practice communal citizenship must meet certain requirements set by the cantons which in turn have to meet national legal stipulations. There is, as befits anything Swiss, great variety in spite of cantonal supervision in the provisions governing citizenship of a *Gemeinde* or commune. In many cases acquiring citizenship involves not only a lengthy period of residence (which varies from canton to canton) but the payment of a very large capital sum. Canton Geneva holds the record with SFr. 75,000 for some communes. In Ticino the canton and the communes can demand as much as SFr. 20,000; SFr. 10,200 is the going rate in parts of Canton Neuchâtel, while Glarus merely requires the administrative costs. There is, so far as I know, no comprehensive list of the fees charged by cantons and *Gemeinden* and it is far from the most admirable of Swiss political customs, since it offers sanctuary to the wealthy tax-dodger and excludes the sons of immigrants who may have been born in the community and speak its dialect. The federal government merely stipulates that a foreigner applying for citizenship must have lived a total of twelve years in Switzerland, and three of the last five years.

In the Swiss passport and on all official forms, the citizenship of the *Gemeinde*, the so-called *'Bürgerort'* or the place where one is *heimatberechtigt* (entitled to be at home), is written large. This communal citizenship remains with the family and its descendants even if they have been living elsewhere for several generations. Most Swiss will instinctively answer the question, 'where are you from?' with the *Bürgerort*, even though they may never have set foot in the place. The home commune today has less significance than it used to, since only about a third of the population now actually live in the *Gemeinde* where they have rights. Nevertheless there are rights of last resort to be claimed. The commune of origin, not the commune of domicile, must support its citizens if they fall on hard times. Commune of origin plays a role in the election of members of the *Bundesrat*, since locality is one of the many elements to be balanced among the members of the seven-man executive. The commune of origin may be one with ancient collective holdings or, in some cases, collective obligations. There may be profits to be collected or dues to be paid. It says something about the rootedness of Swiss identity that this curious yet important, fictional yet very real, form of citizenship should be so instinctively accepted.

The political community is not the same as the *Bürgergemeinde*, the commune of the citizenry. It is usually the much larger *Einwohner-gemeinde*, the 'commune of residents', who have all the usual rights of Swiss citizens in any Swiss community where they may be domiciled. The commune of residents is the political reality for almost two-thirds of contemporary Swiss men and women. Communes vary enormously in size and character. Of the 253 communes in Canton Ticino in 1970, according to the official cantonal statistics, 44 had less than 100 residents, while 3 had more than 10,000. Lugano had 23,051, while Rasa had 12. The 20 least populous communes had collectively only 1,101 residents.[4] The extremes of Alpine depopulation and urban congestion can be found in one canton. Clearly political practice must vary enormously in the small, middle and large communes.

Take the case of a small commune, defined as under 4,000 citizens eligible to vote. There are 107 *Gemeinden* in Canton Luzern. Several of these have intense party political activity, and activity which stretches into areas wholly outside 'politics' in the Anglo-American understanding of the word. Here is a concrete example: the town of Malters lies in the pretty river valley of the Kleine Emme about 20 kilometres west of the city of Luzern. There are 2,717 persons on the electoral roll, so that politics, one would imagine, could be free of organised party interference. The opposite is true. The two main parties, the Liberals and the

Christian Democratic Peoples Party (*Christlichdemokratische Volkspartei*)
are powerfully represented in the commune. The elected *Gemeinderat*
of five members had during the early 1970s a majority of Liberals, three
to two, but the CVP is the larger party in the cantonal parliament and
has a majority in the cantonal executive. Where the CVP has power,
it exercises it, and, where the Liberals retain it, they are no less tough.
Jobs, not policy differences, raise the most heat. Each village, including
Malters, has a *Sektionschef*, a part-time representative of the Swiss army,
whose job it is to keep the records on all eligible male citizens and to act
as local ordnance officer. The *Sektionschef* in Malters and in every other
of the 107 Luzern *Gemeinden* is a CVP member. The Liberals respond in
kind. Malters has to have drains and a water supply. There are two
firms in town which could carry out the work, but they are not chosen
by competitive bidding for each contract as would be the case in
England or America. Instead, the *Brunnenmeister* (the Master of the
Fountains) is elected by the *Gemeinderat* on a straight party political
basis, and the firm which he heads gets the work. The *Brunnenmeister*,
a Liberal elected by a vote of 3 to 2 in 1971, looked forward with some
anxiety to future elections, since the CVP had been unusually active in
Malters and he had put SFr. 4,000 of his own capital into equipment to
carry out his office. He knows that his main competition, a CVP firm,
is sharpening its spanners in readiness. In reply to my amazed question
whether his firm was at least the better of the two, he smiled modestly
and replied, 'I wouldn't say that'.

The heat generated can be measured by the following excerpt from
a letter to the local paper, the *Volksbote*, in August of 1973. It was the
last salvo by the CVP in a fierce campaign for the office of president
of the school board;

It has never been any different in Malters: as soon as somebody has an opinion
of his own and that opinion does not fit the official party line of the Liberals,
the most tremendous hue and cry is raised against it by the very same people
who all year long are talking about democratic rights and freedom and claim
to be questioning this, that and everything. The one thing apparently one
must never do is to put up another candidate. That is a mortal sin.

The election was held on 5 August, in the depth of the vacation period,
but still 52% of the registered voters turned out. Herr Edgar Hinnen,
the Liberal, defeated Herr Hans Burri, the CVP, by 835 to 656 votes. A
Young Liberal activist explained to me that while the school board
victory was encouraging, he was worried about the future. The Malters
Liberals, he argued, were in the hands of three or four traditional

families, too nice and too conservative to fight CVP fire with fire. He looked round him conspiratorially and, seeing a group of four young men at a table on the other side of the room, continued in a whisper, 'We have to be careful. We are not all Liberals here.'

Party politics in Canton Luzern have always been fierce, but the puzzled visitor may find it difficult to see why. Even the activist had to confess that there were few matters of principle that separated CVP and Liberals. As a leftish Young Liberal, he thought the CVP social policy rather better and more progressive than the Liberal. Of course he had CVP friends, though rather fewer than Liberal ones. Yes, his family were solidly Liberal on both sides and always had been. He tried to put into words the differences between the parties and retreated into emotional expressions of a rather vague kind. Liberals were in some way more open-minded, not less Roman Catholic than the CVP, but less clerical, more attached to free enterprise and less attracted to 'etatist' solutions. Malters Liberals feel an affinity with the Liberal party of Luzern city, a certain cosmopolitanism, radicalism even, combativeness. Finally, he urged me not to confuse the Luzern Liberals with the Zürich *Freisinnige* or the Basel Radicals. They were, he said with some contempt, the parties of big business, not a popular people's party like the Liberals in Luzern.

Party history in Canton Luzern is in a curious way a shorthand for social and economic history. The CVP of today is still in many ways the old *Katholisch–Konservativ*, the 'KK' of yesterday, entrenched in certain country districts in Canton Luzern and all-powerful in the *Waldstätte* (the original cantons of Uri, Schwyz and Unterwalden), Valais and Fribourg. Its new 'Christian Democratic' image is an attempt to get out of the Catholic ghetto by following the example of the German Christian Democratic Union; what was a confessional must become a mass party. In Canton Luzern the key to party politics lies buried in the centuries of estrangement between the patrician, cosmopolitan oligarchy who ran the elegant, little city of Luzern and the more backward, democratic, conservative, clerical peasantry of the valleys. In Luzern, unlike the position in Bern, the aristocracy were among the leaders of the Liberal regeneration of the 1830s. The content of Luzern liberalism, its elitism and its 'Josefine' view that the state must control the church, pushed it into a head-on collision with the mystical, violent, peasant-born Joseph Leu von Ebersol, whose democratic, conservative and Catholic *coup* of 1841 began the process leading up to the civil war, the *Sonderbundkrieg*. Again it was the Liberal, rationalist, anti-Vatican, patrician leadership who regained power after the defeat of the *Sonderbund* and who maintained it in distant alliance with the very different sort of liberalism represented in the victorious Protestant cantons until the 1870s. These conflicts, the struggle between city and country, between enlightened, rationalist cosmopolitanism and clerical, pious, democratic conservatism, live on in the shimmering, almost invisible mental structures of the attitude of the Young Liberal in Malters. The continuity of history in Switzerland reproduces these attitudes from generation to generation until both origin and ideological content seem lost in a haze. I have no idea what permutations of historic circumstance, settlement or local condition gave Malters a predominantly Liberal character. Each community will have its own version of the history of the whole, long, complicated and difficult to assess. What strikes the eye here is the rootedness in the past of even the election of 5 August 1973, for the president of the school board in one small Swiss *Gemeinde*. As Johannes von Müller, the great Swiss historian of the eighteenth century, said 'above all, nothing is either large or small, because it looks to be so on the map; it all depends on the spirit'.

The spirit of a community like Grenchen in Canton Solothurn is obviously going to be different. Grenchen, known as the most 'proletarian' city in Switzerland, produces 70% of the internal parts for watches made in Switzerland and contains the headquarters of several of the most famous Swiss watch companies, as well as the administrative centre of Ebauches SA with its central computer controlling the operation of seventeen subsidiary companies. There are many other large and small firms in the watch and allied industries. Its population of 20,000 spreads out over the flat basin of the River Aare and along both sides of an autoroute from Biel to Solothurn. Yet it too is a *Gemeinde* and has all the forms of communal government which Malters has. The issues are different — credits of SFr. 7 million for a new school building, outstanding debts of over SFr. 50 million, new taxes to bring in SFr. 37 million. In the modern industrial community where over a third of the inhabitants have only relatively recently moved in, *Gemeinde* politics simply cannot have the same intensity or personal quality as in Malters. Party politics are more formal if not more obvious. The *Gemeinderat* in Grenchen (the Communal Council) has thirty members (at present 13 *Freisinnige* (Liberal), 11 Social Democrats and 2 *Landesring*, an independent party supported by the Migros firm). There are 12,000 people on the electoral roll, but usually between 40 and 400 show up at the *Gemeindeversammlung*, or town meeting. At a recent meeting, when the issue was a fierce increase of 20% in community taxes, 1,368 citizens showed up, a huge gathering but still only about 12% of the community.

The problem of participation in politics is clearly a function of size. In Wangen an der Aare, not far from Grenchen, with a population of about 4,300 inhabitants, a recent election for the nine-man *Gemeinderat* produced a turnout of 90% of the voters. In Grenchen this is no longer conceivable. The city government of Grenchen realises that the old communalism has become a fiction. It has plans to revise the city's constitution by replacing the present unwieldy *Gemeinderat* with an efficient full-time, five-man executive and the pathetically attended communal assembly with ballots to be sent to the citizens by post. In some Swiss communities the failure to participate in the machinery of democratic life has now become chronic. The city of Geneva is an extreme example of low turnout and listless citizenry in spite of much dramatic political activity. In some cases the communal and city governments have simply been swamped by problems they cannot control and for which local democracy offers few solutions. No visitor to Zürich will be unaware that it has a traffic problem. Yet on 20 May 1973 59% of citizens of the city of Zürich said No to the carefully worked out plan for an Underground from Kloten to Dietikon and a Rapid Transit System from the city centre to Dübendorf. In a leading article in *Die Weltwoche* called 'Muddling On', Ulrich Kägi summed up the exasperating position:

59 per cent of those voting in the city and 57 per cent in the canton of Zürich knew last weekend precisely what they did not want: the Underground and Rapid Transit Systems. Much more questionable is whether they know what they do want. What are the prospects of finding a solution which will save the city and region from death by automotive suffocation? Every solution costs money, which no one wants to pay.

The city and commune of Lugano has been swamped by tourism and the problems of the Italian economy, the latter in some ways the more serious menace. The Via Nassa, Lugano's equivalent of Zürich's Bahnhofstrasse, has become the centre of a semi-legal banking community which has mushroomed out of all control. In the ten years between 1960 and 1970, the number of limited companies registered in the canton went up from 1,476 to 6,440. In 1970 alone 980 new companies worth a nominal capital sum of SFr. 69,826,000 were formed.[5] The flood of legal and illegal lira has launched an enormous number of these 'name-plate companies' and added to the problems of the city administration. A distinguished journalist in Lugano told me that in September 1972 the going rate for urban property was about SFr. 20,000 per square metre. Translating that sum into units comprehensible to English-speaking readers, I calculate that a small bungalow-style house with a small garden would need 1,000 square metres of surface or at these prices SFr. 20,000,000 (roughly just under £4 million at the current exchange rate). The land area required for a hospital or school would yield an astronomical sum, so the city builds none. Instead, the entire *centro storico* of Lugano has been surrendered to those who can pay the price: the banks, insurance companies and foreign firms. And all this in a community with only 23,000 inhabitants.

It is not surprising that city and cantonal authorities have no idea what to do when they consider Lugano's problems, still less the ordinary citizen. Nor is it clear that the traditional devices of direct democracy help much in these matters. In the last ten years Lugano has become a more democratic commune in formal terms, but democratic voting procedures have not stopped the city turning into a safe-deposit box.

The next level of Swiss politics is the canton, and it is on the cantonal level that the workings of Swiss federalism show the strengths and weaknesses of the system. The present division between cantons and federal authority grew out of the crisis of the civil war. It led, as I tried to show in the previous chapter, to a compromise and to a bicameral legislature where the sovereignty of the cantons found its expression in the *Ständerat* or the Council of States. The position is stated in Article 3 of the federal constitution: 'The Cantons are sovereign in so far as their sovereignty is not limited by the Federal Constitution, and, as such, they exercise all rights which are not transferred to the Federal power.' At the heart of every federal system there can be found a statement of just this sort. If one examines this one or Article 10 of the US constitution, where a similar division is proposed between state and federal authority, one sees a dilemma. Sovereignty is another word for political power, and these constitutional provisions try to divide an indivisible fabric. Either a state has ultimate power or it has not. In both the Swiss and the US cases the interpretation of the text depended on the outcome of a civil war. The answer was clear. In Switzerland, the *Bund* or federal union and in the USA the federal government was to have that power. When A. Lawrence Lowell wrote his great study of continental European politics in 1896, he thought that the Swiss had resolved the dilemma very differently from the American approach: 'Instead of assigning to the federal and state governments separate spheres of action, the Swiss, like the Germans, have combined legislative centralisation with administrative decentralisation, the federal laws being carried out as a rule by the cantonal authorities.'[6]

The growth of the modern state in Switzerland changed that. By 1954 when Professor Hughes wrote his commentary on the Swiss constitution, he was tempted to declare the distinction meaningless. All he would concede is 'that there remains in spite of all a very attractive savour of sovereignty about the Cantons, which places them in another class to English countries'.[7] The existence of separate cantons with separate institutions makes Swiss politics and social life fundamentally different from that of a centralised state. Cantonal identity, like the powers of the *Gemeinden*, provides a receptacle for differences. It is the foundation of Swiss multilingual, religious and social peace. Each canton resembles a set of Chinese boxes or, perhaps, a beehive, into which history has built dozens of smaller boxes, the *Gemeinden*, or communes. They in turn are often subdivided into ethnic, religious or cultural sub-units which, while not formally recognised, give the commune its characteristic colour or tone. This cellular political system allows ethnic and other particularisms to flourish side by side. It gives to Swiss political life a marvellous mosaic surface. The residents of the communes 'sous les roches' may be Catholic and anti-Bernese while those 'sur les roches' may be the opposite, but as long as the walls between compartments have been drawn adequately and the larger cantonal box has room for both, no troubles arise. The Jura problems show what happens when the compartments cannot be made to fit; it also shows how the cellular system responds to a fierce conflict directed at itself.

The origins of today's troubles can be seen in the debris left by Napoleon's new order. Before 1789 the Jura districts had belonged to the prince—bishop of Basel. Exiled by the Reformation, the prince—bishop had established his see in the pretty Lilliputian residence of Arlesheim, from which he ruled the poor, remote valleys of the eastern Jura for more than two centuries. In the name of reason and revolution, the French republic put an end to the secular domain of the prince—bishop as they were to do to so many other mini-principalities and tiny kingdoms. For a while the Jura became part of the republican French 'Département du Mont Terrible' only to be reassigned several times during the Napoleonic era. The conservative statesmen who tried to put Europe together again in 1814 and 1815 knew that turning back the clocks would not work, though rulers like the Elector of Hesse—Cassel and the King of Savoy tried to do that by demoting all those promoted and abrogating all decrees sanctioned under Napoleon. The Gracious Lords of Bern wanted their subject territories back, especially the lovely and prosperous Vaudois lands along Lac Léman, but the Swiss Committee of the Vienna Congress considered that too risky. Napoleon's nineteen cantons were sanctioned and the Bernese were compensated for the loss of the Vaud by being given the miscellaneous possessions of the former prince—bishop of Basel. It was a poor deal. 'They have taken our wine cellar and corn chamber', said a contemporary Bernese wag, 'and left us the garret.' As the inset to Map 2 on p. 70 shows, the image is well chosen. The northern districts of Porrentruy, Delémont and Saignelégier are very like the Swiss garret, remote, self-contained and very hard to reach even by today's means of transport. The formal decision of the Vienna Congress could, of course, not be refused and so Canton Bern was notified that it had been agreed 'to procure for it and to guaranty to it Bienne with its territory, Erguel, Moutier and the Porrentruy'.[8] The formal union of the city of Biel—Bienne and the Francophone districts along the lake, the Bieler See, was, on the other hand, a real gain. The residents of the southern districts of the Jura were content for they were largely Protestant and welcomed the union with a large, comfortable Protestant state like Canton Bern. The residents of the northern territories were Roman Catholic, poor and discontented. The nineteenth century saw the religious and geographical divisions harden. By the twentieth century, better economic conditions had eroded the coolness of the north Jura towards Bern but had also complicated the situation by bringing German-speaking immigrants into hitherto purely French territories. In the census of 1880, the whole Jura contained 24% German-speakers while in some of the southern districts it was over 30%. The First World War revived separatism, but as the Protestant Synod noted with deep suspicion in 1917: 'All members of the separatist committee are Catholic; not a single Protestant has taken part. Are we not justified, we Jurassien Protestants, in seeing in the separatist movement clericalism at work in one of its most audacious enterprises?'[9] French-speaking, Jurassien radicals were convinced of it and even welcomed German immigration on the grounds that every Protestant vote was a vote against clericalism. During the 1920s and

1930s the Jura as a whole was so hard hit by the depression that separatism as an issue and the Catholic—Protestant division tended to fade out.

The rebirth of the separatist movement can be dated: 20 September 1947. Bern was one of the few cantons left in which the *Regierungsrat* (Executive Council) was still elected within the *Grosser Rat* (the cantonal parliament) and on that day a member from the Jura was refused election to the executive because he spoke French. The language question temporarily united both Protestant and Catholic, north and south, in the Comité de Moutier. The committee's efforts eventually led to amendments to the constitution of Canton Bern recognising the identity of the Jura in practical and symbolic ways. During the 1950s a new movement, the 'Rassemblement jurassien' (RJ) gained ground in the north and began a popular initiative for a separate canton. The leaders of the separatist movement managed to get 24,000 signatures on the petition calling for a referendum among the Jura people about separation. This amounted to 55% of those eligible to vote. The separatists hoped to demonstrate in the ensuing ballot that the Jura was solid. They knew they would be heavily outvoted by the rest of Canton Bern, but a big Yes vote in the Jura would create a splash. When the votes had been counted not only had the whole canton said No to opening the separation question but so had the Jura by a small margin (Yes: 15,163; No: 16,354). The division was geographical and religious. The three Roman Catholic northern districts (Porrentruy, Delémont and Saignelégier) voted two to one in favour, while the three Protestant southern districts (Moutier, Courtelary and La Neuveville) voted three to one against. The confessional line was particularly sharp in the Vallon de St Imier where the old Catholic communes 'sous les roches' which had once belonged to the bishopric of Basel voted overwhelmingly Yes, while the villages 'sur les roches', which had never been part of the bishopric and were Protestant, voted equally overwhelmingly No. Another attempt at the direct democratic instrument, an initiative of May 1962, was an even more embarrassing failure for the separatists.

The dilemma for the residents of the northern Jura seemed complete. Direct democracy must defeat them. They were a minority of the total population of the canton and even of the historic territories which they claimed. They made up a smaller proportion of the population of Bern in the 1960s than they had in 1900. On the other hand, they refused to abandon their claim to all of the Jura even though the southern Jura resolutely opposed separation. They felt their frustrations and nursed their very real sense of grievance. The slogan of the anti-separatists in 1959, 'Votez non, et on n'en parlera plus!' proved as false as the hopes of the separatists. Almost inevitably, the Rassemblement jurassien moved toward direct action and violence. In 1962, the youth wing of the movement was formed. They called themselves *les Béliers* after the medieval battering rams which became their symbol. Bernard Varrin, their leader, summed up their position recently, 'we use provocation because we believe that it is the only language that the Swiss understand'. In the years since the early 1960s direct action and political moves have been linked in a counterpoint of unrest.

In 1965 the Jura members of the Bern parliament placed before it a seventeen-point programme for an autonomy statute, and after the cantonal elections of 1966 the new *Regierungsrat* worked out plans for both a constitutional revision and a statute of autonomy. In March 1970 the voters of Canton Bern approved an amendment to the constitution according to which a petition signed by 5,000 eligible Jura voters could demand a vote on separation. Only Jurassiens were eligible to vote on the matter. If separation were accepted, individual communes might vote in a second ballot on whether they wished to remain in Canton Bern. The *Regierungsrat* gave itself the right to make this provision operative as soon as an autonomy statute had been passed by the cantonal parliament. Unfortunately the deadlock remained. The separatists, knowing that on those terms they would lose a plebiscite, rejected the constitutional amendment on the grounds that only 'genuine' Jurassiens should have the right to vote. They demanded that all non-resident Jurassiens living elsewhere in Switzerland be included and all 'non-genuine' Jurassiens, in practice, German-speaking residents, be excluded. No democratic regime could possibly agree to a 'cooked' electoral roll of that kind and, knowing that, the separatists refused to look at any solution short of 'Canton Jura' but more autonomous than the existing arrangements. The Union des Patriotes jurassiens founded in opposition to separatism rejected both the initiative or plebiscite and the idea of a new statute of autonomy. The third force', the Mouvement pour l'Unité du Jura founded in 1969, wanted an autonomy statute, which would make the Jura a separate electoral unit for national and cantonal elections, the creation of a Jura regional council and the establishment of a regional capital.

In June 1973, the separatist spokesman in the *Nationalrat* M. Jean

Wilhelm (CVP), the editor of the Porrentruy newspaper *Le Pays*, moved a resolution urging the *Bundesrat* (Federal Council) 'to intervene decisively in the Jura problem, to find a way out of the dilemma and to seek a genuine solution'. He argued that Canton Bern by its own devices could never achieve one. By this stage, the *Béliers* had a membership of about 2,000, organised now in tightly knit paramilitary units. During the previous five years they had concentrated their activities on making the cantonal authorities look silly and in popularising their slogan 'Jura libre'. In 1968 they celebrated Swiss National Day on April Fool's day instead of the first of August. They had dressed as chimney sweeps to demonstrate against the visit of the president of the *Regierungsrat*, the cantonal executive, in Porrentruy. They occupied a police station in Delémont in June 1968, the Swiss Embassy in Paris in 1972 and in a flashy double action occupied the Belgian Embassy in Bern and the Swiss Embassy in Brussels at the same time to show international solidarity with Walloon extremists. Other actions were directed at the army, the national parliament and the city of Bern. They attacked four times in 1972 in acts of provocative violence, pouring tar in the tracks of Bern's trams, trying to nail the door shut to the City Hall and burning old tyres in the public squares.

During the autumn of 1973, the crisis seemed to deepen. The debate in the Bern cantonal parliament enflamed sentiments in all the communities. The Volkspartei (SVP) deputies, representatives of the German-speaking Bernese peasants who set the tone of cantonal politics, enraged the French minority with their complacency. Canton Bern, they argued, had made great concessions in limiting the referendum to the Jura districts and in accepting such provisions in its constitution. On 18 December 1973, the *Regierungsrat* announced that it had decided to put into effect the provisions of the amendment of 1970 and set 23 June 1974 as the date for a referendum on separation.

Once again, the melancholy lesson of the past fifteen years had been confirmed. Violence had worked. The RJ had put themselves on the map in a big way but with the slightly ironical result that the party could only succeed by sacrificing its previous principles. If it accepted the plebiscite as legitimate, it conceded that 'Canton Jura', a united Francophone canton including Biel—Bienne and the southern districts, would never be realised. By participating in the plebiscite it also surrendered the principle that only 'genuine' Jurassiens be allowed to vote. At first the RJ stuck to its old line. Roland Béguelin, the General Secretary of the RJ, a gifted and charismatic figure (and incidentally a Protestant from the southern Jurassien commune of Tramelan) gave a long, exclusive interview to the left-wing *National-Zeitung* in which he predicted that there would have to be casualties before a solution was reached. Violence was the only way. Gradually opinion shifted, and when the party met in May 1974, delegates voted overwhelmingly to take part in the plebiscite. On 23 June 1974, the RJ duly went to the polls along with over 90% of all those entitled to vote. 36,802 voted for separation and 34,507 against, an overall majority of 2,745. The story made the front pages of foreign papers like *The Times* and *Le Figaro* and was universally hailed as another example of Swiss good sense; *Sonderfall Schweiz* had again set an example to the world.

Violence is, however, not so easily laid to rest. What one side starts, another may finish. The 23 June vote shook the southern communities very profoundly. Ancient hostilities revived. Fears of Catholic plots could not be allayed by soothing promises that the RJ would accept the separate identities of the southern districts and that it would be prepared to give them cantonal status as a half canton like the two Appenzells. The active southerners wanted no part of the new canton. In Map 2 the reader can see how the Jura districts voted on 23 June 1974. Those areas shaded in grey voted for separation; those in white opposed it. Nine communes indicated by horizontal lines in the Moutier district voted for separation while five northern communes opposed the separatist trend of their neighbours. In Bonfoi on the French border there was a tie.

In the six months after the plebiscite, an anti-separatist youth movement sprang into life. Its membership grew to 5,000 by the end of 1974. The *Sangliers*, the wild boars, promised to meet the *Béliers* head-on and in language too tragically familiar in Northern Ireland, Jean-Paul Gehler, their leader, warned his opponents that while the *Sangliers* would not strike first, they would retaliate. The remaining elements of the so-called 'Third Force' (Mouvement pour l'Unité du Jura) found themselves ground down between increasingly intransigent separatist and anti-separatist movements. Anti-separatists began to take a violent line, and talk of *Irlandisation* became common on both sides of the deepening divide. After some confusion, anti-separatists in the three southern districts launched a petition calling for a second plebiscite in which the three southern districts could vote to detach themselves from the north. Extremely complicated legal battles began, as the RJ desperately tried to contest the legality of the

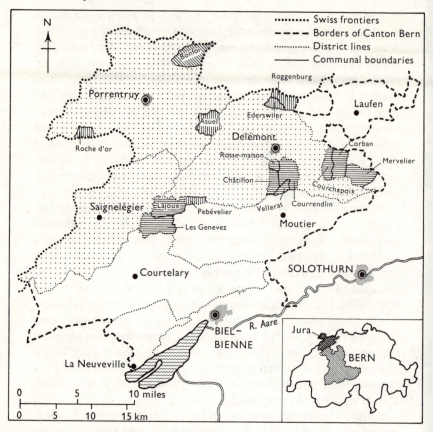

Map 2   Voting patterns in the Jura

initiative. At that point, as tempers were becoming very heated, the *Bundesrat* intervened and appointed three of its members as a mediation group. In January 1975 Dr Furgler, one of the three members, went as far as to meet Béguelin secretly, a meeting discovered only by a chance indiscretion. Petitions, counter-petitions, court judgements and governmental pronouncements on federal and cantonal level gradually began to focus on the issue of the second plebiscite. Attempts to contest the provisions of the amendment of 1970 failed. The Bern government stuck to its right to hold a plebiscite once the petitions by the requisite number of citizens had been duly accredited and verified. Hence on 16 March 1975 a second plebiscite in the three southern districts took place on the issue of remaining within Canton Bern. Table 3.1 shows the results of the voting (the figures in brackets are those of the plebiscite of 23 June 1974).

The vote clarified some but not all of the issues. The narrowness of the outcome in the town of Moutier provoked protests, and in April 1975 the RJ wrote formally to the *Bundesrat* demanding that the results in the district of Moutier be set aside on the grounds that the outcome had been 'manipulated' by the Bernese authorities. During the night of 24 April, a demonstration of *Béliers* in Moutier got out of hand. Eight hundred demonstrators fought a six-hour battle with police in the worst violence of the entire crisis. Militant separatists threw petrol bombs, rocks, paving stones, iron bars and bicycle chains, and ten policemen were seriously injured.

The next stage of the process involved plebiscites on 7 and 14 September, 1975 in each of the fifteen communes which voted differently from the majority of their district in the plebiscite of 16 March 1975. These communes, as a result of the vote, have now either to be made into Bernese enclaves within the new Canton Jura or vice versa. The result in Moutier was even narrower on 7 September 1975 than on 16 March 1975 (2,151 for and 2,540 against joining the new canton) and was followed by the worst rioting in the recent history of Switzerland. Six hundred police were in action against hundreds of separatist demonstrators rampaging through the town. The cantonal police chief Herr Robert Bouder, described the incident as 'not mere clashes but an attack on the constitutional order'. Roland Béguelin promised his supporters in a speech in Delémont on 14 September 1975 to fight

TABLE 3.1

	For Bern	For Jura
Moutier	9,947	7,749
	(9,330	7,069)
Courtelary	10,802	3,268
	(10,260	3,123)
La Neuveville	1,927	997
	(1,776	931)
Total	22,676	12,005
	(21,366	11,124)
Town of Moutier	2,524	2,238
	(2,194	2,124)

on until the whole Jura had been 'liberated'. The results of the plebiscites are in any case not even the end of the constitutional alterations. They must be approved by the Bernese executive and parliament, by the voters of Canton Bern and ultimately by the voters and cantons of the rest of the Confederation, since the creation of a Canton Jura will involve an amendment to the federal constitution. It may be years before the Jura issue settles down.

While the ultimate resolution of the Jura conflict is far from clear, three general features of Swiss political reality stand out. The first is the way the Swiss cellular structure of politics acts to focus issues into ever smaller and more precise geographical units. The very violence in the town of Moutier illustrates the peculiar Swiss attention to micropolitics. It is conceivable that in the end Moutier will be divided by neighbourhood or even by street into Jura and Bernese enclaves. The second has to do with identity. If Porrentruy or Delémont had really been 'French', as at times some extremists seemed to want, they would never have become important. They would sleep the deep slumber reserved by the extreme centralisation of the French state for small, remote, market towns. There is an irony here. These two little towns make domestic and international news because, and only because, they are Swiss. The essence of Swiss identity is the preservation of even the smallest ethnic, linguistic and cultural units. The circle comes round. By granting the Jurassiens their wishes, the Swiss assert the most important characteristic of 'Swissness', the equality of all human communities before the bar of history.

A third feature of the Jura crisis is the peculiar flexibility of Swiss constitutions. The ultimate solution to the Jura crisis, if it is the ultimate solution, was made possible by an amendment to the Bern constitution accepted by the voters in 1970, but Bern is not unique in this. All cantons have constitutions like the federal one. The constitution of Canton Solothurn of 1887, which in its turn had wholly replaced the constitution of 1867, had been revised twenty-three times by 1963, and the process of revision continues merrily. A constitution in Switzerland represents a sort of political ledger in which successive ages write down the results of their compromises. Whereas the US constitution is venerable, sacrosanct and very difficult to amend, the Swiss constitutions are pedestrian, practical and detailed. Constitutions are merely substitutes for the sovereignty of the people and can easily be altered if the sovereign people change their opinions.

Underlying the provisions of a Swiss constitution is the assumption that ultimately the ideal state is the direct democracy or the *Lands-gemeinde*, the assembly of all free citizens in the historic ring. This, the pure form, not the clauses of a constitution or its preamble, is the truly venerable element in Swiss political life. The institutions of collective, communal self-government are very old. Reasonably firm evidence exists for the existence of *Landsgemeinden* as early as the 1230s in Canton Uri. The first *Landsgemeinden* seem to have taken place in Zug in 1376, Appenzell in 1378 and Glarus in 1387. Schwyz, Obwalden, Nidwalden and Uri have had regular *Landsgemeinden* since the early fourteenth century and Ob- and Nidwalden have them today, along with the two Appenzells and Glarus. Similar evidence from neighbouring Graubünden indicates that the first loose alliance or league of free valley communes, the League of the House of God (*Gotteshausbund*), had begun to operate by the latter part of the 1360s. Gradually the independent valley communities united, in the Swiss case in a set of federal treaties, in the case of Graubünden in three loose-knit leagues, but in both associations, sovereignty remained firmly placed at the base. Until the outbreak of the French Revolution, the Republic of the Three Leagues, today's Canton of Graubünden, represented the most extreme form of communal sovereignty. The Republic was made up of three leagues, twenty-six higher jurisdictions, forty-nine jurisdictional communes and 227 autonomous neighbourhoods 'with competitive, overlapping frequently incompatible claims', or as an eighteenth-century traveller put it, 'each village of Raetia, each parish and each neighbourhood already constituted a tiny republic'.[10] The union of these tiny republics was accomplished by a system of referenda in which the village community, not the voter, was the sovereign body. Tiny Bündner villages were consulted on everything from a state treaty with the Habsburgs to the repair of certain barrels and vats in Maienfeld; the equivalent in *Landsgemeinde* regions was frequent and lengthy meetings. Twenty-four took place in Canton Schwyz in 1765. Benjamin Barber believes that these historic circumstances still mould Swiss political attitudes:

To this day, the Swiss seem less interested in the power of offices and the personality of officeholders than the citizens of other less direct democracies. The collegial federal executive with its anonymous rotating presidency continues to embody this predilection of direct democracy for treating the citizenry as the real government and the elected government as powerless attendants.[11]

It is certainly true that representative, parliamentary governments never really took root. There were no Edmund Burkes nor James Madisons in Swiss history. When the ultra-modern liberals of the 1840s tried to impose representative parliamentary structures, they were not entirely successful. The traditions of direct democracy were so deeply rooted that borrowing from the US constitution could not transform the new *Bundesstaat* into a Western, representative republic. In the end, the men of 1848 were Swiss too, sharing certain instinctive assumptions about the 'sovereign' people. They submitted their draft to the people for ratification by referendum, as if that were the most natural thing in the world. They put in clauses making a referendum on revision of the federal constitution obligatory and allowing popular initiative for a 'total revision' of the constitution. It is, I think, equally significant that in the same year, 1848, Schwyz and Zug, two of the oldest cantons, gave up the *Landsgemeinde*, and Schwyz immediately adopted the referendum as a substitute.

By no means all Swiss are enthusiastic about the *Landsgemeinde*. The Liberal Party of Canton Obwalden have made four concerted attempts to have it abolished, losing each time narrowly. They believe that the assembly of several thousand people in Sarnen 'in the Ring' is not only inefficient but malicious. Caspar Diethelm, president of the Liberal Party, told *Die Weltwoche* in late April 1975:

For seventy years the majority party (the Christian Democrats) have used the *Landsgemeinde* consciously as an instrument by which people are easily manipulated. At a *Landsgemeinde*, the government can 'sell' the people things they would never otherwise buy. The Blacks (the Conservatives or Christian Democrats) do what they like with us at the *Landsgemeinde*.

Efficiency is not a feature of the *Landsgemeinde*. A shifting group of people going in and out of the historic Ring make a poor constituency in which to hold elections. The 1973 elections became a farce and lasted for hours because the numbers of those who had or had not voted became muddled. It is certainly not an ideal situation when the 'sovereign' finds itself voting millions of pounds' worth of expenditure late in a long afternoon after the great majority of free citizens have gone home to their TV sets. Cantons, especially those with *Landsgemeinden*, face the same problems as do larger communes. How can semi-direct and direct democracy be made to work when the unit has become too large for the members to know each other?

There are two main categories of semi-direct democratic devices in operation today: the referendum and the initiative, but no reader who has followed me this far will be shocked to learn that within each category and within each canton there is the usual Swiss variety of practice. The Swiss referendum is a device by which either 'constitutional' or 'legislative' matters (and in Swiss practice the two often blend) are submitted to the people for ultimate sanction. Each of the types may be 'obligatory', as is commonly the case in cantonal and federal constitutional questions, but they may be optional ('facultative'). An obligatory legislative referendum means simply that either all laws have to be voted by the people, or some laws of a special kind or some special acts as in the case of the 'financial referendum' on expenditure. Fig. 1 may help to make clear the way laws were passed and put to obligatory referenda in Solothurn before recent changes were sug-

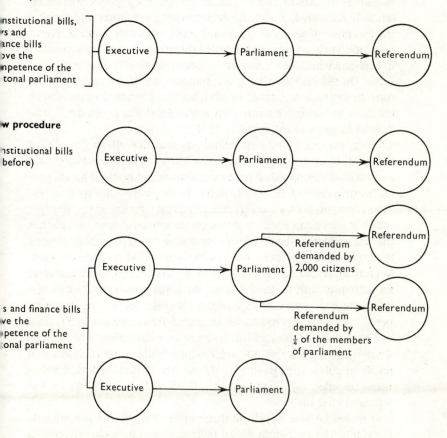

Fig. 1   The passage of a law in Canton Solothurn

gested. The alteration does not abolish the referendum. It merely makes it optional; that is, it puts the burden on the citizens to collect the necessary number of signatures, in this case, the very small number of 2,000.

The other main category is the initiative. The referendum has a purely negative effect. It merely enables the people to reject measures approved by the legislature. The initiative gives the people the right to legislate directly. A certain number of citizens can propose a law either in detail or merely in outline. They must gather a certain number of signatures on a petition to the legislature; 50,000 on the federal level; 10,000 in Canton Ticino (partial reform of 31 May 1970 before which it was 7,000); 5,000 for constitutional initiatives and 4,000 for legislative initiatives in Canton Luzern and so on. Once the petition has been officially registered, which involves checking signatures and the like, the executive department concerned must ultimately make a recommendation to accept or reject it. Then the relevant parliament votes on it. Legislative initiative is now an accustomed part of the Swiss political scene. On federal level the right of initiative for partial revision of the constitution was introduced in 1891, but the attempt to introduce the initiative in legislative matters on federal level was rejected by a substantial majority of the voters in 1961.

Direct democracy in Switzerland has profound effects on political life, but they are not easy to summarise. The study of them has occupied a number of distinguished political scientists and political sociologists for nearly a century. In 1896 Lowell gave the referendum good marks: 'it has certainly been a success in the sense that it produced the result for which it was established. It seems, on the whole, to have brought out the real opinion of the people.' The initiative on the other hand seemed to him 'bold' in conception but 'not likely to be of any great use to mankind; if, indeed, it does not prove to be merely a happy hunting-ground for extremists and fanatics'.[12] Denis de Rougemont cites the case of a referendum in 1961, when the people rejected a law raising the tax on petrol by 7 centimes but allowed an amended one raising it by 5 to pass. My reaction is to think of this incident as a '2 centime' folly, but de Rougemont argues that the referendum 'obliges the authorities to justify in public their intentions, the press to discuss the text, the electorate to reflect on it and to inform itself, and all that keeps up and animates civic life'.[13]

It would be nice to believe that, but the evidence hardly supports the claim. The provisions for an obligatory and optional referendum have an honourable democratic pedigree but lay great burdens on officialdom. The *Staatsschreiber* of Canton Solothurn, the rough equi-valent of the chancellor on federal level, very kindly showed me the books on these matters in his office. A cantonal referendum in March 1972 cost the taxpayers SFr. 83,019. Since there had been thirty-one such ballots in the ten years from 1962 to 1972, the citizenry were paying out at the rate of a quarter of a million francs per annum to allow an average of 40% of their number to say yea or nay to questions such as the following:

The cantonal Constitution of 25 October 1887 will be amended by the follow-ing clause: Article 19*bis*: By means of legislative action and for the protection of the population in the event of catastrophes or warlike events measures may be taken which grant the *Regierungsrat* or the Cantonal Parliament for a limited period powers which deviate from the regulations governing the competence of such authorities in the Constitution.

Meynaud shows that participation in federal referenda and initia-tives has declined from an average of 58.8% in the period 1945—50 to 47.3% for the years 1958—63.[14] For Max Imboden, this was one of the crucial symptoms of what he saw as the 'Helvetic *malaise'*. Imboden divided the voters into groups: the non-voters, the regular voters and the occasional voters. What worried him were the shifts in the groups: 'Today the occasional voters make up 50% to 60% of the active citizenry. The group of those who only go to the polls when they have a special interest is thus twice as large as the number of regular voters. The occasional voter embodies the predominant political attitude.'[15] There is no doubt that this process has continued since Imboden wrote his pamphlet. The reader can see in Fig. 2 what participation in direct democracy looks like in Canton Solothurn in the ten years from 1962 to 1972, and the deterioration of voter participation goes on. The federal referendum on education of March 1973 managed to draw only 25.3% of the citizens to the polls, one of the lowest turnouts since 1848. Since important measures can be rejected by relatively tiny majorities, Pro-fessor Erich Gruner has recently suggested that a quorum be introduced of, say, 33% voter participation. If that level were not reached in a referendum, then the law would be assumed to have the assent of the nearly 70% who had not bothered to turn out. Something of this sort may well be necessary if the public continues to vote with its feet.

The referendum and initiative exercise an influence even if the voters never get to the polls at all. Every piece of legislation in a canto-nal or federal parliament undergoes subtle alterations because a referendum might be the consequence of a given clause, a process

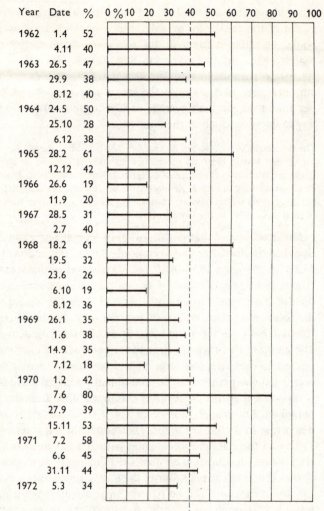

Year	Date	%
1962	1.4	52
	4.11	40
1963	26.5	47
	29.9	38
	8.12	40
1964	24.5	50
	25.10	28
	6.12	38
1965	28.2	61
	12.12	42
1966	26.6	19
	11.9	20
1967	28.5	31
	2.7	40
1968	18.2	61
	19.5	32
	23.6	26
	6.10	19
	8.12	36
1969	26.1	35
	1.6	38
	14.9	35
	7.12	18
1970	1.2	42
	7.6	80
	27.9	39
	15.11	53
1971	7.2	58
	6.6	45
	31.11	44
1972	5.3	34

Average participation, 40 %

Fig. 2   Participation of voters in referenda, Canton Solothurn

which Jürg Steiner has called *Referendumsdrohung* – the referendum threat.[16] The elaborate consultation process which the civil service goes through before drafts of bills even get to parliament is also overshadowed by the moods of the 'sovereign'. Various political scientists have examined the legislative process in detail and others have looked at the consultative machinery, *Vernehmlassung* as it is called, to see where and how far the possible rejection of a bill by referendum has influenced its development. The results seem to be inconclusive. No one doubts that semi-direct democracy effects both procedures. Nobody, on the other hand, can quite establish at which stage or where it did so. The obligation to hold a referendum on state treaties, which are either without time limit or run for fifteen years or more, has certainly affected the conduct of Swiss foreign affairs. In August 1972, the Federal Council announced that it intended to submit the agreement on free trade between Switzerland and the Common Market countries, which had been signed in July in Brussels, to a referendum. A very senior civil servant in the Political Department explained the issue to me. There was some doubt if the government was constitutionally obliged to submit a trade treaty to the voters, but there was no question that it was politically prudent. The experts know that the free-trade treaty is the beginning of a vast and unforseeable process of economic 'integration' into a wider Europe. They know that Switzerland is beginning a new chapter in her history, but they also know that the voters need to be educated to accept these facts. Hence the referendum and the political campaign which accompanied it offered the federal government a chance to explain to the voters what the issues really were. On 3 December 1972, 51.2% of the eligible citizenry went to the polls on the issue. 1,345,057 voted *Ja*, while 509,350 voted *Nein*. All twenty-five cantons voted for the treaty.

The instruments of semi-direct democracy also affect the role of parliament and the activities of political parties. In his fascinating study of political parties in Switzerland, Professor Erich Gruner argues that the referendum is responsible for one of the most striking peculiarities of Swiss parties, their lack of powerful central organisations:

The referendum conceals the solution to the puzzle. It permits the party strategists to get the masses of the people under way easily and quickly without the need for a great party apparatus nor a disciplined group of followers. This rapid mobilisation is only possible because the staff and workers — in contrast to the masses — do not fall back into lethargy. They keep party passions among the closed circle of prominent members cooking over a low flame. In this respect the Swiss party system is a just reflection of our militia system in the army.[17]

By using referenda and initiatives, a party can be in the odd position of being government and opposition at the same time. This practice has become particularly popular with the Socialist Party, since it tends to soothe the irritation of left-wingers who feel that the SPS ought not to serve in a bourgeois executive. The very frequent use of referenda and initiatives, especially on dramatic issues, sucks much of the life out of parliamentary politics. If the great debate will be outside the walls anyway, why listen to what is said inside? If the parties spring to life on issues, the issues capture the public imagination and not the political parties themselves. A paradox emerges. The total politicisation of Swiss life leads to its opposite, a lifelessness in daily politics and indifference to it.

There are certainly reasons for the paleness of Swiss politics other than those which arise from direct democracy. The careers of a Schwarzenbach or a Duttweiler, the retailing eccentric who built both the Migros chain and his own political party to go with it, show that charismatic politics are indeed possible. One cause lies in multiplicity. There are twenty-five different political units, called cantons, and each has its own political party system. François Masnata, who has studied the Social Democratic Party in Switzerland, undoubtedly the most centralised of all Swiss parties, concludes: 'Each cantonal party has the tendency to consider itself the whole and not as a part of an ensemble.'[18] The party which appears in parliament tends to resemble a patchwork quilt rather than a seamless cloth. Since the cantonal party was itself a federation of local parties, the national party turns into a federation of federations. There is, secondly, the tendency to accumulate overlapping offices at various levels and on the same level across various interest groups. The alert member of a Swiss trade federation or craft union or employers' organisation will be well informed by central office as to the doings of 'his' representatives in cantonal and national parliaments; 'his' understood as the representative of an interest group. Since Article 32 of the constitution makes it obligatory that 'the economic groups concerned shall be consulted during the drafting of the laws' the representative of the interests will get his say one way or the other. The work in committee, or even before committee stage in the civil service commissions of 'experts', will be more useful, if less dramatic, than a speech in parliament.

No great careers are to be made in the English or American sense of the word in a cantonal or national parliament. The rise of a Disraeli or an F. E. Smith, a Lyndon Johnson or a Daniel Webster, is not conceivable under the Swiss arrangements. There is no place for grand confrontations and fiery speeches. Proceedings in a Swiss parliament normally resemble a board meeting.

Another feature of Swiss politics at all levels is longevity. It is considered a great insult in most communes, cantons and federal authorities to fail to re-elect a member of an executive. On the level of *Gemeinde* this frequently means that the members stay on until they drop. The Swiss voters have to have unusual provocation to let a sitting member of the executive fall from grace. Periods of service in *Gemeinde*, canton and federal executive of ten or even twenty years are not unknown. The famous Professor Albert Gobat served as a *Regierungsrat* (member of the executive) in Canton Bern for thirty years. It was, his junior colleague Karl Scheurer confided to his diary, a good omen that the executive 'was able to bear so difficult a colleague for so many years'.[19] The long service produces an amiable but rather anonymous atmosphere at the centre of Swiss politics, especially on cantonal level.

The political virtues the Swiss prize most tend to be worthy and unexciting. Christopher Hughes argues that everywhere in Switzerland a predominance of *Sachlichkeit*, 'the executive frame of mind', 'the virtues of the good civil servant' are accorded too much prestige. 'The weakness of the practice of *Sachlichkeit* is that it assumes as best something which is in fact only second best, namely uncontroversial administration.'[20] *Sachlichkeit* is a hard word to convey. 'Impartiality', 'objectivity' 'practicality' all catch a bit of the flavour which arises from the root of the word *Sache* or thing. Work is the key element in this quality. The good Swiss politician is earnest, high-minded, works a seven-day week and leaves his desk spick-and-span each night. Here too the virtue is real but not exciting.

Language is another problem for the Swiss politician of the German area. Debates in most cantonal parliaments and in the federal parliament tend to be in the 'written language', the Swiss version of High German. As Max Frisch's hero puts it in *Mein Name sei Gantenbein*: 'I decide that it's better to take on my role in High German. I always have a feeling of role-playing when I speak High German, and so fewer reservations.'[21] Speaking High German tends to have a similar effect on politicians. They too adopt roles and employ a wooden, pompous idiom known as *Grossratsdeutsch*, the German of the Grand Council chamber.

A final element which makes Swiss politics on the national level less exciting than in many other European countries is the astonishing stability of voting patterns. Table 3.2 illustrates the point. A similar picture including figures for actual votes cast and the percentage achieved by each party is revealed in Table 3.3.

TABLE 3.2   Party strength in the *Nationalrat* by seats

Year	Radicals	Liberal–Dem.	Conservative	Democrats	Socialists	BGB (Peasants)	Pd.A (Communist)	Landesring (Ind.)	Republicans/ National Action	Other	Total seats
1919	60	9	41	7	41	29				2	189
1922	58	10	44	4	43	35	2			2	198
1925	59	7	42	5	49	31	3			2	198
1928	58	6	46	3	50	31	2			2	198
1931	52	6	44	2	49	30	2			2	187
1935	48	7	42	8	50	21	2	7		2	187
1939	51	6	43	6	45	22	4	9		1	187
1943	47	8	43	6	56	22		7		5	194
1947	52	7	44	5	48	21	7	9		1	194
1951	51	5	48	5	49	23	5	10			196
1955	50	5	47	5	53	22	4	10			196
1959	51	5	47	6	51	23	3	10			196
1963	51	6	48	6	53	22	4	10			200
1967	49	6	45	6	51	21	5	16	1	0	200
1971	49	9	44	–	46	23	5	13	11	0	200
1975	47	9	46	–	55	21	4	11	6	1	200

Sources: E. Gruner, *Die Parteien in der Schweiz*, Table 10, p. 186; and *Jahrbuch der eidgenössischen Behörden, 1972* (Bern: Verbandsdruckerei, 1972), pp. 127–31; Swiss Embassy, London.

These figures are astonishing. Modern Switzerland has maintained its political attitudes in roughly the same relationships for fifty years. There are some 'movements within the stability', to cite M. Chevallaz. The smaller ideological parties, the Swiss French Liberals, the Swiss German Evangelical Conservatives, the East Swiss Democrats, are gradually disappearing. The Peasants Party, which now calls itself the Swiss People's Party, has just managed to arrest the decline inevitably associated with the smaller part played by agriculture in a modern economy. Finally, there is movement on the right-wing fringe of political life. Herr Schwarzenbach's tremendous success in the initiative of 1970 led him to chance his arm in the formation of a party, to which I shall return later.

On federal and cantonal levels this stability has made possible what amount to permanent deals to share power. Since 1959, the main

TABLE 3.3 Results of the elections to the National Council

Parties	1943			1947			1967		
	Number of electors	% of the total	Seats gained	Number of electors	% of the total	Seats gained	Number of electors	% of the total	Seats gained
Socialist	251,576	28.6	56	251,625	26.2	48	233,873	23.5	51
Radical	197,746	22.5	47	220,486	23.0	52	230,095	23.2	49
Conservative	182,916	20.8	43	203,202	21.2	44	219,184	22.1	45
Peasant	101,998	11.6	22	115,976	12.1	21	109,621	11.0	21
Independent	48,557	5.5	7	42,428	4.4	9	89,950	9.1	16
Communist	–	–	–	49,353	5.1	7	28,723	2.9	5
Liberal	28,434	3.2	8	30,492	3.2	7	23,208	2.3	6
Evangelical	3,627	0.4	1	9,072	0.9	1	15,728	1.6	3
Democrat	29,627	3.4	5	28,096	2.9	5	14,270	1.4	3
Other parties	35,017	4.0	5	9,282	1.0	–	29,196	2.9	1
	879,498	100%	194	960,012	100%	194	993,848	100%	200

Source: Georges-André Chevallaz, 'La politique intérieure: Le mouvement dans la stabilité' in *Die Schweiz seit 1945*, ed. Erich Gruner (Bern: Francke Verlag, 1971), p. 204.

parties on federal level have operated according to a 'magic formula' by which CVP (Catholic), FDP (Liberal) and SPS (Socialist) have two places and the SVP (Peasants) one on the Federal Council (the *Bundesrat*). Since no significant shift of opinion has occurred in the four general elections since that year, the formula works tolerably well. The *Bundesrat* is quite unlike any other executive branch of government in the world, and Lowell quite rightly saw it as 'the most thoroughly native and original' of all federal institutions. Each Federal Councillor is head (*Vorsteher* or *Chef du département*) of one of the seven main departments of state. They are all elected at the same time by each new parliament at its first session for a term of four years. Both houses vote together in the so-called Federal Assembly or *Bundesversammlung* and each seat is filled in turn; that is, seven separate elections are held on the same day. The members of the *Bundesrat* benefit from that unwillingness to turn out incumbents which we have already noted. In this, as in many other ways, they resemble the executive of a small commune or *Gemeinde*. Normally those members of the *Bundesrat* who wish to go on are allowed to do so, although there have been cases in which, as Professor Hughes points out, men not likely to be re-elected have prudently chosen not to stand. 'The admirable use made of the power, which election by the Assembly gives to party leaders and fellow Federal Councillor, to "take their colleague by the arm" and to call to his mind the pleasures of retirement is a chief justification for parliamentary (rather than popular) election.'[22] Occasionally, as in 1917 or 1953, a member of the *Bundesrat* will resign, and in the 125 years of the modern Confederation there have been three other cases of premature retirement because of a defeat suffered either in the Assembly or in the public performance of duty.

Since neither the distribution of seats on the Federal Council among the parties, 'the magic formula', is likely to change nor are the actual incumbents in danger of defeat, the elections of members of the *Bundesrat* at the beginning of most four-year sessions of parliament have a certain formal quality, but they offer a discreet indication of how members of the Chambers see each Federal Councillor. Since each must be re-elected in turn, attention focuses on the number of votes he gets. Here were the results in 1971:

Hans Peter Tschudi (Soc., Basel, Interior Department)	220
Ernst Brugger (Rad., Zürich, Economic Department)	214
Nello Celio (Rad., Ticino, Finance Department)	194

Rudolf Gnägi (Peasants Party, Bern, Military Department) 178
Roger Bonvin (Chr. Dem., Valais, Transport/Energy
  Department 164
Pierre Graber (Soc., Vaud, Political Department) 114

The *Bundesversammlung* (that is, both chambers meeting together) had 244 members (200 in the lower house, the *Nationalrat*, and 44 in the upper house, the *Ständerat*). The very low vote for M. Graber, the foreign secretary, lower even than the 125 given to Herr Kurt Furgler (Chr. Dem., St Gallen), who was elected to fill a vacancy, amounted to the nearest equivalent to a Swiss vote of no confidence.

One of the members of the *Bundesrat* is elected president and one vice-president of the *Bundesrat* at the same election at which they all stand for re-election. The president of the *Bundesrat* is also president of Switzerland. The term of office is one year and rotates among the members. A long serving *Bundesrat* like Philip Etter (1935–59) may well be able to serve twice as president of Switzerland. New *Bundesräte* wait their turn until all their seniors have filled the office of president but, aside from that, the office moves in strict annual rotation. The powers of the presidency are not great and mainly consist of the chairmanship of the *Bundesrat* and ceremonial functions as head of state. It would be wrong to underestimate the office in spite of this. Its incumbent has general oversight over government as well as a few special emergency powers; in troubled times he can make a difference. Initially the presidency was tied to the Political Department, so that Switzerland effectively suffered a new foreign secretary every year. Under the forceful Numa Droz, the Political Department was separated from the presidency in the years 1887 to 1894 and after several decades of disagreement the 'System Droz' was made permanent. In the modern *Bundesrat* it is not unusual to have a man serve as head of one department of state during his entire tenure.

The *Bundesrat* is not a cabinet in the English sense. The 'government' cannot 'fall' if its measures are rejected by the parliament. According to Article 97 'members of the *Bundesrat* while in office may hold no other official position either in the service of the Confederation or of a Canton, nor may they follow any other career or exercise any other profession'. Unlike the English cabinet minister, they may not be members of either house of the legislature, and in this sense resemble the position of members of the American 'administration' who may not sit in Congress. Unlike the US president, they may and in fact usually do take part in debates in parliament and have the right to speak and to introduce resolutions. Chairs are set aside in the *Nationalrat* chamber for members of the *Bundesrat* to use as they choose. Normally the head of the department in whose bailiwick some legislation falls attends as a matter of course, but he speaks for the entire *Bundesrat* rather than for himself. Custom asserts that the *Bundesrat* has one voice and one opinion.

If the *Bundesrat* is not precisely a cabinet, it is also not exactly an 'administration' either. Certainly the *Bundesrat* has some of the aura of the president of the USA. The Bern press corps rises respectfully when a *Bundesrat* enters the room and hard, direct questions are rarely put. Frequently, as one very senior political correspondent told me, the press knows exactly where each of the members stand on an issue but well established custom forbids them to use it. The notion of a collective identity has never been entirely plausible. There have always been members of the Federal Council who stood out by sheer force of personality, men like Motta, Hoffmann, Pilet-Golaz or Minger. Most recently, the clever and eloquent Nello Celio enjoyed a prestige so widespread that in cantonal elections his party, the Radical Democrats (Liberal), could campaign simply as 'the party of Nello Celio'.[23] Mass communications have begun to take their toll of the traditional remoteness of the Federal Council. In late 1973 Celio and two other members of the *Bundesrat* retired together. The ensuing elections took place in what for Swiss circumstances amounted to a blaze of publicity, complete with a 'little Watergate' scandal involving the official candidate of the Christian Democrats, Enrico Franzoni. It was alleged that he had 'bribed' the proprietor of a boat-hiring company to abstain in an election years earlier in the commune of Muralto of which Franzoni was then mayor. Transcripts of trials were produced and allegations of payments of hush money made. Most remarkable of all was the actual morning of the election, 5 December 1973. In spite of the ungodly but very Swiss hour of 7.30 a.m. at which the elections were held, all the seats in the visitors' gallery and the overflow rooms in a nearby hotel were occupied and the chamber of the *Nationalrat* was brilliantly lit for television. Expert panels had assembled to comment on the elections and press men seemed to be everywhere. It was, as Frank A. Meyer described it in the *National-Zeitung*, very 'un-Swiss':

Yesterday and today were in conflict. *Bundesrat* elections will never again resemble a conclave to elect a pope. The elected and the defeated had to face the press, to pass microphones pushed toward them, to answer questions on radio and television, to communicate their feelings of disappointment or joy. Very 'un-Swiss', almost like other countries.

The 'greatest show in Switzerland' had an unusual script too. All three candidates who had been nominated by the parliamentary party groups, Arthur Schmid of the Socialists, Enrico Franzoni of the Christian Democrats, and Henri Schmitt of the Radical Democrats, lost to 'unofficial candidates', Willi Ritschard for the Socialists, Hans Hürlimann for the CVP and André Chevallaz for the Radicals, and lost on the first ballot in each case.

This curious outcome reflects not only the complexities of Swiss political life at every level but their federal, cellular character. Article 96 of the constitution states that 'not more than one member may be elected from a given canton'. Custom stipulates that there must always be one member of the *Bundesrat* from the three most populous cantons of Bern, Zürich and Vaud and that there ought to be never less than two Swiss French and/or Italian. Cantonal citizenship is determined by *Bürgerort* in theory but in practice members may claim residence as well as commune of origin. Finally, the 'magic formula' requires that there always be two Socialists, two Christian Democrats, two Radical Democrats and one Swiss People's Party member on the *Bundesrat*. Vacancies are filled in order of the seniority of the retiring member and require an absolute majority of the 244 members of the joint session of both chambers. If no candidate has a majority, a second ballot takes place, followed by more ballots until an absolute majority is reached. From the third ballot on, the candidate with the lowest votes drops out of the running. This system offers the added peculiarity that, not unlike the open primary system in the United States, political opponents ultimately choose a given party's representative, since each of the main parties is too weak to elect 'its' candidate on its own. The makeup of the *Bundesversammlung* in December 1973 was as shown in Table 3.4.

In effect, the 'official' Socialist, Herr Arthur Schmid, needed 73 votes from other parties to become a *Bundesrat*, the 'official' Christian Democrat, Signor Franzoni 62, and Monsieur Henri Schmitt, the 'official' Radical 59. Each of the three official candidates had barely obtained a majority within his own parliamentary party, Herr Schmid and Signor Franzoni in three-way contests and Monsieur Schmitt in a straight fight. Each suffered under various disabilities. Franzoni had been harmed by the 'little Watergate', Schmitt by his reputation as a 'law and order'

TABLE 3.4

Radical Democrats	64
Christian Democrats	61
Social Democrats	50
Swiss People's Party	28
Landesring (Independent)	14
Liberal and Evangelical	11
Republican/National Action	11
Parti du Travail (Communist)	5
Total	244

Director of the Police and Justice Department in his native Geneva and by the fact that he had finished last of the five Radicals in the election for the Genevese equivalent of the *Bundesrat*. Herr Schmid had suffered a similar embarrassment in his home canton, Aargau, and he had both the reputation of being too weak and too left-wing. Several of the outsiders were better known and more charismatic. The Christian Democrat, Dr Leo Schürmann, was extremely well known as Swiss Prices Commissioner and in the words of the Basel-Land Christian Democratic Party in a telegram to the federal party stood for 'the successful break through from the traditional milieu and a new approach by Christian Democracy to urban problems'. The right-wing Socialist, Willi Ritschard, had the advantage of being the first working man (he had begun as a plumber and steam fitter) to aspire to the Federal Council. He enjoyed the respect of the bourgeois parties for his success as Solothurn's Director of the Finance Department. The handsome young Andreas Gerwig of Basel, a splendidly charismatic figure, who was later to be defence counsel for the big sit-in on the site of an atomic power plant, was the hero of the younger and more left-wing Socialists. Claims for the importance of other candidates in the two other parties were fervently made. The whole thing, wrote Alfred Peter in the *National-Zeitung*, was a 'lottery', but a better image might have been a parlour game with very complicated rules. The election of any given candidate must automatically favour some and harm others. The first ballot was that to fill the vacancy of the retiring Socialist Herr Tschudi. Unexpectedly, Willi Ritschard collected just enough votes on the first ballot, 123, to win outright. Since his canton was Solothurn, Leo Schürmann, also from Solothurn, was automatically out of the running for the vacancy created by M. Bonvin's retirement, the vacancy allotted to the Christian Democrats by the 'magic formula'. Hans Hurlimann, a steady, conventional cantonal politician from Zug in central Switzerland, suddenly found himself catapulted past Franzoni into the *Bundesrat*, and the witty historian and former mayor of Lausanne, André Chevallaz, easily beat the controversial Genevan police and justice minister, Schmitt.

Bells rang out all over Canton Zug, and the public seemed pleased by the unexpected drama on the screen. Leader-writers praised the independence of the members of the 'Militia Parliament', but party officials were very cross indeed. Richard Müller of the SPS called it 'a box on the ear' and other Socialists threatened to reopen the question of the 'magic formula' if the bourgeois parties refused to accept the SPS's true representatives. Urs Reinhardt, the general secretary of the Christian Democrats, attacked 'the hyenas and beetles of the mass media' who had smeared his party's candidate. While a public opinion poll in Geneva showed that most people interviewed thought that what went on in Bern never affected them anyway, Genevan politicians criticised the injustice done to Geneva, which had not had a Federal Councillor for over fifty years. Italian Switzerland reacted bitterly. Writing in the Christian Democratic *Popolo e Libertà*, Attilo Grandi struck up the familiar litany of complaint and neglect of Swiss Italian sentiment: 'We had deluded ourselves into thinking that the presence of Nello Celio in the Federal Council had reinforced in the parties and in the members of the chambers our convictions, but once again we have to accept bitterly the fruits of an historic, atavistic incomprehension . . . a political insensitivity.' Even the liberal *Corriere del Ticino* mourned the defeat of the 'other formula, that is, an equality of ethnic representation, which we thought had won universal sympathy'. Celio interviewed by Radio della Svizzera italiana had to admit that he too was disappointed. Representation of Italian Switzerland, while not necessary, was desirable, because 'we bring to the highest executive body of the country something different'.

There must be losers in any electoral system and with only seven seats on the Federal Council, not all cantonal, linguistic, religious or political elements can be satisfactorily represented. Some cantons (Uri, Schwyz, Nidwalden, Appenzell Inner Rhodes and Schaffhausen) have never had a Federal Councillor and others only one in the years since 1848. A more fundamental objection is that the elections are a game. After a similar, though less dramatic, upheaval in 1966, Nationalrat Breitenmoser (CVP, Basel-City) observed: 'Federal Council elections are rather like games of chance based on the formula: at the right moment find the right man with the right language from the right canton. The one elected is a very lucky fellow.' Perhaps there ought to be more Federal Councillors, more than one permitted from a given canton or no consideration given to commune of origin (*Bürgerort*). Certainly one or all of those alterations would loosen the automatic couplings by which candidates seem to drop into or through the right slots. Another, even more fundamental alteration would be direct popular election of Federal Councillors by the citizens. Good precedents exist for electing the executive directly; most cantons have direct elections of members of the Executive Council (*Regierungsrat*). All of these devices would make the election of Federal Councillors less like a pinball machine through which candidates drop on to the right or wrong cushions, but it would not resolve the much deeper *malaise* about the institution itself. Seven diligent honourable men do not constitute a political as opposed to an administrative focus. A president by rotation reduces the chance of genuine national leadership. In his latest novel, Giovanni Orelli likens presidential orations on festive occasions to frozen food. The citizenry eats lunch while the president alone is talking. In fact his patriotic sentiments 'have been stored for a week in a cupboard, in a sort of strongroom, cut on to tape before being served: just like a food which looks as if it had been cooked to order but has really been waiting there for weeks or months in the store-rooms and refrigerators of the big stores'.[24] Perhaps the Swiss can confront the turbulence of the 1970s with the traditional pieties, now wrapped in cellophane and stored on tape, but there are those who doubt it. Among them is James Schwarzenbach, one of the few Swiss politicians to have made an impact abroad. Schwarzenbach has ridden to notoriety on the exploitation of the enormous political implications of the foreign worker question. By comparison with that, the machinery of *Bundesrat* elections may seem quaint or trivial. Yet the *Bundesrat* is the only executive the Swiss have, and it remains to be seen if it can regain the initiative in the explosive emotional issues generated by the huge foreign population.

The first, and in some ways the hardest, thing to do is simply to grasp the scale of the problem. The tables below may help. Table 3.5 shows the growth of foreigners as a proportion of the total Swiss population. One in five of all persons employed in Switzerland is foreign. The resident foreigners constitute one problem, but the foreigners who work in Switzerland on a daily or seasonal basis constitute another. Table 3.6 shows the changes in the numbers of foreign workers by

TABLE 3.5   Foreigners in Switzerland

Date	Total	Percentage of total population
1 December 1950	285,000	6.1
1 December 1960	585,000	10.8
31 December 1965	810,000	13.8
31 December 1967	891,000	14.8
31 December 1968	933,000	15.3
31 December 1969	972,000	15.8
31 December 1970	983,000	15.9
31 December 1971	999,000	16.1
31 December 1972	1,080,000	17.2
31 December 1973	1,094,000	17.2
31 December 1974	1,102,000	17.3

category of work permit. Within the categories shifts are considerable. The resident group grew by 12% as more long-term foreign workers achieved the necessary number of consecutive months of residence to qualify. The other group to grow was that of *Grenzgänger* or *Frontalieri* workers who live in France, Germany or Italy but cross into Switzerland to work each day. Frontier-crossing workers are particularly prominent in Canton Ticino where in August 1974, 32,577 were employed. Geneva with 24,467 and Basel with 19,777 come next. The overall concentration of foreign workers, resident or otherwise, is heaviest in the Zürich area, where about a sixth of all foreigners are employed, followed by Geneva. At the end of August 1974, Italians made up 41% of all employed foreign workers (excluding holders of resident visas) followed by Spaniards 20% and French 11%, Yugoslavs 8%, Germans 7% and other nationalities less than 3%. Roughly two-

TABLE 3.6   Foreign workers by type of visa

End of August	Resident	Annual visa	Seasonal	Frontier crossing (*Grenz-gänger*)	Total
1970	174,723	429,956	154,732	74,797	834,208
1971	204,748	391,814	180,828	87,838	865,228
1972	242,373	355,150	196,632	97,203	891,358
1973	276,568	322,513	193,766	104,573	897,420
1974	309,650	288,575	151,962	110,809	860,996

fifths of the Italian nationals, regardless of category of visa, found employment in Ticino and about a fifth in the Zürich area. Naturally enough, Italians made up over 90% of foreign workers in Ticino, 39% of all foreign workers in German Switzerland and 28% in French Switzerland.[25] The importance of foreigners to Swiss industry can be seen in the figures for employment in the 10,351 enterprises officially classified as industrial. Foreigners (both holders of permanent and temporary permits) made up 37.7% of all employed persons in industry in September 1974. In the clothing and cleaning industries more than half and in the earth and stone processing enterprises just under half of all workers were foreign.[26] No other European country comes near this dependence on foreign workers.

While the *Bundesrat* has been able to maintain control over the number of permits for work, it cannot control fertility rates in the resident population of foreign workers. There were in 1972 100 live births per 1,000 foreign women between the ages of fifteen and forty-nine, compared to 55 per 1,000 for Swiss women.[27] The overall population of foreigners in Switzerland has stayed high in spite of the effects of the depression. Social tensions have, if anything, been sharpened by the change in the economic climate, rather than lessened, as many Swiss hoped might happen.

Herr Schwarzenbach entered this scene in 1967, elected to the *Nationalrat* as the non-partisan representative of the 'Aktion gegen Ueberfremdung von Volk und Heimat', a pressure group to limit the number of aliens in the country. By profession a publisher and journalist, he directs the Thomas Verlag in Zürich, has written novels and biographies, and serves as a divisional propaganda officer in the army with the rank of major. A comfortable man, who smokes a pipe and exudes an easy-going, patriarchal authority, he would have enjoyed peripheral notoriety, had it not been for the opportunities for agitation inherent in Swiss democratic procedures. Schwarzenbach may have been the only member of the *Nationalrat* in the late 1960s to represent his movement but he could use the initiative as well as the main parties. His 'Aktion' demanded a reduction of the total number of foreign workers by a third and a limit on the percentage of foreign workers in each canton to 10% of the native population. He allowed Geneva a unique position as headquarters of so many international organisations by granting it a limit of 25%. Had Schwarzenbach's initiative of June 1970 been accepted by the voters, some 300,000 registered foreign workers would have been forced to leave Switzerland. The *Bundesrat*, industry and commerce were greatly alarmed and a campaign of anti-Schwarzenbach propaganda began which must have cost more than the cost of all previous initiatives and referenda combined. Glossy propaganda pamphlets pointed out how essential were foreign workers. On 7 June 1970, 74.1% of all Swiss entitled to vote went to the polls. The absolute majority needed was 606,181 and the pro-Schwarzenbach voters numbered 557,517 or 46%. He had nearly won a startling victory. He had also carried six full and two half cantons (Bern, Luzern, Uri, Schwyz, Fribourg, Solothurn, Nidwalden and Obwalden).

Analysis of the results yielded interesting insights into the mood of Switzerland on the threshold of the 1970s. Majorities for Schwarzenbach had been achieved primarily in Roman Catholic, predominantly agricultural cantons. With the exception of Bern, all those giving the Schwarzenbach initiative a majority belonged to the more traditional and anti-federal cantons. It was almost the *Sonderbundkrieg* again with Solothurn in place of Valais. In Canton Luzern there was a topographical pattern: the narrower and more remote the valley the more voters for Schwarzenbach. Clearly, foreign workers were not the great issue there but general hostility to the trends of modern Swiss life. Schwarzenbach became an international figure and now began to build a basis for a new political party, the Republican Party. At the same time a group with similar aims called the National Action formed on his flank. In the national elections of autumn 1971, the two parties gained 7% of the vote and sent eleven members to the *Nationalrat* in Bern. It was the most significant shift in voting patterns for decades. Peter Gilg has examined the actual results in detail.[28] The areas of strongest support are (in percentage of votes cast) listed in Table 3.7. A quick glance shows that in 1971 the most industrialised areas were the most profitable for the two parties. Much more difficult is an analysis of voters by class. Gilg concluded that the districts most susceptible to right-wing appeals were those with the highest proportion of employees and workers, traditional left-wing voting areas and those with a high proportion of foreign workers or, in other words, the Swiss working class.

The new 'National Opposition' of seven Republicans and four deputies of the National Action made itself felt from the first session of the new legislature in 1971. Their opposition was loud, vituperative and 'un-Swiss'. They spoke on every issue from the budget of the state railways to federal contributions to university institutions in the cantons. No matter what the issue they turned it into propaganda in the campaign against the foreign population. Again and again they attacked the *Bundesrat*. Georges Breny of the National Action, the only Swiss French deputy in the group and a tram driver in Bern, even tried to blame the city's traffic problems on the presence of foreigners. It became clear that Schwarzenbach, the group's leader, could not always control the more extreme demagogues and on occasion had to dissociate himself from them. The *Bundesrat*'s reaction to the provocations and to the wider challenge posed by the movement was hesitant. Swiss executive members are not accustomed to stormy scenes and violent language. *Sachlichkeit* alone was no answer. The 'magic formula' by including the four big parties in the executive had created a vacuum at the legislative centre. The style of Swiss politics made its conventional practitioners easy targets for the demagogue. Every concrete step taken by the *Bundesrat*, lowering the number of foreign workers permitted to each firm in 1968 and 1969; setting overall national limits for all foreign workers in 1970; the so-called *Plafonierung* of 1973, and eventually specific control of the number of seasonal workers in 1974, could with some truth be credited to the account of the 'National Opposition'.

On 3 November 1972 the National Action submitted a petition with 68,000 signatures demanding a vote on a bill to reduce the total number of foreigners in Switzerland to 500,000 by the end of 1977. This initiative, the third on the question of foreign workers, went beyond Schwarzenbach's 1970 proposals. The government worked out that 540,000 foreigners, men, women and children, would be expelled from Switzerland and not only the temporary permit holders. The threat to the

TABLE 3.7

Canton	Republican	National Action	Total
Zürich	10.4	6.0	16.4
Thurgau	8.8	4.2	13.0
Basel-Stadt	4.9	8.0	12.9
Neuchâtel	10.1		10.1
Basel-Land		10.0	10.0
Aargau	5.8	3.4	9.2
Vaud	2.9	4.2	7.1
St Gallen	7.0		7.0
Schaffhausen		6.4	6.4
Bern	2.1	3.7	5.8

Swiss economy was terrifying. Cantons with heavy concentrations of foreigners, Zürich, Vaud, Ticino and Geneva, faced the collapse of entire branches of the public service, hotel and building trades and other service industries. White collar and skilled personnel would also be hit. CIBA–Geigy in Basel reckoned that they might lose 333 academically trained people, about 23% of the total research team, and Sandoz estimated that they would lose 775 year-permit holders and 675 border-crossing workers or 15% of the total work force. A public opinion poll commissioned by *Die Weltwoche* and published on 13 March 1974 showed that 40% of those interviewed would vote Yes, 46% No and 14% were not sure. It also showed that 82% announced that they would vote. Nervousness grew especially as the *Bundesrat* offered no counter-proposal. The debate in the *Nationalrat* in mid-March was acrimonious and in one respect sensational. James Schwarzenbach announced that 'his conscience would not permit him to support proposals which would lead Switzerland to the brink of a catastrophe'. He rejected the 'methods of Idi Amin' which his erstwhile colleagues were promoting. Naturally relations worsened between the two wings of the 'National Opposition' and on 29 May 1975 the parliamentary union of Republicans and National Action was formally dissolved. Schwarzenbach submitted his own initiative for a milder limitation of foreigners which the NA countered by an initiative to limit the rights of cantons and communes to grant citizenship at their own discretion (*Einbürgerung*).

The squabble within the right-wing undoubtedly weakened the campaign of the National Action more than any government propaganda. Many potential Yes-voters must have followed Schwarzenbach's advice. In the vote on 20 October 1974 the National Action in fact did less well than Schwarzenbach had done in 1970. Only 69.8% turned out in 1974 compared to 74.1% in 1970 and only 34% voted Yes compared to 46% in 1970. The proposal failed to obtain a majority in any of the twenty-two cantons in strong contrast to 1970 when Schwarzenbach had carried six full and two half cantons. The elections of October 1975 seemed to confirm the decline of the extreme right, although a system which can permit more than 2,000 candidates on 170 different lists for only 200 seats is not easy to interpret. The two parties of the right lost five seats and the Socialists gained nine. In Swiss terms a landslide. It may be that the workers who voted radical right in prosperous 1971 have returned to their traditional allegiance in depressed 1975, but so many personal and local factors play a part that analysis is tricky. How important was anti-feminism? The one Communist loss was a woman. Lise Girardin was defeated in her bid for re-election to the upper house. Several other prominent women were defeated. How important was the poor turnout of registered voters? Has parliament lost prestige?

Swiss politics seem to be entering a period in which direct action rather than parliamentary debate will dominate the national area. The Jura conflict continues. The small but energetic Communist Party (Parti du Travail) has several initiative campaigns well under way. At Easter 1975 15,000 people occupied the site of a proposed nuclear power plant at Kaiseraugst near Basel and refused either to vacate or behave in a decorous, Swiss manner. The occupation which I discuss at length in Chapter 6 continued for eleven weeks. Extra-parliamentary radicalism of the left has become a noticeable element of daily politics, producing underground journals, sporadic violence and scandals. Switzerland is growing more 'normal' as the artificial unities of the *réduit national* dissolve for ever.

Yet there are limits to what extremists of right or left can do with the Swiss electorate. The voters reject the new-fangled, the unexpected, the expensive. Part of the impetus behind the Yes vote in 1970 and 1974 to the initiatives against foreigners was an intensely conservative reaction to the changes of the last twenty years. The battle lines in the Jura conflict go back two centuries; only the techniques have changed. The occupation of the building site at Kaiseraugst, in spite of its modish appearance, represented the exasperation of the citizens of a *Gemeinde* and a region whose local autonomy and democratic procedures seemed to be mocked by big companies and the federal government. Even the Communist Party is very Swiss. The Parti du Travail is basically a regional grouping, largely confined to French Switzerland. Its four deputies are exclusively from Geneva and Vaud and with the exception of M. Roger Dafflon, once a building worker, relentlessly middle-class and professional. The position of women in politics is another sign of the conservatism of the Swiss electorate. Four years after the vote of 7 February 1971, which introduced universal suffrage on the federal level, there were still no women members of the *Bundesrat* or of any cantonal executive. Of the ten largest *Gemeinden* Zürich had two women out of nine Executive Council members, Geneva, Bern and Biel−Bienne one each out of five, seven and nine members respectively; the other six none at all. In legislatures there was a little more representation of women. There were only fourteen women members of the

Nationalrat between 1971 and 1975 and a scattering of female deputies on cantonal level with Basel-Stadt and Geneva having the highest proportion (16%) while Appenzell Inner and Appenzell Outer Rhodes had none. The general secretary of the Socialist Party is a woman, and until 1975 there was one female member of the upper chamber, the lively Mme Lise Girardin, former mayor of Geneva. Her defeat eliminated the only Swiss woman with a national reputation in politics and certainly the only one who might have had a chance in the *Bundesrat* elections of 1973. The under-representation of women in politics reflects the intrinsic conservatism of the electorate and politicians, for it is not now the case that women go out to work in markedly lower numbers in Switzerland than elsewhere in Europe.

These reflections lead me to err on the side of caution, and hence by a roundabout route to return to the politics of the *Gemeinde*. We have seen the set of 'do's and 'don'ts' at work in Malters and in Bern. You don't force people out of office and you accept the rules of the *proporz* game. Everything is 'political', but limits to fair political action are instinctively accepted. Similarly, the world the Swiss citizen sees is profoundly conditioned by historic continuity. 'It has always been so' is deeply felt to be a justification for trying to keep it so for the future, and I can think of a great many less agreeable political philosophies. Most of this is wholly unreflective, simply assumed as part of the texture of daily life. The Swiss know intellectually that things are changing and fast. No one can fail to see signs of inadequacy in the political institutions on all three levels, in the behaviour of the citizenry, in the disorder and confusion within the parties and in the existence of extra-parliamentary left-wing groups and in the emergence of the 'National Opposition'. Yet beneath these changes there are layers of Swiss consciousness which bind and control political behaviour in subtle ways. One of these layers of awareness is attitude to language, and that is the subject of the next chapter.

4. Language

English-speakers rarely think about their language. Unlike the French who poured millions into propagating the French language overseas, the English in their empire (and the Americans in theirs) never worried much about the language as such. There is no recognised academy in any part of the English-speaking world to defend the purity of the language. As a world language, English is casual, slovenly and varied. In Switzerland, and in most European countries, language is a very different thing. By excluding those who cannot understand, it sets the outer limits of membership in a certain type of community. The precise meaning of that membership will depend on the status of the language: written or unwritten, used in a wide geographical area or restricted, spoken by all social classes or only by some. It will also depend on the economic, social, legal, political, religious and ideological structures in which it is used, for example, the language acceptable in a court of law. Language can change social and political institutions. It can help to alter the productive forces of an economy and can enlarge or contract markets. A startling example of life imitating speech is Italian unification. In his fascinating study of language in the history of Italy, Tullio de Mauro estimates that in 1861, the heroic epoch of Italian unification, only 2.5% of the total Italian population could speak Italian. The other twenty-five million inhabited what he calls a 'forest of dialect' so dense that when the Visconti-Venesta brothers walked down the streets of Naples speaking Italian they were thought to be Englishmen.[1] Modern Italy first took form in language, and this may be said of modern Czechoslovakia, Slovenia, Romania, Serbia and, for different reasons, modern Israel. Perry Anderson is right when he observes that 'spoken language, far from always following material changes, may sometimes anticipate them'.[2]

Language is not a colourless fluid through which reality is refracted but a thick, viscous substance like tar. It has its own ebbs and flow which never leave the surrounding environment utterly unchanged. Political frontiers, accidentally imposed, may dam its currents. The accumulating liquid at first stagnates; then separated off from its original main stream, it literally becomes another language. Slovak differs from Czech, because the border of the medieval Kingdom of Hungary divided hitherto undivided west Slavic-speakers. The differences among German, Alsatian, Dutch, Swiss German and Luxemburgisch all began as historical lines on the map and deepened into separate dialect or language currents. The process works in the other direction too. Italian, Ukrainian, Croatian, Serbian and at an earlier date English, French and Spanish spread out to submerge and ultimately absorb other languages and dialects. The Scottish language was largely destroyed by political repression, the Irish reduced by economic and social change. This is the context in which the precise position of language in Switzerland must be seen. There are other multilingual states in Europe, for example Yugoslavia; there are bilingual states like Belgium; there are linguistic minorities on the 'wrong' sides of borders, as in south Tyrol. Switzerland is not special simply because it has four 'national languages' but because language itself has a special place in Switzerland. Language defines and at the same time denies Swiss identity; it reinforces the peculiarities of political practice and reflects them. Above all, it contributes to the bewildering variety in a small area which makes it hard to say anything general about Switzerland. In Chapter 1 I first offered one or two examples of that variety; now I should like to look at it in greater detail. First the dimensions of the question. The 1970 census figures are shown in Table 4.1.

The impact of foreign migration between 1950 and 1970 accounts for the doubling of the percentage of Italian-speakers and for the appearance of 4% 'other' (Spanish, Turkish, Croatian, etc.).

The largest of the groups is still the Swiss 'German' but the inverted commas around the word suggest that there is more to the reality than the noun conveys. Technically what Swiss Germans speak is *Schwyzerdütsch*, a rather artificial term to describe an astonishing number of dialects in a small geographical area. It falls into three broad linguistic groups, Low Alemannic, High Alemannic and Highest Alemannic, dialect groups of the wider Alemannic family whose relatives can be found beyond the borders of the present Confederation in Swabia, Austria and in the southern parts of Baden and Alsace. Technically the

TABLE 4.1   Residents of Switzerland by mother-tongue (in %)

Year	German	French	Italian	Romansch	Other
1950	72	20	6	1	1
1960	69	19	10	1	1
1970	65	18	12	1	4

distinguishing feature of High Alemannic which marks it off from the other Alemannic dialects is a collection of distinct sounds or phonological features,[3] but equally important is the social and political position of the dialect. *Schwyzerdütsch* in its three forms is the normal language of the Swiss Germans in daily life and at all levels of society. All users of High Alemannic can understand all other users, although there are occasional difficulties. The one main Low Alemannic dialect, the *Baseldütsch* of the city of Basel, can also be understood by all Swiss Germans, although the traveller from Basel who finds himself in a remote valley may have to refute the charge that he is German and not Swiss. About 100,000 people still use Highest Alemannic, the dialects of the very high Alps, Oberwallis and the Bernese Oberland in particular, and there the normal *Schwyzerdütsch*-speaker may not understand conversations among native users. Swiss Germans seem to relish that fact, and I have often noticed the extreme gusto with which tales are told of how thick the dialect is up there.

Dialect for Swiss German-speakers is identity, and the pleasure in Oberwalliser archaism is a kind of self-satisfaction, a delight in one's own *Eigenart* or special nature. Dialect is a constant subject of discussion among Swiss German-speakers and a distinct form of instant recognition. The Swiss like the English feel that 'you are how you speak'. The moment a Swiss German opens his mouth, every hearer knows where he comes from. As the English hear class characteristics, so the Swiss notice regional ones. Different dialects produce different reactions. Zürich dialect has a reputation for harshness, some say, 'aggressiveness', while the broad, lava-like flow of *Bärndütsch* gets high marks for a kind of genial, folksy, homely quality. The Baseler enjoys a reputation for witty use of words, and the Luzerner for liveliness and emotionalism. Linguistic and social perceptions tend to merge. I have heard resentment expressed by some Swiss in central and eastern Switzerland that the radio is dominated by the Bern, Basel and Zürich variants. The resentment of the sound reflects the history of the place. Zürich's aggressiveness is an historical fact, smoothly and unconsciously folded into the sound the listener hears.

Dialect is identity but it is also a form of social communication. The easiest way to start a conversation with a stranger at a party is to say 'Ah, I hear that you come from Zug. Do you know . . .?' Once names have been exchanged, the next step is to examine family. 'Are you a relative of the Burris in Hergiswil?' The location becomes more precise and the contact is established. Swiss German-speakers make contact easily with each other, when abroad. More tell-tale than the passport is the characteristic sound of *Schwyzerdütsch* in the London Underground or on Madison Avenue. Since virtually no one but a Swiss ever speaks the language, and hence no Swiss remotely expects anyone else to understand it, Swiss travellers are more prone to chatter away in public than English, French, German or even American travellers would be. It is the private language of some four million people, not a very large group in the wider world, and they value it as the most personal mark of identity. A recent congratulatory article on the eightieth birthday of a well-known Basel civic leader remarked as a matter of course on the fact that after more than fifty years in the city, he still spoke an absolutely pure *Bärndütsch* not out of pride but simply because 'one should preserve one's mother-tongue in foreign parts'.

It is important to be clear precisely what is meant by dialect here. It is not accent as in the case of Yorkshire or Texas. Nor are dialects simply 'debased, corrupt forms of standard. This is, of course, not so. Rather, it is standard which has risen from the dialects to its level of social and cultural prestige.'[4] The opposite idea is also false. Dialects do not necessarily preserve ancient forms of the language. They are no older nor younger than standard German. They have developed differently, feel the iron grip of norms less acutely and in remote areas have preserved a different mix of old and new. Dialects are not necessarily more vulgar than the 'high' speech although they are usually more 'popular' and less literary. Standard or High German can be vulgar in a vulgar mouth, and *Schwyzerdütsch* as refined as its speaker. What is true, as both a strength and a weakness, is that for Swiss Germans, *Schwyzerdütsch* is the mother-tongue, above all, the language of childhood, family, the heart. It is more direct and more intimate. If an ad-man wants to get his message across, he will slip a little *Mundart* (a folksier word for the foreign *Dialekt*) into the copy, as in this advertisement for an apple juice, 'Ova Urtrüeb bsunders guet' or this one for a Swiss cigar, 'Neu Rössli Rund . . . e rundi Sach'. Typically, the homey, intimate articles of daily use are fitted out with copy in dialect, while advertisements for life insurance or analogue computers use the language of high seriousness: *Schriftdeutsch* or written German. The only really successful Swiss pop group, the five-man Rumpelstilz, made a much bigger impact when they switched to dialect song texts. Dialect was their natural monopoly unavailable to the Rolling Stones or the Pink Floyd.

Schwyzerdütsch has a grammar very different from that of High German. There is only one relative pronoun (*wo*), no present participle, no praeterite and no construction 'in order to . . .' There is no verb 'to love' and there are a whole series of common German words, which do not exist in it: *wobei, irgendwie, sondern,* although some urban dialects now use the German words very frequently. The sentence structure is entirely different and, of course, the pronunciation utterly so. For historical reasons *Schwyzerdütsch* has a limited vocabulary. Written German has remained the language of higher culture and also the *spoken* language of elevated discourse. A university professor will lecture in German and conduct his oral examinations and seminars in that language too. He will probably speak dialect in the privacy of his study to an individual student. The Swiss German Radio distinguishes with great subtlety between the occasions for German and those for *Schwyzerdütsch,* not always comprehensibly to the foreigner. The early morning music and traffic news in the now defunct programme 'Auto-radio Schweiz' was in chatty dialect, an odd usage, when one considers the number of drivers in any Swiss city who are foreigners. International news and weather always come in German but sport normally in *Schwyzerdütsch.* Advanced discourse of any kind tends to be in German, as, indeed, are most prayers and, until recently, most sermons. The 'Our Father' is always said in German and the language of prayer and religious discourse cannot really escape the immense impact of the German Bible.

The result of all this is to force the Swiss German back to the German language and to put him at a special disadvantage in the world of commerce and industry. He cannot speak his native language with any foreign customers nor with domestic ones from the other language areas of Switzerland. He has to compete in sales meetings with men whose native languages have international distribution. The successful Swiss businessman takes these facts for granted and makes sure that he remains competitive. I remember my interview with Dr A. M. Schütz, the President of Eterna Ltd, an important Swiss watch company. Dr Schütz strode briskly to his seat and in High German offered me my choice of four languages for our interview, as if he had been offering me coffee, tea or milk. At more modest levels of society, High German tends to falter a little and emerges in that thick Swiss accent so beloved of the German and Austrian musichalls. The average Swiss speaks German woodenly. His prose is stilted, heavy and lifeless. He never makes a joke and by comparison with a witty German or Austrian seems about as lively as the grumpy dwarf in 'Snow White'. The same man using dialect in his 'local', chatting away and laughing, is simply another human being, easy, often very funny and spontaneous.

Spoken Swiss German is full of 'foreign words', especially French ones. Many Swiss German say *merci viel mal* not *danke schön*. A conductor on a tram is a *conducteur* not a *Schaffner*, and so on. There are obvious historical reasons for the prominence of French. For more than two centuries French dominated European culture and for many patrician Swiss families French was the language of civilised discourse. The French were very present politically during the Helvetic Republic and Napoleonic era. French cultural influence varied geographically and also socially. Some communities, especially Bern and Basel, absorbed more French into daily speech than Zürich or St Gallen. During the nineteenth century, the growth in political and cultural prestige of German began to right this imbalance, but uniformity of usage never became as characteristic of written or spoken German as it had been of French. Two great literary contemporaries illustrate this variety neatly. Theodor Fontane and Gottfried Keller were both born in 1819, but the 'German' writer, Fontane, wrote a prose so frenchified that modern editions require elaborate notes to explain words like *Affront* or *Eklat* for contemporary readers. The Swiss author Keller wrote a more germanic German using traditional words like *Base* for *cousine* (cousin) and *Muhme* for *tante* (aunt). Keller's prose probably reflected the smaller influence of French on the underlying Zürich version of *Schwyzerdütsch*. The gap between written and spoken usage also permits the survival of words like *Ilp*, the Basel German word for elephant now obsolete elsewhere. There are specifically Swiss usages, such as *Besammlung* for an assembly of persons and the verb *äufnen* to accrue, neither of which occurs in standard German dictionaries. It is arguable that because *Schwyzerdütsch* is not normally written, it may be less resistant to foreign imports than written languages are, but other explanations, not least Hitler's campaign against 'foreign words' during the 1930s, also account for the higher proportion of them in Swiss German daily use than in High German.

The most remarkable characteristic of *Schwyzerdütsch* is its variety. Dr Ludwig Fischer in a study of Luzern dialect distinguishes five groups among the 289,000 inhabitants: the dialects of the Mittelland, the Hinterland, the Luzern and Hochdorf, the Rigi area and, finally, the Entlebuch. In isolating the character of each he emphasises the crucial geographical elements. In the Entlebuch Valley, for example, there is practically no linguistic influence from neighbouring Obwalden, because until the 1940s the roads were not always passable. 'Earlier isolation, history, cultural life, economic development and the character of the population all helped to erect dialect borders.'[5] Even in the less mountainous regions, this linguistic diversity is marked. Each village or region has its own characteristic vowel sounds, speech rhythms and frequently its own vocabulary. As a result, the Swiss look puzzled if one asks whether dialect can be learned. The idea that dialect can be acquired is clearly alien to them. If they accept, for the sake of discussion, that dialect might be learned, they are quick to point out that there is no generally accepted dialect so there would be no use in trying. It is not surprising that there are only three or four courses in dialect in all of Switzerland. To teach dialect would mean to make it formal and to give it a grammar. The relationship of written German to *Schwyzerdütsch* is very like that of Latin to the vernacular Romance languages in the early Middle Ages, as Dr J. A. Cremona describes it:

It was not simply a question of there being no grammatical codification of the vernaculars: in the forms in which they were known, the vernaculars were believed not to be amenable to grammatical analysis. They were too irregular, too protean and variable, for analysis to be possible. These notions were encouraged by the diverging structures of Latin and vernacular.[6]

It would appear that the first attempts to provide grammars for Romance languages arose from the need to teach the vernaculars to foreigners and to serve as models of 'best' usage for vernacular poetry. Several grammars of this sort appeared in the thirteenth century. The presence of foreigners has not had the same effect in Switzerland. Even the intrusion of mass communications, especially television from the Federal Republic of Germany, has not done more than 'corrupt' dialect by introducing words from the written speech into the spoken one. The tension between *Schriftdeutsch* and *Mundart* continues without either displacing the other. Swiss German linguistic usage rests on an uneasy equilibrium between the decentralising pull of dialect and the pervasive centralising impact of High German. The explanation for this uniquely Swiss balancing act can be found, in the first place, in politics.

Schwyzerdütsch binds Swiss Germans together, especially in the face of the Germans, and is particularly precious to them. Swiss tell you that they 'love' their dialects in the way that people elsewhere love their homes. Spiritually the dialect is a home in the narrow sense and a national home in the wider. Dialect variety reflects and reinforces political and communal variety. The *Gemeinde*, the district, the canton and the federal government may all be said to have a linguistic reality to flesh out the civil forms. A striking example is Canton Bern where, for profoundly political motives, the members of the Grand Council, the cantonal parliament, insist on using Bern dialect. It reinforces the peculiar identity of Bern but at the same time irritates those citizens of the canton who speak French as a mother-tongue. It is well understood in Switzerland that you can expect the *Welschen*, as Swiss Germans often call Swiss French, to try to understand written German but not dialect. Hence by using *Bärndütsch* the Grand Councillors spread themselves more broadly across the political scene and assert their political dominance over the unruly Jurassiens. The dialect includes but it also excludes.

Dialect excludes foreigners very effectively, whether the 'foreigners' are other Swiss in Oberwallis or in Romansch-speaking Graubünden. More than any other single factor, dialect makes it hard to get 'inside Switzerland' or to get to know Swiss Germans. The foreigner who tries to approach the Swiss through the German language gets a misleading impression. Swiss Germans instinctively respond to a High German-speaker in their version of it. They find it psychologically very difficult to hear the one language spoken to them and to respond in the other. In a group, the presence of one non-dialect speaker can kill the spontaneity of a conversation. The moment the Swiss German-speakers remember the alien presence, they tend to throw the language switch back to High, leaving it there until they forget again.

If *Schwyzerdütsch* establishes identity, it does not do so simply nor without a considerable price. The price is seen in the ambivalence of virtually all Swiss about the written language, *Schriftdeutsch*. Its use is a tricky operation. Swiss Germans suspect any fellow Swiss who uses High German too well and are embarrassed by anyone who uses it too badly. A native German-speaker will recognise at once that radio announcers on Swiss radio have accents, but to the Swiss they sound too German to be real Swiss. Not the least of the accusations levelled at the poet Carl Spitteler in 1914, when he urged his fellow Swiss Germans to be less pro-German, was his constant use of High German. The ironies multiply. It was, after all, the prestige of literary German and the achievements of German and Austrian culture in the nineteenth century which made Jakob Burckhardt rejoice that *Schwyzerdütsch* had never become a literary language. The educated Swiss shared the international culture of the most advanced of the European peoples. When in the twentieth century that people reverted to a modern form of barbarism, Swiss Germans found themselves culturally caught up in the German catastrophe. Their literary language could not be spoken without shame in any non-German continental country, and many Swiss travellers in the 1940s suffered great embarrassment because Dutchmen or Danes jumped to wrong conclusions.

The extraordinary situation of German Switzerland is most poignantly revealed in the schools. Swiss German children have to learn to read and write what is effectively a foreign language. The Czech philologist, Olga Neversilova, has compared it to asking someone to learn to play the piano and drive a car at the same time. In her studies of the behaviour of children, she noticed that the children coped with the alien written language by creating home-made High German: *ich bin gesein, Zeuge* for *Züge* and so on. What seems to happen is that the children draw natural analogues from one system and place it in the other. For adult Swiss Germans the written and spoken languages tend to be wholly dissociated. What is written is simply different and pronounced differently from what is spoken. Public lecturers and preachers will tell you that if they wish to speak to an audience in dialect, they cannot use a written manuscript but must rely on key words or phrases. The moment a proper text appears, the mind apparently switches into the channels which control the written language. These problems multiply what is already a complex and much discussed process: learning to read. In Miss Neversilova's view the present practice in Swiss schools is distinctly unsatisfactory and should be reconsidered:

In the first classes at primary school written German is taught with the aid of Swiss German. As far as the Swiss German is concerned, there is no attempt to convey a 'theory' of Swiss language, which might lead to the formation of a meta-language or to thinking about the language or even to an awareness of Swiss German as a system with rules of its own ...[7]

The children have problems moving from dialect to High German, but so do writers. They write in a language which is not exactly foreign but not their mother-tongue either. Some Swiss writers evade the issue by weaving in the odd dialect word or phrase and by giving the timbre of dialect to what is basically pure High German. Others, like Peter Bichsel, achieve their effects by radical innovations in German prose. In 1964 Bichsel published some brilliant short stories entitled *Eigentlich möchte Frau Blum den Milchmann kennenlernen*, in which the literary language was reduced to its simplest building blocks. The title, drawn from one of the stories, is actually a typical sentence in both length and content. Even in translation something of Bichsel's style comes through. Here is a specimen from his controversial *Des Schweizers Schweiz*:

I come out of the boring *Nationalrat* onto the crowded street. The many cars drive past each other. I stand there for ten minutes and don't see a single collision. The autos do not collide because they drive on the right. Some time or other this parliament decided that automobiles must drive on the right. That is why there are no collisions. Parliament has ordered my world for me; it fulfils its task; my world is ordered.[8]

Literary German more remote from that of, say, Thomas Mann can hardly be imagined. Subordinate clauses, heavily modified adjectival phrases, the long, dangling sentence, have been cut away with a scalpel. Bichsel has a considerable reputation and was awarded a prize by the famous German literary group, the 'Gruppe 47'. How does he see his own very idiosyncratic language in relation to German literature?

I never heard the charge in Berlin that Swiss authors could not write High German but often the accusation that they wrote too high a German; they were prissy and fussed about grammatical exactness, they had contributed very little to the German language. I sometimes suspect that some Swiss authors come from Hanover rather than Zurich ... I too lack the guts. I too am very concerned to be understood by north German readers.[9]

A Swiss writer cannot escape his dilemma by writing in dialect, although some pretend to do so. Ernst Eggimann says in commenting on his poetry, 'All I had to do was to sit under the broad roof of our farm house on our porch and listen. I could surrender myself to the language. The language made the poetry . . .'[10] No poetry is written like that, not even dialect poetry. A dialect poet's head is full of German literary history and tradition; his normal reading will be largely in High German. Hence his dialect poetry comes out of the same two-tiered consciousness which enfolds the High German writer. Hermann Burger sums up the recent success of the dialect poets by drawing a parallel with pop art: 'In museums things are suddenly to be seen that would not have been seen there a few years ago. If one took away the frame, the museum atmosphere, one would see the same things with very different eyes.'

The problem of writing dialect as a literary language can be seen in theatre as well as in lyric poetry. A perfect example is the case of Paul Haller, who wrote a great deal of second-class lyric poetry in High German but also two tragedies in dialect. Many critics think Haller's *Marie und Robert*, written in 1915, the best play by a twentieth-century

Swiss author. Haller himself was so embittered by the play's lack of success that he gave up dialect as a literary medium. A few years later he took his own life at the age of thirty-eight. The play was either forgotten or performed only by *Volkstheater* and amateur groups until 1958, when for the first time an important professional company attempted the work. In the spring of 1975, the critic Peter Ruedi discussed a new production at the Baseler Komödie in a review which superbly illustrates the problem of dialect theatre. 'The Basel production shows in an exemplary fashion the strains in handling such dialect material, above all, the language struggle. Haller wrote Aargauer dialect. Where could one find, within the confines of the professional stage, a complete Aargau cast? Where could one even find nine pros who speak the same dialect?'[11] The producer forced his actors to speak a common approximation to Aargau dialect. The result, wrote Ruedi, was 'devastating'. The enforced Aargau *Mundart* turned out to be a more artificial speech than stage German could ever have been. The spontaneity of dialect was lost.

The dilemmas of dialect literature arise because dialect is both general to all Swiss Germans but by its very nature rooted in a specific locality. The history of the country and the particularism of its politics find reinforcement in the habits of its speech. There is no Swiss dialect, but lots of Swiss dialects, no Swiss German language but German. The Swiss writer, whether in High German or dialect, cannot escape the confines of the two sets of conflicts: the conflict between dialect and the written language and between local and national identity. Swiss writers seem to be condemned by the paradox that there is no such thing as Swiss writing. A perfect example is the recent study of Swiss literary outsiders by the poet Dieter Fringeli. He manages to insist that 'there is no autonomous, no typical Swiss literature'[12] in the introduction and then to plead for its existence in the individual essays. I counted the word *unschweizerisch* (un-Swiss) five times in the first thirty pages. The very fact that Fringeli selects neglected Swiss authors and not just neglected German authors underlines the dilemma.

Two questions easily become confused here. Is there a Swiss literature as such, that is, what have Swiss Italian, French and German writers in common? And is there a Swiss German literature distinct from the larger world of German writing? The broader question is harder to answer. Undoubtedly, writers like Orelli, Plinio Martini and Piero Bianconi share themes with Swiss German writers, village life, peasants, depopulation and so on, but it is hard to go beyond that. The answer to the second question seems to me clear. Yes, there is Swiss German literature and it includes all those caught up in the special Swiss form of bilingualism. I emphasise the special character of Swiss bilingualism, because many English-speaking people are unaware of how widespread bilingualism is. De Mauro provides figures for Italy which indicate that in the early 1950s a third of the Italian population had abandoned the use of dialect as the sole instrument of communication but only half of those (that is, 18.5% of the total population) used Italian exclusively.[13] The remaining two-thirds of the population use dialect normally in all social situations. The difference, and it is absolutely crucial, between Swiss German and Italian dialect usage is class. In Italy, the use of dialect is a matter of class. The higher the educational and social level the more likely it is that Italian only will be spoken. This phenomenon was well known in Switzerland in the nineteenth century. Gottfried Keller's protagonist in *Der grüne Heinrich* observes that his father's aspirations and new style of life included wearing shirts with ruffles and speaking 'purest High German'.[14] In the twentieth century, the situation reversed itself. It became a matter of national pride to speak dialect and an assertion of Swiss political independence. I get the impression, although I have seen no figures to support it, that educated young people today are more firmly committed to dialect than their parents were. At any rate, dialect shows no signs of dying out nor has Swiss German literary production shown any sign of faltering. The tension and the ambiguities are unresolved, but the Swiss Germans seem to survive it. Indeed, they flourish in its peculiarities. In literature since 1945, they have been unusually creative: Max Frisch, Friedrich Dürrenmatt, Otto F. Walter, Adolf Muschg, Peter Bichsel, Urs Widmer and E. Y. Meyer are just a few of the names that come to mind. Frisch and Dürrenmatt have probably been the most successful writers in the German language during the past thirty years. Only Günter Grass and Heinrich Böll have had an equivalent international impact.[15] Certainly Frisch and Dürrenmatt are much better known to English readers than are most of the big names of contemporary German literature: Martin Walser, Uwe Johnson, Peter Handke, Hans Magnus Enzensberger and Siegfried Lenz.

The linguistic situation of Swiss Italians really belongs to the general history of Italian linguistic development, although it has many similarities with that of Swiss Germans. The written language called Italian, like the written language called German, is not, on the whole, what Swiss Italians speak. Their position, on the other hand is closer to that described by de Mauro in that, like the Italians across the frontier, their literary language was for all practical purposes a dead language until the early nineteenth century. The establishment of the Tuscan dialect of the thirteenth and fourteenth centuries as a vehicle for national awakening owed its success to the prestige of Dante, Petrarch and Boccaccio and also to geography. 'As a central Italian dialect Tuscan had enough points of common development with both northern and southern dialects to serve as a bridge between them.'[16] The interesting difference between German and Italian Switzerland is that, while the Germans have two levels of speech, the Swiss Italians have three: the local dialect, the general Lombard dialect or *koiné*, and the literary or High Italian. The Lombard dialects belong to the family known as the *gallo–italici* and are very close to French in both pronunciation and vocabulary. On the basic level, the local variants are enormous, as in Alemannic. A man from the valley of Bedretto in the extreme north of Canton Ticino will not understand the local dialect of the Valle di Muggio in the extreme southern tip of the canton, the Mendrisio. The general *koiné*, or Lombard patois, saves them from embarrassment and acts as the medium of communication. All Swiss Italians are effectively trilingual, and move from local to Lombard to Italian with almost unconscious ease.

Italian and German remain 'high' languages in both parts of the country but with subtly different significance. Dialect is less universal in Italian Switzerland and runs along the edges of social divisions, age, sex and class in fascinating and complex ways. Two acquaintances meeting on the street in Zürich would speak dialect at once, but in Lugano they would speak Italian. Going from Italian to dialect is a little like moving from the polite to the familar form, from the *lei* to the *tu* in Italian, and presupposes a degree of familiarity. Dr Federico Spiess, of the Vocabolario dei dialetti della Svizzera italiana in Lugano, describes it this way:

If I have to go to the window of a post office and I speak Italian, I make the postal clerk understand that I want to ask for some information or to buy a stamp and that I want our relationship to remain at this strictly official level. If I have to go back to the same window two or three times, and, if in addition to the few indispensable words exchanged, even a single allusion to the excessive heat or cold, to head-ache or sniffles, to the health of wife or children, the war in Viet Nam or an earth-quake in Peru, the price of meat or the latest referendum, should insinuate itself into our exchange, dialect is immediately used to underline the new sort of relationship between us.[17]

Dialect is the language of neighbourliness and the ward, but here too its use reflects very subtle canons of social behaviour. The country man or woman in a city shop may use dialect with impunity, but the middle-class city dweller will use Italian, certainly at first, lest the shop girl feel insulted by such excessive familiarity. Similarly the middle-class city dweller who returns to the village of his origin would give even greater offence if he did *not* speak dialect from the beginning.

It is in family or school that the use of Italian shows its most remarkable features. In traditional middle-class families, parents speak dialect with each other, as do the children, but children speak to parents and parents to children in Italian. Respect and distance imply the use of the literary language as in the quotation from the famous Ticinese poet and novelist, Francesco Chiesa, which heads this book. To show respect is to speak Italian. Similarly, as Dott. Rosanna Zeli has found in her study of dialect usage in schools, the dialect means intimacy or equality of status. Teachers chat in dialect in the common room but speak Italian to pupils in the classroom and in all other encounters. Children speak dialect among themselves and, of course, Italian to teachers. Dott. Zeli found that in secondary schools the boys spoke dialect among themselves but Italian to the girls, and the girls dialect among themselves but Italian to the boys. The uncertainties of teenage sexual relations push them into Italian as the language of distance. Adult men use dialect more often than women, especially in towns and cities. A similar pattern is clear among French-speaking peasants in the Pyrenees. Women adopted the urban back 'r' in place of the local front rolled 'r' more rapidly than men.[18] This may reflect women's greater responsiveness to fashions, or possibly a more positive reaction to modern life in general.

Italian is the language of public life and dialect the language of private social relations. Hence it is not surprising that, as soon as a political organisation or government body becomes larger than, say, twenty people, which it will generally not do on village level, Italian replaces dialect as the means of communication. Radio and television are almost wholly in Italian, although dialect is occasionally spoken, when a country man is being interviewed. The presence of foreigners in large numbers has also played a part in the development of language in Italian Switzerland. From the 1880s to the present day, there has always been a large Italian colony in the canton. In 1910, for example, the 41,869 resident Italians made up 28% of the total population, still the highest percentage of foreign residents in the canton's history.[19]

The influx of Swiss Germans as tourists, hotel owners, retired persons, industrialists and commercial people has added to the mix of population. In 1960, over 11% of the overall population came from other cantons, mostly German-speaking. Italian naturally gets a boost from these two factors since energetic German Swiss will want to learn Italian but not dialect, while the Italian-speaking foreign workers, unless they are Lombards, will not be familiar with the local dialect variants. In addition, the figures which I gave in the previous chapter about communes with tiny populations were drawn from Italian Switzerland. As the mountain and high valley communities die out, their local dialect goes with them. Many dialects have already simply become yellowed research cards in the capacious card index of the Vocabolario in Lugano which issues the definitive guide to dialect. The dialects die out more rapidly than the director, Dr Federico Spiess, and his colleagues can publish volumes. By the time the vast multi-volume study of the dialects of Italian Switzerland is complete, many of the local dialects will long since have ceased to be used. As a final irony, Dr Spiess and his colleagues, in spite of years of collaboration, speak Italian not dialect in their office.

The Italian-speaking areas of Switzerland belong physically to the Italian world. They lie to the south of the Alps, and their borders with Italy have historical rather than geographical origins. The rivers empty into the north Italian lakes and in general the actual valleys themselves face toward the south. Swiss Italians speak of the rest of Switzerland as *oltre Gottardo*, beyond the great Gotthard Pass. Italian television is received in Ticino and in the three Italian-speaking Graubünden valleys. Swiss Italian television enjoys a high reputation in the areas of Lombardy which can receive it. The cultural capital of Ticino is Milan, which is less than an hour by car from Lugano and Locarno. The natural Lombard affiliation, proximity and the size of the public have had a tendency to suck the writer and scholar from Italian Switzerland into the Milanese orbit. The most famous of modern Ticinese poets, Francesco Chiesa, who died at the incredible age of 102 in June 1973, wrote many of his most important short stories and poems for the *Corriere della Sera* of Milan and had his works published by Italian firms. The wonderful collection called *Racconti del mio orto* (1929) ('Stories from my Garden'), originally published in the *Corriere*, are so written that there is no trace of 'Swissness' about them. The main character is a philosophical bookkeeper and passionate gardener. The place where he lives could be anywhere in northern Italy. The one reference to something concrete, to the cost of an article, is given in lire not in Swiss francs, as if Chiesa wished to underline the non-Swiss character of the work. Shortly after his death, the Rome newspaper, *il Tempo*, devoted a very long two-column obituary to Chiesa's place in Italian literature, which closed by citing his considerable achievement, 'which granted him not only a pre-eminent position among Swiss Italian writers but reserved one for him not much inferior to his distinguished contemporaries in Italy'. *The Times* in its brief obituary noted that Chiesa had celebrated his 100th birthday by publishing a collection of sonnets. *Die Weltwoche* in Zürich failed even to report the death of one of Switzerland's most important writers.

The sense of being ignored gives to the culture of Italian Switzerland a certain edginess. Some residue of the centuries of involuntary membership in the Confederation lingers on in the culture and attitudes of the 'Third Switzerland'. The Swiss Italian expects to have to learn German and French to cope with his fellow citizens from the other regions but he never expects them to return the compliment. On the other hand, he knows that his contribution to the Swiss identity is indispensable in spite of the small proportion of the population who speak Italian. If the Italian component had not survived the French Revolution and the ensuing wars Switzerland would not have become multilingual. A state composed only of one-fifth French-speakers and four-fifths German-speakers would have been less resistant to the centrifugal pull of cultural and linguistic nationalism. The 'Third Switzerland' represented a kind of cement, proof that a multi-national state could survive and flourish even in the nineteenth and twentieth centuries. This indispensability is reflected in the disproportionate frequency with which Swiss Italians serve in the *Bundesrat* and other high positions. Overall, while only 4% of the entire population are Swiss Italian, as opposed to Italian-speakers, 7.6% of all federal administrative employees, 6.0% of postal employees, 11.9% of railway employees, are Swiss Italians. Only at the upper levels of the administrative grade of the civil service is the proportion of Ticinese and Swiss Italians from Graubünden precisely equivalent to their share of the population.[20] Nevertheless, the Italian Swiss have the feeling that they are not taken seriously. As Dott. Flavio Zanetti puts it, the other Swiss tend to look at Ticino with eyes full of folklore, as 'a little paradise where carefree people live solely from the warmth of the sun, and whose only contribution, in the opinion of other Swiss, is to produce scandals and quaint customs'.[21]

The Raeto–Romansch-speakers who make up 1% of the population are edgy too but for different reasons. They are engaged in a struggle for ethnic survival whose outcome is pretty uncertain. The history of Raeto–Romansch reaches back to the Roman Empire when the Raetian people inhabited a huge mountainous area from the Rhine to the Adriatic. The Raetians became fully latinised and remained so until the barbarian invasions fragmented their unity. By the end of the period of barbarian incursions, Raetia had become three utterly separate, linguistic islands, an eastern or Friulian group in today's Italian province of Udine, a middle group in the Dolomites and a western group in the area of today's canton of Graubünden. The incursions of the Walser and other Germanic speakers in the thirteenth century further divided Romansch-speaking communities so that large differences began to develop within Raeto–Romansch. Romansch dialects came to resemble coloured bits in a larger mosaic rather than a broad patch of ethnic reality. The communal autonomy of old Graubünden enabled German and Romansch *Gemeinden* to live in peace. The commune had the right to adopt whichever language they wished. In this process the Ladino of the Engadin and the Val Müstair grew apart from the Surselva of the Upper Rhine Valley and both developed into written languages with different orthography and pronunciation. The other two idioms, Surmeirisch and Sutselvisch, became written languages only in modern times.

By the twentieth century, Alpine depopulation seriously threatened the Romansch communities. The language faced extinction and there was no allied culture beyond Switzerland to which the Romansch community could turn. In 1919 the Lia Rumantscha (Romansch League) was founded to unify under one roof the various small organisations which fought the good fight for linguistic survival. The rise of fascism and nazism gave Romansch an unexpected boost. As the Swiss became more conscious of the threat to their continued existence, they listened to each others' grievances more intently. In 1938 Romansch was elevated to the status of a national language, and the federal authorities granted a subsidy to the Lia Rumantscha, which by 1974 had risen to 450,000 francs a year. Swiss German Radio (SRG) broadcasts a certain number of hours each week in Romansch, which the cantonal government of Graubünden and Romansch-speaking activists regard as wholly inadequate. The cantonal government have asked SRG for a studio in Chur, the cantonal capital, and for a minimum daily programme of an hour of

Romansch broadcasting on radio and not less than five minutes on television. SRG, while expressing sympathy with such demands, have so far rejected them all on the grounds that the audience, actual and potential, will not justify the cost. There are weekly newspapers in Romansch but no daily. Some sixty kindergartens have been set up for the children of both Romansch- and non-Romansch-speaking parents. The teachers help to guide the children toward the comfortable use of Romansch in daily life. The trouble begins in primary school. After the 3rd or 4th class, Romansch ceases to be the language of instruction and is gradually replaced by German until it remains merely an optional extra at secondary level. The facts of life compel all Romansch-speakers to learn German, without which they cannot survive. They usually tend to pick up several other languages as well. I saw an example of what this means in practice in a shop in Dissentis-Muster. A charming young lady serving in a small supermarket spoke six languages within a quarter of an hour: Romansch, *Schwyzerdütsch*, High German, Italian, French and English. She assured me that this was not unusual for anyone in a public job. Such virtuosity cannot by itself save Romansch, as the melancholy figures in Table 4.2 suggest.

The struggle to save Romansch has many of the features of the great linguistic efforts of the nineteenth century to revive the Slavic languages. The Lia Rumantscha has concentrated on devising decent grammars, preparing dictionaries such as the *Dicziunari rumantsch grischun* and encouraging poetry and prose. In precisely this way Slovak, Slovenian, Ruthenian and Czech were lifted from peasant dialects or archaic literary idioms and made into the vehicles of

TABLE 4.2

	Swiss population	Swiss Romansch	%
1941	4,265,703	46,456	1.1
1950	4,714,992	48,862	1.0
1960	5,429,061	49,823	0.9
1970	6,269,783	50,339	0.8
	Population of Graubünden	Romansch	%
1941	128,247	40,187	31.3
1950	137,100	40,109	29.2
1960	147,458	38,414	26.1
1970	162,086	37,878	23.4

nationalist movements. In Switzerland and in Canton Graubünden much of what Slovaks and Slovenes had to fight for has always existed: self-determination. No German chauvinists threaten the future of Romansch. There is no need to blow up power stations or daub walls with patriotic slogans. Perhaps Romansch is more threatened because it is politically without external foes than it would be if Canton Graubünden had the power to refuse Romansch-speakers privileges. The real enemy of Romansch is the modern world. People go where the jobs are, and the jobs are no longer in Romansch-speaking areas. Dictionaries and grammars cannot prevent emigration from the Alpine fastness. For those who have never seen Romansch physically here are some proverbs taken from the two main variants:[22]

Engadin (Ladino):
Basdrinaglia — la pü bella parantaglia.
(The more distantly related the better.)
Chi serva ad sumün, nun agradesch'ad ingün.
(He who will serve everyone, serves no one well.)
Id ais meglder da magliar tuot quai chi's ha co da dir tuot quai chi's sa.
(Better to eat everything one has than to say everything one knows.)

Surselva:
Il pur en la lozza mantegn il signur ella carrotscha.
(The peasant in the mud feeds the lord in the coach.)
In crap che rocla fa buca mescal.
(A rolling stone gathers no moss.)

The most important linguistic minority is, of course, the French-speaking Swiss, the *Suisses romands*. They comprise just under 20% of the total population and are the dominant linguistic group in five cantons and a vociferous minority in a sixth. Unlike the other Swiss groups we have looked at, the Swiss French do not, on the whole, speak dialect. In the three Protestant French-speaking cantons, Vaud, Geneva and Neuchâtel, the dialects are just about extinct. In their place there has grown up a regional French whose characteristic inflexions reveal to the philologist the underlying dialect which once existed. Swiss French is, then, French with a regional flavour, like the French spoken in Belgium. Like the Belgians, Swiss French say *septante, huitante* or *octante* and *nonante* instead of the more cumbersome 'proper' French *soixante-dix, quatre-vingts* and *quatre-vingt-dix* for 'seventy', 'eighty' and 'nincty'. The French *traineau* (sledge) becomes the Swiss *luge* and so on. There is the sort of vocabulary and accent difference which exists between American and English use of the English language. In the more remote, Catholic areas, the French-speakers of Fribourg, Valais and the Jura still use dialect, but it is rapidly dying out. In a recent study of the village of Hérémence in Valais, one of those astonishing villages tucked away in the very steep and remote valleys above Sion, it was found that no one under the age of thirty used dialect as a regular means of communication. In a generation the dialects of the high Alps in the Catholic cantons will be as extinct as they are in Protestant ones. The Swiss French belong unequivocally to the cultural world of France, and, while they may have to swallow the accusation of provincialism, they share that with other French-speakers unfortunate enough to live elsewhere than Paris.

The relations between the French-speaking and the German-speaking Swiss have always been complicated, not least because while Swiss Germans are confined, but also defined, by the world of dialect, the Swiss French have the advantages and disadvantages of the absence of dialect. What is 'Swiss' about French Switzerland is less obviously defined by language than in the other cases we have considered. Certainly Protestantism played its part in creating a sober, industrious, thrifty, God-fearing type of citizen. A frugal and industrious Protestant population was very much part of French life until the revocation of the Edict of Nantes in 1685, when French Protestants were forced into exile or discreet withdrawal from public life. As Denis de Rougemont says in his brilliant little book on Switzerland, the common theme of his childhood was 'work': 'How often in the Neuchâtel of my childhood have I read engraved on a tombstone or printed on the funeral card of the deceased in place of the usual biblical citation: 'le travail fut sa vie'.[23]

These bourgeois, Protestant virtues, well known in Scotland, the north of England and in the American states are the virtues of a puritanism which represented 'another France' as much as it reflected general Swiss values. Historically, then, French Switzerland is defined in opposition to France as much as in union with it. De Rougemont offers five ways in which the Swiss French differ fundamentally from their French neighbours:

1. Culture in our cantons has never been tied to the state and has never been an instrument of state power;

2. Culture among us had its existence in little compartments either natural or historic — the city of Geneva, the country of Vaud, Neuchâtel or La Chaux-de-Fonds ... which have never been unified, united by a central power or made uniform as was the case of the French provinces under successive regimes;

3. We are old republics founded on the autonomy of the communes;

4. Protestantism is dominant in French Switzerland; it has determined the greater part of our customs, our profound moral concerns and our distrust of ceremonies . . .

5. We are not only neighbours of a Germanic world; we are in a state of osmosis with it much more so than many of us realise or would like to admit.[24]

Unlike the Swiss Germans, the 'Swissness' of the *Suisses romands* is not primarily based on language. History, not an exclusive dialect, has made them Swiss and religion, politics and economic forces have kept them that way. Hence the Swiss French are free of the coils of one identity problem (they are part of a great world linguistic community) but tied up in another (since they are culturally French, is there any Swiss culture?).

French Switzerland has difficulty in establishing an identity, not least because it is too simple to talk of the *Suisse romande*. The *welsche Schweiz*, which looms so large in the imaginations of German Swiss, is a myth. The most striking characteristic of French-speaking Switzerland is its diversity. To begin with, the six territories are geographically divided, look toward different compass points and follow rivers which, unlike those of the German areas, do not all empty into one great central valley. They are divided by religion, which, in turn, means that they are divided by culture, education and social custom. They are divided politically, including the most radical and most conservative communities in Switzerland. Each canton has its own school system, its own university and higher secondary systems and its own tax laws. In a sense the Romandie is the most intensely federalist of areas in Switzerland. An example of what this means can be seen in the newspaper world.

In 1970 there were more than 300 newspapers in Switzerland as a whole, of which more than 100 were dailies, and this for a population of just over 6 million. Even more remarkable is the scale of these papers. In December, 1969, 220 Swiss papers reported a circulation of less than 2,500; 60 others up to 10,000; 30 more, among which are some of the most famous, did not reach 20,000; only 11 reported between 50,000 and 100,000 and only 2 over 100,000.[25] If the daily papers are divided by language one gets a picture which looks like that in Table 4.3.

According to official Swiss press statistics for 1975, only four French Swiss newspapers had circulations of more than 50,000 copies (*24 heures/Feuille d'Avis de Lausanne, La Tribune de Genève, La Suisse,*

TABLE 4.3   Circulation of Swiss dailies by language

	German		French		Italian		Total	
	No.	Circul.	No.	Circul.	No.	Circul.	No.	Circul.
1939	82	913,170	27	317,350	9	32,600	118	1,263,120
1943	79	935,588	24	341,140	6	29,138	109	1,305,866
1950	84	1,086,777	26	356,049	6	46,100	116	1,438,926
1955	87	1,091,167	29	387,806	6	39,736	122	1,518,709
1960	84	1,242,526	27	434,485	6	44,193	117	1,721,204
1965	91	1,645,269	26	485,956	6	50,497	123	2,181,722
1968	86	1,700,812	21	502,475	6	56,528	113	2,259,815

Source: Pierre Cordey, *Die Schweiz seit 1945*, p. 248.

Tribune de Lausanne/Matin) but two (*La Suisse* and *Tribune de Lausanne/Matin*) had Sunday editions which exceeded 100,000 copies. These four papers come closest to being 'national' dailies for French Switzerland, but underlying the statistics there are fascinating patterns of distribution. The figures in Table 4.4 for the *Tribune de Lausanne* before the merger with *Matin* show good sales in the Catholic, rural areas of Fribourg and Valais but in neighbouring Geneva, all of thirty minutes away by car, it might as well have saved the effort. It sold more papers in German and Italian Switzerland than it did next door in Geneva and Neuchâtel.

The intensely regional character of each paper and obvious economies of scale have led to several mergers. Interlocking ownership through a holding company link three of the biggest four dailies today, but even the one independent, *Tribune de Genève*, shares correspondents with *24 Heures*. Middle-sized papers of strong political colour, such as the Christian Democratic *Courrier* in Geneva, are in trouble and even the famous *Journal de Genève* in spite of its venerable history can barely make ends meet on an 18,000 circulation. M. Claude Monnier, the foreign editor, told me that the staff think of it less as a newspaper than as 'un miracle quotidien'. A logical merger would be that of the historic *Gazette de Lausanne* and the very similar *Journal de Genève*. Attempts to fuse have so far failed. The two staffs could not reconcile their different points of view. Apparently the world looks different in Geneva and in Lausanne. In more remote regions the world looks even more idiosyncratic, and 31,500 citizens of La Chaux-de-Fonds see it through the eyes of *L'Impartial*, while the *Gruyères* is read by 8,500 residents of the valley of the same name in Canton Fribourg.

There is, then, no 'national' newspaper for French Switzerland,

TABLE 4.4   Sales of *Tribune de Lausanne*, in 1968

Vaud (of which Lausanne 18,265)	32,571
Valais	8,753
Fribourg	5,368
Neuchâtel	1,907
Jura bernois	1,296
Geneva	935
German Switzerland and Ticino	6,094
Abroad	430
Total	57,354

Source: Pierre Cordey, *Die Schweiz seit 1945*, p. 249.

because French Switzerland as an entity does not exist. There is no capital and no single centre of culture. Hence the different regions and cities cling to their papers. They know a great deal about the wider world but little about the neighbouring village or canton. In this the *Suisse romande* is very Swiss, even if many French-speaking intellectuals dislike having to admit it.

If French Switzerland is an abstraction, it becomes a reality of a kind only in contact with German Switzerland. French-speakers are a minority of the whole country but they are a large enough minority to have claims. These claims matter, not because there is such a thing as the *Suisse romande* but because over a million Swiss citizens use French as their native language. In the canton or city the French-speaker is untroubled by the existence of other language groups. It is at work, if he is employed by a large company or in the federal civil service, that problems arise. In the federal civil service there are directives governing the employment of persons from the different linguistic groups. Italian-speakers are over-represented as a whole, while French-speakers have roughly their share of posts at all levels. They are lightly over-represented in the Political Department, no doubt as a historical survival of the idea of French as the diplomatic language and partly because French candidates for the upper ranks of the civil service tend to gravitate toward diplomacy and away from the customs and excise. Swiss Germans dominate the boiler rooms of government. The director and the five vice-directors of the Federal Financial Administration are Swiss Germans and in the BIGA (the Federal Office for Industry, Trade and Labour) there is only one vice-director who speaks French as his first language.

In the economy as a whole the same pattern reveals itself. There are large international businesses whose headquarters are in French Switzerland, Nestlé, for one, but the great weight of economic power, the chemical giants, the machine tool firms and the big banks are all essentially Swiss German enterprises. Upper levels of trade and commercial associations tend to be dominated by Swiss Germans. Spokesmen for industrial concerns and lobbyists tend to be Swiss Germans. The hotel trade is dominated by Swiss Germans and even watchmaking is far more Swiss German than the names of firms would lead the outsider to believe. The machinery and parts side of the business is generally in the hands of Swiss German firms. They dominate the whole range of activities summed up in the word *Feinmechanik* or precision engineering, while Swiss French dominate finished products, the jewel, case and artistic sides of the trade. Swiss French banks tend to be smaller, to serve a more exclusively private clientele, and to specialise in more traditional forms of asset management than do Swiss German private banks. It is characteristic of the differences between the economies of the two language areas that while only one of the big ten machine tool companies is Swiss French and only one of the big five printing and publishing companies, four of the five biggest subsidiaries of foreign banks are in Geneva alone: the Banque pour le Développement commercial, Discount Bank (Overseas) Limited, Banque pour le commerce Suisse–Israelien, and the Banque de Paris et des Pays-Bas (Suisse). The fifth is the Banco di Roma per la Svizzera in Lugano.

It is hardly surprising that such economic and demographic preponderance gives rise to resentments and that frequently such resentments take the form of Swiss French v. German. These resentments are further inflamed by the entirely different approach to language itself in the two groups. The Swiss French do not, as a general rule, speak German. In most of my interviews in French Switzerland I found that my conversation partners normally spoke French everywhere in Switzerland and expected to be understood. Some confessed to the fact with embarrassment; others announced it with indifference or even a certain pride. 'They all speak French in Zürich, or try to', one man airily informed me. They do not all speak French there, but the man was right in emphasising that they try. Swiss Germans take language learning with deep seriousness. The moment a Swiss German finds himself anywhere or with anyone on whom he can practise and 'improve' his French, English, Italian or whatever, he does so. A senior, German-speaking member of a large Swiss company told me a characteristic anecdote. He had to entertain a vice-president of the firm from Lausanne. Being a dutiful Swiss German he made great efforts all evening to speak French, which he does badly and hence dislikes. Much wine was consumed. As the two executives parted, he suddenly felt compelled to ask the sort of direct question which normally Swiss never put to one another. He turned to his vice-president and asked, 'Are you pleased that I spoke French all evening?' 'Why should I be?' shrugged the vice-president. 'You Swiss Germans just like to practise on us.'

Swiss French, even if they have the best will in the world, find the language problem difficult. They must, to begin with, learn two Germans, High German and *Schwyzerdütsch*. If they learn the latter, they can use it only within Switzerland, and in any case, since it is so rarely taught, learning Swiss German is not all that easy. They find themselves forced to learn High German and hence run into precisely the same linguistic barriers that any foreigner does in making contact with Swiss Germans. Both sides are conversing in a foreign language. Many Swiss French reckon that they are, after all, flattering the hearer if they talk French right from the start. At least that way one of them is using his mother-tongue. Mme Lise Girardin, as a rising national politician in the Radical Party and the most prominent woman in Swiss politics, has to travel and speak all over Switzerland; she sees this difficulty at various levels. She speaks good German and is perfectly prepared to use it at meetings. The moment she begins, she told me, her Swiss German hearers ask her to use French instead. On the other hand, in committee or executive meetings of the Radical Party, the opposite problem arises. Documents have been prepared all too frequently in German only, and she finds herself trying to inter-vene in a debate while translating the text under discussion at the same time. Official published papers are always trilingual but at the draft stage, much more often than mythology admits, the work has been done in German. Her experience is that Swiss Germans are, perhaps, overly conscious of the need to placate the linguistic minority in some respects and forgetful of it in others.

Another difficulty is the strong centralism of French culture or, more precisely, the power of its norms. Several centuries of French preoccupation with the normative elements in language teaching have had their effect on the Swiss French too. *Dialekt* is a good word in German Switzerland, while patois has negative overtones. The purity and perfection of written and spoken French is important in

Swiss French schooling. Swiss French-speakers instinctively look for 'best' usage and, very characteristically, refer to High German as *le bon allemand*. Swiss French also share the instinctive prejudice against dialect as vulgar or low speech which I tried to disperse earlier in this chapter. *Schwyzerdütsch* is by definition 'bad German'.

Finally there is Paris, which for the Swiss French is, in its way, as important as it is for French-speakers generally. Roberto Bernhard, one of the great intermediaries between the two Switzerlands, points out that for the Swiss French Paris is the 'living stream of cultural development'. The cultivated French-speaking Swiss is far more likely to read a French paper regularly than he is to see a Swiss German one, and there is a certain sort of snobbery which expresses itself in *only* reading French newspapers and journals. Membership of a great cultural, Paris-centred world gives French-speaking Swiss an aura of superiority over their more provincial Swiss German cousins, who no longer even have Berlin to offer in reply. On the other hand, for the Parisian French, the Swiss are hopelessly provincial, 'les petits Suisses'. Swiss French live in an ambivalent position toward both their fellow citizens of different language and their fellow French-speakers of different citizenship.

Multilingualism is a fact about the Swiss as a people; it is much harder to say if and to what extent it is an attribute of individual Swiss men and women. Surprisingly, in view of the amount of talk about the problem, there has been very little research done on bi- and multilingualism in Switzerland. So far as I know, it is impossible to establish the most elementary facts —how many Swiss speak more than one language? To what level of competence? How many read more than one language? How often? The spread of a splendid system of cable radio and television has made it possible to receive without interference all three languages on radio and increasingly so on television in all parts of the country. It might become possible to calculate how often Swiss Germans listen to *Suisse romande* news or watch French entertainment programmes. There is evidence of a vague kind, as one would expect, that Swiss Germans tend to do so more often than Swiss French. In all three language areas, there is always the choice of radio and TV from across the border, which naturally reduces whatever urge the Genevois has to listen to radio or watch TV from Zürich or Basel. French and Swiss news bulletins in the evening are so phased that a viewer in French Switzerland can catch both without difficulty.

One experiment in bilingualism is the city of Biel—Bienne on the southern edge of the Jura. An historic German town which never quite made the grade to cantonal independence, Biel filled up in the nineteenth century with French-speaking watchmakers and craftsmen from the Jura, so that today about 30% of its 65,000 inhabitants use French as their daily language. All street signs are in both languages and every city employee and elected representative must be bilingual. Of its 326 electoral districts there is not a single one which is exclusive to one or the other language group. The inhabitants are well known for replying without thinking in one language to a question in the other. Below the surface there is less genuine bilingualism than the town propaganda would have one believe. The school systems remain rigorously separate. The *Gymnasium*, which until 1955 was bilingual, has now split into French and German sections. The one bilingual newspaper folded after only two years of life.

The greatest difficulty in discussing conflict and cooperation between the language groups is to know whether what looks like language conflict may not be class or economic conflict. This is particularly true of the three cantons where French and German Swiss are supposed to live together in peace. The German minority in Canton Fribourg suffer a degree of discrimination. The French-speaking majority makes up about two-thirds of the canton's population of 180,000. Both languages enjoy equality in law and the rights of both groups have been written into the constitution. In practice very few of the judges and court personnel use German, and often hear cases in French even if both parties speak German. There was no training college for educating German-speaking teachers until 1962, and there are other examples of petty thoughtlessness of which German-speaking residents complain. In the Valais, similar incidents are recounted and there is even a language protection league for the German-speaking minority called the *Rottenbund* (the League of the Rhone), which resolutely insists on using archaic German terms for all place names, 'Martinach' for 'Martigny' and so on. In both cases the groups concerned express in linguistic terms issues which are at least as much economic and social. Canton Fribourg and Canton Valais are, perhaps, the two most conservative cantons in the Confederation. Both are strongly Roman Catholic and, in the case of Fribourg historically rather anti-democratic. Fribourg was the last and most reluctant canton to introduce direct democracy and one of the last of the large cantons to accept the 'magic formula' approach to sharing power on the cantonal executive among the parties. In both cantons the German areas are more backward, more conservative and more clerical than the French-speaking areas, and hence some of the linguistic resentment is also regional conflict. In Valais the resentment is deepened by the historical reversal of roles. Until 1798 the *Oberwalliser* were top dogs and forced German down the throats of their French-speaking subjects. Children were beaten in the schools of Sierre if they were caught whispering in French. Now that Oberwallis has become a distressed area living on subsidies for inadequate peasant plots, the French majority has the upper hand. General resentment at this state of affairs finds its release in linguistic chauvinism of an intemperate kind.

The Jura conflicts offer an interesting example of inflamed linguistic sentiments. As I suggested in the previous chapter, the deepest fissures are those which divide French-speaking Jurassiens, but Bern and the dominant German-speaking majority in the canton stood for the other enemy, an enemy as much cultural as political. The *Jura libre*, a weekly separatist paper which appears in Delémont, defends pure French against 'outrages to our language'. Here is an excerpt from the column 'Parlons français':

Many subsidiaries of large firms established in French Switzerland receive publicity and advertising texts from head office which are completely German in thought . . . The firm Voegele posted a series of price tags in its Delémont shop recently, which read 'X. francs chaque pièce'. In French one should say: 'X. francs *la* pièce'. The other day in the shop front of the same store one saw with amazement the following inscription: 'Toujours à la hauteur du trend de la mode juvenile'. What is that jargon? (*Jura libre*, 23 August 1972)

No affront is too trivial nor grammatical lapse too slight for attention. Behind every mistake lurks the 'imperialist' and 'heavily teutonic' spirit of the oppressor.

The Jurassien separatists are not simply unreasonable when they fight the battle against linguistic outrages. Hard economic facts shimmer through the bad French of the Swiss German chain store. By attacking the one, they see themselves preventing further encroachments of the other. Should a stable Canton Jura emerge from the crisis, the Jurassiens will have political power to make an impact on firms trading within the canton and may develop educational institutions to train French-speaking managers and technicians. Through a combination of historical circumstance, geographical isolation, religious tradition and linguistic nationalism, they will have created a new small state. In this process the defenders of French will see themselves as vindicated, and, once again, as so often in the last two hundred years, economic and political realities will have been profoundly influenced by the intangible forces of language and culture.

The process is clear in the Jura. It is less so in the case of Switzerland as a whole. Minds conditioned by two hundred years of nationalist propaganda find it hard to think of a nation without a national language. Can there be a Switzerland which is more than the sum of its particular parts? No one who has visited the place could doubt that there is something more, but what is it? In the previous chapters on history and politics I tried to underline common historical experiences and political institutions which all Swiss share. In the next chapter, I shall offer evidence from the economy which points to the same conclusion. It may be that the combination of history, politics and economic development provides a sufficient explanation and that Switzerland survives as a state in spite of linguistic variety. The only common linguistic experience of all Swiss would then be the absence of a common language. A case, paradoxical at first sight, can be made for such a view. It is certainly true that the cumbersome forms of multilingual courtesy have become unifying elements, which reinforce the cellular structure of politics. People learn to be good pluralists in the 'language laboratories' of government institutions and large companies.

It could also be true that the question is wrong or that some of the assumptions underlying it need to be looked at. History offers lots of examples of 'ideas of the age' so widely accepted that only cranks and outsiders dared to question them. Take the case of social darwinism in the nineteenth century or social class in the twentieth. The 'unconscious mind' is a good example in our own day. Most of us now accept without further thought that human personality has two levels: a 'conscious' and an 'unconscious' layer. None of us has ever seen the unconscious and there is no proof that it exists. Yet we rear our children, improve our prisons, interpret our actions and words as if it did. The idea of the unconscious pervades our thinking so totally that we have lost the distance necessary to see it all. I believe that the link between a language and a nation is just such an idea. The French are those who speak French, the Danes Danish. And the Swiss?

The connection between a language and the people who speak it is an obvious one and appeared early in European history. In the late thirteenth century, the Florentine scholar Brunetto Latini evidently thought that he had better explain why he had chosen to write a major work in French: 'And should any ask why, because we are Italian, this book is written in Romance according to the idiom of the French, I would answer that it is for two reasons: one, that we are in France, the other because its speech is more pleasing and more common to all peoples than Italian.'[26] Goethe reflected the same attitude to language five centuries later, when he observed 'the German went to school under the French to learn how to live well and under the Romans to learn how to speak well'.[27] Both passages are really saying that Italians should speak Italian and Germans German. Between Goethe's time and our own, the idea of 'a people' has undergone a subtle but crucial change. The man most responsible for the change was Goethe's great contemporary Johann Gottfried Herder, who published a study in 1772 called *Ueber den Ursprung der Sprache* (Concerning the Origin of Language). The work became the bible of nineteenth-century linguistic nationalists. Herder believed human languages corresponded to distinct peoples. Those who shared a common language were a *Volk*. Each *Volk* had a *Seele* or soul, which in turn expressed itself in a *Sprache* or language. Herder's *Volk* was, of course, not Hitler's. For Herder *Volk* meant those who spoke a language and the idea of a *Volk* without one was an *Unding*, an impossibility. Herder thought of *Volk* as a category in the nature of all men, more or less, present from the beginning. Herder's definitions have a dialectical relationship to each other: *Volk* defines *Sprache* and vice versa. Their impact on the contemporary world was powerful. Educated men in Slavic countries literally rushed into the countryside to find the *Volk* with its *Sprache*, and found what they were looking for. As a Polish landlord grumpily observed in 1848, the Ruthenian people had only been 'discovered last year'. In due course Herder's cultural categories filled up with nastier fluid; biological and racial definitions seeped into the idea of *Volk* but even in Hitler's Reich, where racial definitions were most powerful, the link which Herder first postulated between *Volk* and *Sprache* remained largely unquestioned. It still exists in the automatic assumption that the French are those who speak French.

Switzerland raises questions about both terms of Herder's equation. What is a language? The great complexity of Swiss dialect usage, the variety of its forms, the geographical spread of its influence, in short, the whole tangle of issues abbreviated by the word *Schwyzerdütsch*, make a nonsense of Herder's romantic verities. The same applies to

Volk. This great shimmering abstraction dissolves when you approach it. It can be applied to no specific cases and supported by no concrete evidence. In so far as individuals feel themselves part of a people', they assert a political or historical or regional reality as much as a linguistic one. Language is certainly a part of that reality but not all of it. In Herder's terms the Swiss may be an impossibility (an *Unding*), a *Volk* without a *Sprache*, but this is only because Herder's terms are too narrow. The Swiss are a *Volk*, because geography, history, political structures and linguistic diversity have made them one, but also because all Swiss, whether French, German or Italian in language, participate in one national economy, whose features reinforce the other characteristics. It is to that economy that I turn now.

5. Wealth

The first, and possibly the most important, economic fact about Switzerland is that it is a very rich country. No visitor to any Swiss town can fail to notice the glitter of wealth from behind shop windows. Everything looks solid, well-made and expensive. In late 1973, the *National-Zeitung* published figures which gave statistical support to the impression of the eye. In terms of gross national product per head of population, Switzerland was then the richest country in the world (Switzerland $6,890, Sweden $6,510, Federal Republic of Germany $6,260, USA $6,090). No doubt the oil states along the Persian Gulf can beat any industrialised country today, but Switzerland is still one of the three or four richest developed countries, no matter how the word 'rich' is defined.

The Swiss collectively have been rich for a long time. Habits associated with the acquisition and management of wealth reach back continuously into the later Middle Ages. Some areas of the country have been wealthy almost without interruption for nearly five centuries, others with interruptions for some of that span and yet others have been relatively poor well into the twentieth century. Reliable numbers for the late medieval and early modern epochs are hard to come by, but in Chapter 2 I cited the case of Niklaus von Diesbach who at his death left a fortune of 70,000 gulden and was known as the richest Bernese of the age.[1] One rich man is not an aggregate; indeed, individual rich men surrounded by starving people is the mark of today's very poorest states. Besides, how much was 70,000 gulden in the fifteenth century?

Hektor Ammann did a good deal of research on just that question in his study of the cloth-making canton of Schaffhausen in the later Middle Ages. His figures for the period from the middle of the fifteenth to the first quarter of the sixteenth century show that the largest fortunes recorded in what was certainly a prosperous textile centre at the time fell between 13,000 and 19,000 guldens. His league table of wealth and class in Upper Germany (to which Switzerland still belonged) shows that fortunes of the Diesbach size were rare, possibly occuring only in the Basel trading community. In Augsburg and Nuremberg, on the other hand, the Fuggers, the Welsers, the Höchstetters, the Tuchers and the Imhofs, were much richer. Jacob Fugger, who died in 1525, probably left a fortune worth several millions, depending on how you assess the marketable value of the castles, settlements, the mines in the Tyrol and Hungary as well as the trading capital, loans to princes and so on. Fortunes of 200,000 gulden were not unusual in late medieval Augsburg and Nuremberg. By these standards, the Swiss belonged to the second division in wealth. No Swiss family or trading company approached the magnificence of their German neighbours. On the other hand, wealth seems to have been rather widely distributed. The structure of capital ownership, measured by taxes paid, was not all that far from modern standards of tolerable (at least so far) inequality. Of Schaffhausen's 4,000 inhabitants, some 800 had assets which the city taxed. The top fifteen taxpayers owned a third of the wealth, and the next sixty-four taxpayers owned another third, while the remaining 600 owned the rest.[2] Most late medieval Swiss cities studied by Ammann show the same general features, especially the smaller ones. Schaffhausen's 4,000 inhabitants must have been comfortable if almost every fifth individual (roughly every head of a family) earned enough to pay tax.[3] The guild constitution adopted in 1411 fits this social and economic structure neatly. The small wealthy establishment corresponded to the self-perpetuating, mercantile, political leadership described in Chapter 2.

The most important thing about Swiss fortunes was not size but survival. By the time a century of religious war had swept over them, the great cities of Upper Germany were ruined. The Swiss fought each other but not to the point of mutual destruction. Even Zwingli accepted the rights of his Papist opponents to share in the government of the Confederation, in effect, their right to exist. Later on Swiss neutrality in the Thirty Years War paid fat dividends and by the eighteenth century accumulations of capital were impressive. The abbot of St Gallen, Cölestin II, spent half a million gulden in adorning his Lilliputian absolutist state but in 1767 still managed to leave his successor, abbot Beda Angehrn, another quarter of a million, mostly in cash.[4] An equally important invisible asset was the continuous tradition of mercantile enterprise. When the European economy began its great expansion after 1730, the Swiss city-republics took advantage of the upswing. The tiny city-republic of St Gallen (total population under 8,000) had sixty substantial mercantile houses during the eighteenth century engaged in the manufacture and sale of cotton, muslin and embroidery. About 100,000 spinners, weavers, calico printers and embroiderers worked for the city companies, mostly in the famous *Webkeller* (the weaving cellar) in each of the peasant houses dotted up and down the mountains of Appenzell and among the valleys of the Rhine, the Thur and the Linth. East Switzerland became one of the richest and most thickly settled parts of Europe. The commercial activities of St Gallen had deep historical precedents. As early as the fifteenth century, the *Mal*, the first quality seal in European economic history, stamped St Gallen linen cloth as merchandise of prime quality. By the eighteenth century, the same political structures and the same economic organisation were directed to the same end: quality production for export markets.[5]

The structure of textile manufacturing in eastern Switzerland underlines a second very important feature of the Swiss economy: a high degree of specialization. The little town of St Gallen with its 8,000 inhabitants resembled the central nucleus of a complex nervous system. Almost alone of great European trading cities of the eighteenth century, St Gallen had no agricultural hinterland. The baroque 'Vatican City', the Abbey, in its midst and the prince—abbot's territories beyond its walls forced the city to specialise ever more exclusively in commerce. The pastor of the French church in St Gallen wrote in 1813:

St Gallen is an entirely commercial city. That unity of occupations facilitates our examination. From commerce is born avarice, not the sordid and bizarre avarice which forms skin-flints but the fatal habit of weighing sentiments on the scales of gold . . . Business absorbs them and they devote themselves exclusively to those studies most indispensable for their state . . . The revolutions which occur in the republic of letters do not disturb their sleep.[6]

Culture, habits, political institutions and religious injunctions combined to produce an utterly devoted merchant capitalist, a man, as one observer put it, born to be a 'commercial traveller'. This high degree of specialisation has its chroniclers in the uncomfortable few who did care about the republic of letters, and their complaint was always the same from Zwingli's days to those of Max Frisch. Switzerland is 'narrow', 'philistine', 'materialist', in other words, unusually highly specialised for economic survival.

Another feature of Swiss manufacturing in the eighteenth and nineteenth centuries caught the eye of Karl Marx: its decentralisation. In Chapter 12 of Book One of *Das Kapital* Marx discusses the origins of what he calls *Manufaktur*, the classical pre-industrial form of manufacturing. He distinguishes two main types, 'heterogeneous' and 'organic', and chooses the Swiss watchmaking industry as his example of the perfect specimen of *heterogene Manufaktur* (he could just as well have used St Gallen textiles). The main feature of heterogeneous manufacturing is that the capitalist assembles bits and pieces made simultaneously in no determined order and in different workshops, while organic manufacture involves a continuous flow of products in which each worker's finished product is the raw material of the next. 'Out of a temporal side-by-side grows a spatial side-by-side',[7] and hence the assembling of the continuous processes under one roof, i.e. the factory. Neither the Swiss watchmaker nor the textile worker escaped factory labour entirely but for the most part the work was done by the 'putting out' system, in German called the *Verlagssystem* and in watchmaking *établissage* (from the watchmaker's table, *un établi*). The capitalist or *établisseur* had little capital himself and needed little, because the decentralisation of production was so great that he needed only a tiny staff to assemble the finished product. (Marx lists over a hundred specialised stages of production: engravers, engine-turners, case makers, gilders, escapement makers, watch-hand makers, case finishers, pendant makers, mainspring makers, case spring makers, polishers, etc.[8]) He paid the hundreds of different tiny firms and individual craftsmen twice a year at the so-called *termes*.[9] The decentralisation of watchmaking continued into the twentieth century and R. A. G. Miller estimates that about half of all persons employed in watchmaking at the turn of the century were still 'travailleurs à domicile'.[10] Alongside the outworker stood the tiny firm, highly specialised but employing less than five people, and both categories survived into the twentieth century. In the industrial census of 1965 six out of every ten firms in the watchmaking industry employed less than ten persons. Characteristically, the 1974 wage table shows the average hourly wage of watchmakers at SFr. 9.22 for men, the second lowest in all Swiss industry.

Some important features of watchmaking (and by extension textiles, the other great Swiss industry of the nineteenth century) should be underlined. Decentralisation meant that while there were proletarian conditions, there was little class consciousness. Adhémar Schwitzguébel, himself a watchmaker and leader of the anarchist Fédération jurassienne, had to apologise at a party congress in 1874 for the failure of class consciousness to develop among his 'half bourgeois workers, living a bourgeois existence'.[11] Prince Kropotkin in his *Memoirs* wrote that the watchmakers were 'federalist in principle. . . each separate region, and even each local section, had to be left free to develop on its own lines'.[12] The economic development of the two most important Swiss export industries did not, as in Britain and Germany, destroy the cellular structure of the old political framework but reinforced, indeed reinvigorated it. The communal political unit, the kinship network and the economic unit fused to form a powerful whole. Kropotkin described the Jura in May 1871:

In a little valley in the Jura hills there is a succession of small towns and villages of which the French-speaking population was at that time entirely employed in the various branches of watchmaking; whole families used to work in small workshops. In one of them I found another leader, Adhémar Schwitzguébel with whom, also, I afterward became very closely connected. He sat among a dozen young men who were engraving lids of gold and silver watches. I was asked to take a seat on a bench, or a table, and soon we were all engaged in a lively conversation upon socialism, government or no govern-ment, and the coming congresses.[13]

Kropotkin was enchanted by the sturdy independence, literacy and devotion of his anarchist watchmakers, men who walked five or six kilometres in blinding snow to attend socialist and anarchist meetings. Like Francesco Chiesa's experience with the Alpine shepherd (cited at the beginning of the book), Kropotkin found the peasant workman remarkably literate, informed and articulate.

General conditions were very nearly ideal for the development of light industry in Switzerland during the nineteenth century. The Swiss emerged from the Napoleonic Wars with a modernised system of government, with capital surpluses so abundant that the private bankers in Basel and Geneva had begun to invest heavily abroad as early as the end of the eighteenth century and with a labour force already well adapted to light manufacturing. Thousands of rushing streams provided cheap power to turn spindles, and Zürich rapidly became the capital of a flourishing cotton textile industry. The number of spindles rose from about 400,000 in 1830 to about a million in 1851.[14] As Zürich specialised in cotton, St Gallen took up embroidery and by 1913 embroidered goods at SFr. 215 million stood at the top of the list of Swiss exports, followed by watchmaking at SFr. 183 mil-lion, with other textiles and machine tools well behind.[15] Cotton and embroidery, like watchmaking, partly because mills grew up where nature had put the running water, left the basic cellular structure of Swiss communal life intact. When mechanisation came, it came less brutally and with less concentration of people than in Britain or

Germany. In fact, embroidery produced the paradox that mechanisation actively fostered decentralisation. Instead of taking the worker to the factory where the machines stood in great rows, the machines were installed in the peasant worker's cottage. Here the traditions of the *Webkeller* of the eighteenth century renewed themselves in the nineteenth and twentieth. At the time that embroidery topped the list of Swiss exports, only two firms used more than one hundred machines. Embroidery, like watchmaking, depended on decentralisation and the putting out of work.

The Swiss variant of nineteenth-century economic development, which I think of as 'micro-capitalism', had enormous advantages for the capitalist. The smaller the units, the less the percentage of production which could be subject to factory legislation. By putting the machinery into the peasant's cellar, the employer evaded the terms of the 1877 factory law and reduced wages at the same time. Child labour was very widespread in cotton and embroidery, less so in watches, and in many ways children in the Victorian cotton mill were better off than in their parents' homes in St Gallen. Parents proved to be more thorough, more ruthless and more insistent exploiters than a millowner could ever have been. Here is a passage from the diary of a twelve-year-old; 'After supper, I have to ravel until ten o'clock; sometimes, if the work is pressing, I have to ravel in the cellar until eleven. Afterward I say good night to my parents and go to bed. So it goes every day.'[16] The children rose again at five or six to get in a few hours of work before school. The myth of the happy peasant with roots in the land, actively propagated by liberal publicists, lost its meaning as the nineteenth century went on. The *horloger paysan* turned into an anxious, harrassed exploited outworker.

Apart from the brief flurry of anarchism, working-class organisations were slow to develop and one can easily see why. In Schwitzguébel's terms, the worker remained necessarily a 'half bourgeois'. When the Fédération des Ouvriers sur Métaux et Horloger was founded in 1915, it tended to concentrate on bread-and-butter issues and shun the more violent forms of class conflict. Anarchism had fizzled out and now piecemeal achievements were to do the job instead. The great excitement of the General Strike of 1918 masked the essential conservatism of the Swiss working class, as I suggested in Chapter 2. Two other elements in the Swiss situation worked against labour militancy. First was democracy itself. The radical constitution of 1848 put Switzerland in the enviable position of being the most democratic country in Europe. The improvements in the revised constitution of 1874 and the introduction of referenda and popular initiative during the 1890s kept a step ahead of potential popular unrest. Only when the advance toward greater representation lagged during the First World War did resentments begin to accumulate. The concession of proportional representation in 1919 tapped that pool by making the Socialist Party one of the four main groups in parliament. The militants were tamed by the government's timely surrender on social welfare issues and soon accepted the *status quo* as more or less unalterable. The anarchists who had seen that danger never found the answer. To abstain from the many elections on all three levels of Swiss politics was futile; to participate was to accept the *status quo*.

The second element was the pervasiveness of libertarian ideas at all levels of Swiss life. Decentralisation and putting out fostered the myth that, as a Genevese watchmaker put it in 1798, 'watchmakers work as free men. They are all more or less artists . . .'[17] The sturdy Appenzeller peasant could believe the same thing, even if he had to work a sixteen-hour day. After all, he owned his house, his land, perhaps, even a share of his machinery. He was in the literal sense a 'half bourgeois', both peasant proprietor and capitalist worker at the same time. *Travail à domicile* and small-scale production remained unusually prominent in Switzerland until well into the twentieth century. 1910 was the first year that the number of workers employed in factories exceeded outworkers and those employed in units too small to fall under the factory laws.[18] This 'arrested development' caught Marx's eye too. The failure of Swiss industry to get beyond what he saw as the random (*zusammenhanglos*) or heterogeneous stage of *Manufaktur* to the mature processes of factory production reflected the nature of the products. The main Swiss products had two characteristics which were 'obstacles' to factory methods: 'the smallness and delicacy of the work and its luxury character, that is, its variety'.[19] Mass production, Marx believed, demanded uniformity of product, and, in fact, the development of the *Roskopf* or simple pinlever watch, selling at SFr. 20, led to factory production of movements, the *ébauches*, still the most mechanised, capital intensive stage in watch manufacture.

Marx was certainly right to put his finger on the luxury trade as the main source of Swiss wealth, but there was an irony there, which he failed to notice. The Swiss made luxury articles because their natural environment was poor and their transport costs high. Of the 41,287 square kilometres of modern Switzerland 23.6% is called 'unproductive', mainly the areas of the higher Alps, which in early modern times and prior to the growth of tourism had very little economic value. Another 23% belongs to forest, 27.0% to grazing and pasture, 19.4% to animal feed crops and only 6.3% to cereal crops and viniculture.[20] These statistics reflect, of course, the modern, very high degree of specialisation on milk and dairy products, but Ammann has evidence that Switzerland had become dependent on cereal imports by the fifteenth century.[21] In Chapter 2 I quoted the case of Canton Schwyz which no longer had grain seeds by the beginning of the sixteenth century, so it is not unreasonable to think that the specialisation on the export of dairy products goes back a long way. There was no mining in medieval Switzerland and even today Switzerland lacks almost all of the raw materials of modern industry. Transport costs, in spite of the rivers, have always been high, especially when Swiss products competed for foreign and overseas markets. In the middle of the nineteenth century, J. M. Hungerbühler, one of the first economic historians of modern Switzerland, reckoned that textile products from the Toggenburg or Watwil arrived at the nearest seaports bearing ten times the freight charges of their competitors, and that Swiss goods remained competitive only because Swiss wages were 15% lower than those in neighbouring Germany and hours 15% longer.[22] Hard work by itself could not overcome the natural disadvantages of geography. A steady supply of sturdy, relatively well educated but poor mountain boys helped to keep costs down, but the real key to success on world markets (and effectively world markets were the main markets for Swiss products) was quality. The more the value added by Swiss skill the greater the chances of profit. High costs of imported raw materials and high transport costs pushed Swiss merchants and manufacturers into luxury products, where the margin created by specialised skill between costs and prices was bound to be greatest. The watch and the small piece of embroidery used little raw material, were light and easy to transport and very expensive to buy.

By the middle of the nineteenth century, Swiss manufacturers had developed recognisably modern attitudes to their enterprises. They spent money and time, developing and improving the quality of the products, and even more time on exploration of the market. In Keller's largely autobiographical *Grüne Heinrich*, there is a scene in which young Heinrich's mother visits a cotton manufacturer about a possible job for her boy. The date must be the middle of the

1830s. The manufacturer is delighted to hear that the boy wants to be a painter, which he regards as a most agreeable activity:

But this urge must be directed into solid and sensible channels. Now you, my dearest lady and friend, will be aware of the character of my not insubstantial enterprise. I make cotton prints and, in so far as I achieve a tolerable income, I do so by seeking always to bring the latest *Dessins* as attentively and quickly as possible and to outbid the ruling taste by offering something entirely new and original. To this end I employ some designers, whose only task it is to find new *Dessins* and sitting in this comfortable chamber can sketch flowers, stars, tendrils, dots and lines to their hearts' content... He [young Heinrich] shall abstract from the riches of nature the most wonderful and delicate forms and drive my competitors wild.[23]

Part of the training would be apprenticeship in Paris to learn the language, the techniques and, above all, to study the market.

As cotton textiles conquered Zürich, another industry began very modestly in Basel: the dyestuffs manufacturing industry. Between 1857 when J. R. Geigy and W. Heusler set up their small plant to extract dyestuffs from wood products and 1900, only the Swiss firms of Binschedler & Busch (later reincorporated as the Society for the Chemical Industry in Basel or CIBA), Kern & Sandoz, F. Hoffmann–La Roche, and J. R. Geigy SA were able to keep up with what David Landes has called the 'leap to hegemony, almost to monopoly' of the German dyestuff industry, a leap without parallel in the economic history of the nineteenth century and 'Imperial Germany's greatest industrial achievement'.[24] By 1900 only the Swiss were left with a vigorous, competitive dyestuff and organic chemical industry in the face of the overwhelming power of the great German giants later to be consolidated in the I. G. Farben cartel. The achievement is the more remarkable because, as always in Swiss economic history, none of the raw materials were native to the country and very large amounts of raw and semi-finished products had to be imported to sustain Swiss chemical production. Even more remarkable, and from our point of view more interesting, is the compartmentalisation of the industry. Like watches in the Jura, embroidery in St Gallen, and cotton textiles in Zürich, the new chemical industry was, and still is, exclusive to Basel. How did a wealthy but quiet mercantile community of about 27,000 people in 1847 become the centre of one of the greatest industries of the twentieth century?

No one answer will do but some elements in the history of Basel stand out as plausible parts of a tolerable one.[25] There was a great deal of capital in Basel. When it joined the Confederation in 1501, it was already the richest city-state in the region. In 1862, there were twenty substantial private banks investing at home and abroad. The local silk ribbon industry, the so-called *Posamenterie*, had a demand for colouring and dyestuffs, which assured the infant organic chemical companies of a safe market. It is worth noting too that the ribbon-makers, like the watch and embroidery workers, worked at home, outside the city's jurisdiction and hence in earlier times outside the restrictions of the guilds. The *Bändelherren* or 'ribbon lords', the equivalent of the *établisseurs* in the Jura, lived in town where, as in St Gallen, they supplied the mercantile venture capital for the industry. The introduction of the bar loom in the seventeenth century had greatly increased productivity. By the middle of the nineteenth century there were about 4,000 bar looms in peasant cottages in the country-side around the city. Silk-dyeing for the ribbons had become a separate branch of the industry and here a factory system had begun to emerge. In these respects, Basel was not all that unusual among the Swiss cities we have looked at; where Basel differed was *Kultur*. Basel had always had aspirations toward higher things. During the fifteenth and sixteenth centuries, Basel had been home to Erasmus and to Paracelsus and to Johannes Froben, one of the greatest printers (or what we should today call publishers) of the age. Erasmus's New Testament in the original Greek text printed at Froben's works in 1516 is, perhaps, the most important single work ever published in Switzerland. The first revised edition of Galen, the first edition of Vesalius, and the first edition of the *Book of Herbs* by Fuchs all appeared in the fine editions of the Basel printers. Woodcuts prepared by Dürer, drawings by Hans Holbein the Younger and frontispieces of the greatest opulence adorned the books printed by Froben, Cratander, Bebel, Herwagen and Isengrin. There was also the only Swiss university, founded in 1460. Basel could claim, along with Geneva, to be a metropolis.

Printing is by its nature a radical trade. It flourishes where censorship is lax and public tolerance well developed. Renaissance Basel welcomed the alien, the eccentric and the heretical with more insouciance than most other European cities. Basel naturally became the home of a native Swiss tradition of free thought and in the eighteenth century the Enlightenment took deeper root in Basel than in any other Swiss canton save Geneva. It is no coincidence that the radical moving spirit of the Helvetic Republic, Peter Ochs, and many of his most passionate supporters, were Baselers. During the late seventeenth and eighteenth centuries Basel and its university claimed the Bernoulli family, who, like so many of the city's craftsmen, preferred the tolerant patrician atmosphere of the city to the absolutist repression around it. The Bernoullis, rather like the Bach family in music, produced four generations of brilliant mathematicians, scientists and scholars, almost all of whom taught at the university of Basel. Johann Bernoulli (1667–1748) pioneered a great deal of modern pure and applied mathematics, was the first to use the 'integral calculus' as a concept and wrote the first textbook on differential calculus.

This rich cultural and scientific background helps to explain the spectacular expansion of chemistry. As early as 1845, Christian Friedrich Schönbein had produced the first man-made material. A professor at the University of Basel, Schönbein investigated the effect of sulphuric and nitric acids on various substances. He saw that cotton underwent a chemical transformation while retaining its fibre structure. The cellulose of the fibre became cellulose nitrate. Schönbein's new cotton (he called it *Schiessbaumwolle* or 'guncotton' because it was so inflammable) later became the basis of the first plastics.

In spite of this lively tradition Basel seemed very narrow to the young patrician Jakob Burckhardt when he returned to his native city in 1843. After Berlin, Paris and, above all, after the literary intoxication of the 'Ladybirds – A Society not for Philistines', which he had joined at Bonn University, he was struck by what I have called the cellular qualities of Swiss life: 'How much a city like this silts up without stimulating life-giving elements from outside. There are learned people here but they have turned to stone against everything foreign. It is not good nowadays if such a tiny corner is entirely left to its own individuality.'[26] Yet the very individuality which Burckhardt deplored turned out to be the precondition for the most general of developments, the growth of an international dyestuffs industry. That 'tiny corner' had specialised in economic survival for centuries and now, as Landes says, by 'concentrating on special tints, requiring the highest production skills, and offering customers the latest technical advice',[27] Basel on its own competed with that greater Germany to which young Burckhardt was so partial. In the process, it may be argued, the tiny corner ceased to be what it was and became the capital of a vast empire of plastics, drugs, hormones, dyestuffs and glues which have literally transformed the physical circumstances of all mankind. Today the three biggest Basel chemical companies, CIBA–Geigy, Hoffmann–La Roche and Sandoz, have an aggregate turnover which is larger than the

Swiss federal budget. Hoffmann—La Roche, with a turnover of over SFr. 5,000 million (equal to just under SFr. 1,000 for every man, woman and child in Switzerland) has become the largest drug manufacturer in the world but by no means the most popular with other governments. Its two most famous products, librium and valium, two widely prescribed tranquillisers, have attracted the attention of ministers of health in several European countries on grounds of monopoly pricing. The company has been under investigation by the anti-monopoly section of the European Commission about alleged violations of the fair practices code in marketing animal vitamins. Here again, Hoffmann—La Roche by extreme concentration of effort on a few products has become the largest supplier of animal vitamins in the world.

Until very recently, the great chemical companies believed that all publicity was bad publicity. It used to be said that the only number in the Hoffmann—La Roche annual report was the date. Its shares were tightly held by family trusts and the few traded on Swiss exchanges fetched prices as high as SFr. 200,000 per share. Now the blanket of secrecy around Hoffmann—La Roche has pretty well disappeared. Dr Jann, the chairman, gives interviews and, unthinkable even twelve months ago, has graced the cover of the American magazine *Businessweek*. This sudden conversion to the sunlight after a century of shade was much influenced by the reaction within Switzerland to Hoffmann—La Roche's troubles. The Swiss press had no reason to leap to the defence of the company. One leader-writer remarked that 'if Hoffroche had shown more skill and less arrogance in its public relations in years past, it would never have had a conflict with Great Britain at all'. As a result of these recent experiences, Hoffmann—La Roche, Sandoz and CIBA—Geigy have begun to publish more informative annual reports in the American style, complete with details of their cash flow and other useful information for the security analyst.

Part of the trouble about publicity arose because Swiss company law is so feeble that companies are obliged to disclose little of their true profits, losses and reserves. The government recognises that to demand more would cause real difficulties. The managing director of a large company explained to me that if Swiss firms had to present true balance sheets, as do English and American companies, the vast 'still reserves' of concealed capital would be so shocking that the state would simply have to tax them. Part of the reason for 'still reserves' is historical. Swiss companies have never used the formal mechanism of the stock exchange to anything like the extent that English and American companies have. The 'still reserves' took the place of a public capital market. Hence there was no equivalent to the American Securities and Exchange Commission which could compel a company to reveal its true finances before it got listed on the New York Stock Exchange. Continental banks are also stockbrokers. They had other ways of finding out about company finance than the annual report and, since continental banks also dominate the market in publicly quoted securities, they had no reason to worry. The attempts by the Swiss security analysts to achieve better reporting of company finances have not been unsuccessful, merely slow. A few years ago they reported that the twenty-four biggest Swiss companies reported less than half of the internationally accepted facts: cash flow per share, reserves of liquidity, earnings per share, production levels, inventory changes and interest receivable. Since then, the chemical Big Three have dropped the veil, and no doubt others will follow as they see their best protection in frankness.

The Justice Department has accepted the fact that Swiss company law is too weak for modern conditions (company reports are merely one symptom of this) and has set up a committee of experts under Dr Hans Tschopp, vice-president of the Federal Court, to revise it. Their first, interim report appeared in 1972 with a view 'to encouraging the exchange of ideas and to enable the committee to assess whether their suggestions meet the needs of the time'. Many lawyers doubt if they do. 'Still reserves' will not be 'forbidden' according to the report of the committee nor will any change be made in the rights of banks to vote shares they hold as trustees. What this means in practice is that the banks, who in any case are already heavily involved in the big companies by systems of interlocking directorships, simply vote with management the enormous number of shares held in trust by them. On the other hand, the Tschopp Committee have suggested very substantial improvements in the reporting of earnings, in the laws governing shareholding and types of shares and the character of capital structures permitted. The trouble now will come in the long process of *Vernehmlassung*, or obligatory consultation, which I described in Chapter 3. Years will go by before the Tschopp Committee report takes legislative form.

Both the old secrecy and the new candour express different responses to the same reality: the dependence of Swiss industry on exports. The Basel companies protected their affairs so anxiously because they knew that, however strong they might seem on paper, they were vulnerable to foreign attack. Unlike any of their competitors, they had no domestic market to fall back on nor a Swiss state with a lot of international force to protect them. That vulnerability has now led them to try the opposite tack: 'see what friendly, local, multi-national giants we are' seems to be the present defence. Neither attitude alters the fact that 90% of chemical and pharmaceutical production goes abroad. The chemical industry is not unique in this respect. Between 70% and 90% of all textiles, between 70% and 80% of all machinery and engineering products and about 97% of all watches and watch parts are exported. The extreme disproportion between the volume of turnover and the size of the domestic market makes big Swiss companies uneasy. They know the line between wealth and ruin can be thin. The very specialisation which brings the fat profits makes the specialised company vulnerable to changes in the market, costs of technology. The basic realities of Swiss economic life can be summed up in two linked paradoxes: because they were poor, they specialised in luxury goods, and because they specialised they were easily ruined. This 'fragility', as Jean-François Bergier puts it, grew out of the hard realities facing Swiss businessmen. Two examples may help here. According to official government figures, between 5 May 1971 and the end of December 1974 the Swiss franc appreciated against the currencies of the fifteen leading trading countries by 41.3%.[28] The 'floating franc' has hit the watch industry hard, an industry which at the beginning of 1974 could claim nearly 40% of world production, two-thirds of world exports in volume and more in terms of value. During the first quarter of 1975 exports of the pinlever models (*Roskopf*), which account for half total exports, fell by 42%. 99% of this particular type of watch are sold abroad. Pierre Waltz, general director of the Société Suisse pour l'Industrie Horlogère, told a press conference in the early spring of 1975, 'with the dollar at SFr. 3.40 we find ourselves in a more or less normal recession like everybody else. With the dollar at SFr. 2.70 the situation becomes critical. With the dollar at SFr. 2.40 the struggle is hopeless and we shall lose more and more of our markets over the next few years.' The evidence so far supports M. Waltz. In some markets, such as the British, the battle is nearly lost. While the franc has gone up by 40% plus, the pound sterling has gone down by nearly 30%, and allowing for price increases in Switzerland's domestic economy at about 8–10% per annum, it is hardly surprising that the price of Swiss watches in the UK has gone up since 1971 by over 100%. Much more serious is the potential loss of the US market where the price of Swiss watches has gone up by nearly 90%, while the price of Japanese watches has gone up by only about 50%. Roughly 55% of all Swiss watches and watch parts exported go to the dollar area, an area whose currency is depreciating. As a result, not only are Swiss watches more expensive in the USA but American watches become cheaper abroad. The 'floating franc' gives every advantage to the foreign competitor and none to the Swiss watchmaker. He also suffers because he adds so much value compared to the cost of raw materials; probably roughly 90% of the value of a watch is actually attributable to work done domestically. Since the value of the watch is created in Switzerland, the watchmaking industry gains nothing from the fact that the higher franc can buy more raw materials. The chemical or engineering company which imports a large part of the raw materials can gain on the cost roundabout what it loses on the price swings; the watchmaker cannot. The watchmaking is the third largest export industry of the country; SFr. 3,702 million worth of watches (approximately £617 million pounds) were exported in 1974, 10.5% of total exports.[29] That very large sum of money, which for purposes of comparison is about twice the value of UK exports of aircraft and aircraft engines, has been put at risk by a sudden shift in one of the delicately balanced elements of the economic environment. In any other country, an industry so powerful would be able to force the national government to protect it. The Swiss government simply cannot intervene. The government of the USA is not willing to do anything about the downward drift of its currency. By itself Switzerland is too small to fight back the flood of surplus dollars; to try to do so would swamp the domestic economy with huge sums of unwanted liquid balances and court a serious inflationary risk. In the end the government would fail. The watch industry turns out to be fragile, precisely because it is so specialised, adds so much value at home, exports so much of its product, and operates in a luxury market where price matters. The 'fragility' is also Swiss in the wider sense, because the government cannot help watchmakers any more than it can fight the battles of Hoffmann—La Roche.

Another more striking example of 'fragility' is the collapse of the embroidery industry of east Switzerland. The most successful export article in the two decades before 1914, embroidery dominated the economy of St Gallen, Appenzell and Thurgau. The federal industrial census of 1905 revealed that 49.5% of all employed persons in Canton St Gallen worked directly in embroidery (28,967 in factories, mostly small, and 33,547 in homes) and that the total number of persons employed in the industry in the north-eastern cantons approached 100,000.[30] As in watchmaking and chemicals, production was concentrated in certain areas which had become wholly dependent on one product. The specialisation which made the industry competitive also made it, and the economy of north-eastern Switzerland, vulnerable. The First World War hit the industry hard but the end of the war destroyed it. Not only were important export markets like the German and Austrian utterly ruined, but even in the prosperous ones like the USA there had been a huge change. The war acted as a giant social mixer. It mobilised the population, and that included women. During the war, the huge floppy hat, the stays and corsets, and the long skirts went into the cupboards and with them went the taste for embroidered articles. Swiss embroidery production fell from 9,157 tons in 1913 to 2,830 tons by 1921. The value of exports declined from SFr. 215 million in 1913 to 147 million in 1921, to 65 million in 1930 and to 26 million in 1937. An industry which had employed 117,375 people in 1910 had shrivelled to 32,626 by 1930.[31] In the middle of the 1930s St Gallen had become a ghost town. The pompous office blocks in *Jugendstil* which had housed firms with English names like 'Atlantic', 'Union', 'Ocean' and 'Worldwide' were empty. The misery in the countryside was unimaginable. The tens of thousands of small-holders who had adapted their lives to the outwork system of the embroidery industry were destitute. The fragility of the Swiss economy had never been more evident: an entire region ruined by a change in fashion.

The year 1945 marked a break in Swiss history not unlike 1648 but with this difference. Where the end of the first Thirty Years War ruined the Swiss economy, the end of the second 'Thirty Years War' (1914 to 1945) opened a period of unparalleled boom. After a short pause, as Table 5.1 shows, the Swiss achieved rates of growth among the highest in modern history. These were the 'golden twenty years', as Peter Rogge has called them.[32] In spite of expectations, Europe recovered rapidly. Through Marshall aid and other sources, capital was pumped into reconstruction of heavy plant, rebuilding of ruined cities, resurfacing of gutted roads and twisted railway tracks. Incomes rose sharply and with them the demand for consumption goods, specialised products such as drugs, vitamins, prepared foods and the like. Switzerland with its intact industry and its unique blend of products was ideally placed to supply the Nescafé, the vitamin B, the new wristwatch or office calculator which the reviving Europe demanded. Price

TABLE 5.1   Gross national product in nominal and real terms (1938—71)

Year	GNP (nominal)	%	GNP (real)	%	Degree of inflation	Real per cap.	GNP %
1938	9,580	–	18,345	–	–	4,376	–
1948	18,975	–	22,480	–	–	4,906	–
1949	18,755	–1.2	21,685	–3.5	–2.3	4,673	–4.7
1950	19,920	6.2	23,245	7.2	–1.0	4,952	6.0
1951	21,935	10.1	25,130	8.1	2.0	5,292	6.9
1952	23,020	4.9	25,330	0.8	4.1	5,261	–0.6
1953	24,090	4.6	26,465	4.5	0.1	5,425	3.1
1954	25,555	6.1	27,955	5.6	1.1	5,672	4.6
1955	27,265	6.7	29,445	5.3	1.4	5,913	4.2
1956	29,285	7.4	31,215	6.0	1.4	6,178	4.5
1957	30,870	5.4	32,105	2.9	2.5	6,263	1.4
1958	31,520	2.1	31,520	–1.8	3.9	6,063	–3.2
1959	33,840	7.4	33,795	7.2	0.2	6,426	6.0
1960	37,055	9.5	35,770	5.8	1.0	6,671	3.8
1961	41,490	12.0	38,390	7.3	4.7	6,985	4.7
1962	46,050	11.0	40,335	5.1	5.9	7,126	2.0
1963	50,370	9.4	42,190	4.6	4.8	7,312	2.6
1964	55,540	10.2	44,330	5.1	5.1	7,547	3.2
1965	59,985	8.3	46,255	4.3	4.0	7,780	3.1
1966	64,625	7.7	47,585	2.9	4.8	7,932	1.8
1967	68,825	6.5	48,435	1.8	4.7	7,978	1.4
1968	74,220	7.6	50,365	4.2	3.3	8,193	2.7
1969	80,930	9.0	53,128	6.2	2.8	8,530	4.0
1970	88,850	9.8	55,925	4.6	5.2	8,800	3.2
1971	100,760	13.4	58,330	3.9	9.5	9,223	4.8
1972	116,095	15.2	61,713	5.8	9.4	9,665	4.7
1973	129,370	11.4	63,873	3.5	7.9	9,932	2.7
1974	139,490	7.8	64,384	0.8	7.0	9,966	0.3

Source: 'Die schweizerische Konjunktur im Jahre 1974', Mitteilung No. 231, *Kommission für Konjunkturfragen* (Bern, January 1975).

seemed to be no obstacle to the buyer and profits soared. Such rapid, Japanese-style economic growth began to cause huge social and structural changes in Swiss life. The last reserves of surplus domestic labour were simply sucked off the land as Table 5.2 shows.

The backbone of Swiss life, the peasant small-holder, disappeared from the economic arena. Many areas of the mountains depopulated rapidly. By 1970, 22% of the Swiss population lived in communes of less than 2,000 people, as opposed to 48.5% in 1900. On the other hand

TABLE 5.2   Percentage of all employed persons

	1888	1960	1970
Primary sector (agriculture and forestry)	37	11	8
Secondary sector (industry, mining building, electricity, etc.)	41	51	48
Tertiary sector (service, tourism, commerce, trade, etc.)	22	38	44

Source: *Schweizer Brevier, 1972*, p. 42.

45.3% lived in cities of over 10,000 in 1970, compared to 6% in 1900. The Swiss were rapidly becoming a nation of city dwellers and office workers in a political and economic system designed for country men and tillers of the soil. At the same time, the booming economy began to outstrip the natural sources of energy, especially the hydro-electric power drawn from the thousands of fast-moving rivers. By 1975 electricity from all sources supplied only a fifth of the nation's energy needs, and of that a third came from nuclear power. Oil accounted for 80% of all energy consumed in the Confederation. Here too the Swiss economy rested on fragile foundations, as the country discovered when the price of oil was quadrupled during the winter of 1973–4.

Neither labour nor capital shortage interfered with the hurtling progress of the great post-war boom. After 1950 an endless supply of cheap labour flowed into the country from southern Europe. As we have seen, capital from domestic sources was already plentiful. To this was added the large sums transferred by anxious Europeans unable to believe in the reality or stability of the new post-war currencies. The Swiss government, whose contingency planning had been dominated by fears of another post-war depression, a kind of St Gallen complex, awoke to the new reality slowly, but managed to do so just in time to make the situation worse. Government departments at all three levels suddenly realised that the 'infrastructure', the roads, power plants, water and sewage systems, were inadequate for the booming private economy and hurriedly began to make up for lost time. Public works which had stood at about SFr. 1,200 million in the middle of the 1950s reached SFr. 2,000 million by 1961, 3,000 million by 1963 and 4,300 million by 1966. The federal budget tripled between 1960 and 1970, and the cantons and communes were not far behind. In 1961, all three levels spent SFr. 7,630 million, in 1971 they spent SFr. 24,230 million and by 1975 an estimated SFr. 39,100 million. Perhaps the most significant way to measure the change is to notice that in 1961 government expenditure on federal, cantonal and communal level equalled 18.6% of gross national product; by 1975 it amounted to 28%. Finally and inevitably, deficits began to appear in federal, cantonal and communal budgets, rising from SFr. 446 million for all three levels in 1971 to SFr. 2,063 million by 1973.[33]

Deficits of this order are precisely what any sensible counter-cyclical policy would seek to avoid, but the Swiss finance minister is in a difficult position. The structure of Swiss federalism works against him. The cantons themselves differ enormously in size and wealth. The central government assists the 'financially weak' cantons to survive and even offers subventions to those in the two higher categories. Such contributions may amount to about 20% of the income of the rich cantons, about 30% of the moderately well off but over 50% of the very poor ones. As Federal Councillor Celio, the former head of the Finance Department, said in a speech to a civic society in Luzern in 1971, 'any global financial policy will inevitably weaken the position of the cantons. That must be compensated for by a strengthening of the equalisation of finance among cantons . . . Financial equalisation in a federal state is so complex because economic, financial, political and social considerations meet and overlap.'[34] The federal government itself relies on direct taxes for about a third of its revenues, but on indirect taxes on consumption for about two-thirds.[35] The spectacle of rich men and huge companies paying little tax while the average man pays more for his daily bread has prompted the Socialist Party to press for wholesale reform of the system. They have proposed an overall tax burden, including all three levels of the federation, of not less than 27% for taxable incomes of SFr. 100,000, 35% for incomes of SFr. 200,000 up to 50% at a level SFr. 1 million. These minima would prevent any canton from allowing its tax level to drop too low. Minima are also suggested for a wealth tax. The Socialists demand an end to the great variety of tax levels on income and capital in the various cantons, but prospects for what is called 'material harmonisation' are not good. The cantons have been unable to agree, after fifteen years of consultation, on harmonising the dates of the school years, and tax reform is a more difficult matter.

The most serious difficulty facing a Swiss finance minister is not federalism but democracy. In no other country in the world can the ordinary voter say Yes or No to fiscal measures as detailed as, for example, the package put before the voters in June 1975:

1. to raise petrol taxes from 20 to 30 centimes per litre;
2. to raise duty on heating oil from 30 centimes to between SFr. 1.10 and 2.00;
3. to raise turnover tax from 4.4% to 5.6% on retail, and from 6.6% to 8.4% on wholesale, transactions;
4. to raise the maximum rates of direct federal tax from 10.45% to 11.5% on individuals and from 8.8% to 9.8% on the profits of corporations.

Of those eligible 36.5% went to the polls and a majority of them voted Yes to all the measures save the tax on heating oil, which was narrowly rejected. It says a lot for the maturity of the Swiss electorate that it should vote to tax itself by an additional SFr. 1,400 million, but the same 'sovereign' had rejected a different fiscal package in December 1974. Whatever the virtues of Swiss semi-direct democracy, they do not make either for fingertip control of aggregate demand nor for fundamental reform of the fiscal system.

This structure of the Swiss state is a framework uniquely favourable to the operation of the giant companies which dominate the economy. Its traditions are against intervention in private affairs, and there is a majority within the chambers and, it would appear, in the country at large against any significant attack on inequalities of wealth. There is a Swiss welfare system, which works reasonably well. Welfare came second only to defence in the 1974 federal expenditure. Accident, invalid, old-age and survivors insurance are compulsory, but not health insurance. The Swiss have no national health system and the private and semi-public schemes have a variety of gaps in them, which, as in the case of taxation, has prompted much reforming activity, so far not very definitive. The burden of the state in Switzerland rests more lightly on the well-to-do and on companies than in any other developed society, and taxation is correspondingly low. The Swiss top executive is thus very well off. Figures for 1974 show that the managers of Swiss firms with a turnover of more than SFr. 1,000 million (roughly £160 million) earn annually SFr. 240,000 *after tax*, while the equivalent American, French, Italian and British managers earn respectively SFr. 228,000, SFr. 165,000, SFr. 120,000 and SFr. 90,000. Several Swiss banks publish purchasing power tables which work out in detail whether a female office worker is actually better off in Zürich or San

Francisco, but for our purposes it is clear that she is very well off too, if not as markedly so as her boss. Wages in Swiss factories are high. Average money wages for manual workers amount to SFr. 24,011 per annum in 1973, which at about SFr. 6 to £1 works out neatly at £4,000. According to official figures (*Die Volkswirtschaft*, August 1975, p. 384) the total tax burden (federal, cantonal and communal) for a married factory worker with no children was 7.7%, for an office worker 9.8%, of gross earnings in 1974. Inflation takes more but even here real wages (that is, wages corrected for price rises) have nearly doubled since 1949. In 1974, the average male factory worker earned SFr. 11.96 (at present rates of exchange about £2) *per hour.*[36]

In this economic environment, perhaps the most characteristic of all Swiss industries, the banking business, flourished like the bay tree. The Swiss are not the only bankers in Europe, but there is no other country in which banks are so numerous. A recent official survey reported that there was a grand total of 1,629 independent banking companies which operate in 4,480 branches. There is roughly one bank for every 1,400 people. There are more banks (4,480) than dentists (3,568). In addition to the big commercial banks, which conduct every sort of business under one roof there are the twenty-eight cantonal banks, one or two of which have active international businesses. There are some fifty or so private banks specialising in portfolio management, as well as a great many small, local banks, savings and loan associations, foreign banks and representative offices. Basel is the headquarters of the Bank for International Settlements, a legacy of the great currency crises of the German mark in the late 1920s but still today a most important international agency regulating payments among member states. Banking like watchmaking or chemicals, chocolate and tourism, is a very characteristic Swiss industry.

Most people think that Switzerland became rich on other people's money but the reality is more interesting. Banking grew out of trade in the late Middle Ages, and because, as we saw in Chapter 2, in a sense, the late Middle Ages continued in Switzerland longer than elsewhere, the mercantile banking houses continued as well. Neutrality helped to make Switzerland attractive to foreigners but the real sources of capital were the savings of a thrifty, prudent people. Today the Swiss own twice as many foreign assets as foreigners hold in Switzerland. Since Swiss companies tended to be as prudent as their employees, they too saved for a rainy day and, as we have seen, concealed large sums of surplus capital in darker corners of their balance sheets. Since

Swiss banks had less to do with industrial finance than their German competitors they had to find other outlets for these pools of domestic savings. During the period of fascism, when great risks and massive currency restrictions burdened international payments, and after 1945, when many of these restrictions, such as the UK Exchange Control Act of 1947, went on posing problems, Switzerland was the only absolutely free market in Europe. Anything could be done — at a price —and nothing was too complicated for the agile minds of Zürich's Bahnhofstrasse, the Swiss Wall Street. Only in Switzerland could non-convertible Czechoslovak–Brazilian clearing dollars be used to finance the coffee imports of a Hamburg merchant.

During the late 1950s a new world currency began to appear. It began modestly. Managers of European banks noticed surplus dollars in their New York accounts and tried to think of ways to use them. Gradually an international telephone market sprang up in which surplus dollars were loaned out for short periods among banks. The borrowing bank would then sell the dollars against the domestic currency, and buy them back by a future contract timed to coincide with the day of repayment to the lending bank. It could lend the sums thus released to its domestic customers for the same time span. Dollars were on offer so cheaply that, even after subtracting the cost of selling and repurchasing them at the future date, the borrowing bank could still charge its customer a rate below that in the domestic money market. The lending bank was happy, since it earned more for three months' dollars in Europe than it could do on Wall Street. The Eurodollar was born. Europe was still rebuilding after the war, and needed this new source of capital. At first money-market men distrusted a system which looked more like a chain letter than sober banking practice. They assumed that it would be a temporary bonanza. In time it became clear that the real source of Eurodollars was the vast balance of payment deficits of the United States. During the 1960s and early 1970s the deficits became so permanent a feature of world trade that the pool of Eurodollars turned into a chartless sea. The official estimate was about two hundred billion dollars in 1975. Swiss banks were not the first to see the possibilities of the Eurodollar (merchant banks in the City of London were), but the Swiss invented the 'Eurobond', a fixed interest security denominated in Eurodollars. Characteristically, the Swiss banks found a specialised corner of the market, which they soon dominated. Their best customers were American companies who borrowed dollars for five to ten years in Europe more cheaply than they could borrow them at home and used the proceeds of the issues of Eurobonds for their foreign operations. Zürich came to be the nearest thing to a proper stock market for Eurobonds, and the Union Bank estimates that between the early 1960s and the early 1970s thirteen thousand million dollars of Eurobonds were underwritten and issued by Swiss banks.

Zürich is the Swiss financial capital, not Bern, and it is in Zürich, especially on the Bahnhofstrasse, that the legendary gnomes dwell. Gnomes are by the light of day just foreign exchange dealers, that is, men who trade one currency against another. The Swiss Germans are unusually good at it, because they are unusually well prepared for a profession which requires the simultaneous use of different languages. Early in life, as we saw in the preceding chapter, the Swiss Germans become bilingual in *Schriftdeutsch* and *Schwyzerdütsch*. Any Swiss who has ambitions for a life of commerce spends time in French-speaking Switzerland (even typists think in such terms) and they learn English as a matter of course. A dealer will sit in a room surrounded by telephones and a telex by his side. 'Open lines' amplified through little speakers will stand on his desk and he may wear a headphone too. A dealer may have an open line to a London broker connected to his headphones. He speaks English to London, French to Paris and German to the dealer at the next desk, while punching numbers into his desk calculator and from time to time looking at the telex. The foreign exchange dealer regards his Tower of Babel as normal.

What dealers do is very complicated, requires good nerves, a stout digestion and a love of games, but it is not mysterious. Essentially foreign exchange dealers make it possible for us to be paid in our own currency when we sell goods and services abroad or return from holidays. The bank collects the various sums required, passes them to the dealing room and there the dealers buy or sell currency as required to meet obligations. In fact, the dealer is really buying and selling large round lots of currency in accounts in New York or London or Paris, as the case may be. That is the so-called 'spot market'. A sum traded today in dollars will be delivered two business days later, that is, one New York bank will pay to or receive from another a sum in the name of and for account of the dealing bank in Zürich. The scale of these transactions can be very large but the margins are small. A prudent dealer, and here I have to simplify, keeps his 'position' balanced by attempting to match assets in each foreign currency against liabilities. If a dealer buys a million dollars at ten in the morning at SFr. 2.4850, he will try to have another million sold by closing time at SFr. 2.4890, a profit on the transaction of four-tenths of a centime per dollar, equal to SFr. 4.000. His position will be closed on the day with dollars balanced in his book. Reality is much more complicated than this. There is a futures market in which currencies are bought and sold now for delivery in a week, a month, three months, six months, a year or longer. It is the overall position, which the chief dealer has to balance (rather like three-dimensional noughts and crosses). People forget that both parties to a sale cannot each be right. The dollars which our dealer bought could have gone down to SFr. 2.4810, and, if he had balanced his books that day, he would have lost the four-tenths of a centime per dollar or SFr. 4,000.

Until 1971, by guaranteeing the parities of their currencies against all other currencies, governments provided a fail-safe net for foreign exchange dealers. The dealer knew that ultimately he could always buy from or sell to the central bank at the 'intervention points'. In our hypothetical case, with a fixed parity of SFr. 2.50 = $1, and a 2-centime margin each way (from SFr. 2.48 to SFr. 2.52), our Swiss dealer would know that at SFr. 2.4810 the central bank would soon be in the market. He could afford either to take the small loss of SFr. 4.000 or wait for the central bank to prod the rate closer to the SFr. 2.4850 he had paid. When currencies began to float, there was neither floor nor ceiling to what could be made (and lost) in foreign exchange. The last few years have seen some spectacular examples. The collapse of the German Herstatt Bank in 1974 was the most flamboyant. In the previous year, Herstatt had reported net earning from foreign exchange of DM 55,000,000. The reader may try to work out for himself what volume of business would be needed to earn that sum if the margin on each transaction had been the modest 4 pro mille of the hypothetical deal we looked at. The resulting sum is so astronomical that even the laymen will see instantly that much greater margins were being achieved, margins only possible by not covering prudently each purchase by an equivalent sale. A dealer can make a lot more money on the $1,000,000 he has bought at SFr. 2.4850 by not selling it until the dollar reaches SFr. 2.4950. Profit has more than doubled to SFr. 10,000, although the dollar has only improved a centime against the franc. Suppose he then sells 'short' four additional millions at SFr. 2.4950. If the dollar goes down to SFr. 2.4750 he can repurchase his speculation, having made SFr. 80.000. The profits are really beginning to roll, and the dealer is a step nearer to the DM 55,000,000 or bankruptcy. A further element in the picture is volume. As the American balance of payments deficits widened, speculation against the dollar began. The volume of turnover in relatively modest trading rooms during 1972 and 1973 reached 50 and then 100 million dollars a day. Individual transactions of 5, 10 and even 20 millions began to take place; the dollar fluctuated wildly bringing even bigger profits. The bubble burst in 1974 and since that time a number of renowned financial institutions have confessed to the mortal sins which destroyed Herstatt. Lloyds Bank's branch in Lugano managed to achieve the staggering loss of £33 million, and the losses of the Hessische Landesbank and Girozentrale reached £50 million. Finally, in April 1974, the Swiss had their first major casualty. The Union Bank dismissed its head of the foreign exchange department, Dr Robert Strebel (the author, incidentally, of the best work on foreign exchange), and announced that a sizeable loss (later revealed to be over £20 million) had been sustained.

The Union Bank of Switzerland with total assets of over £6,000 million could bear the loss of cash and prestige. More serious was the underlying situation which had produced the currency storms in the first place: the collapse of the exchange rate of the dollar. How far successive American administrations have allowed the huge trade deficits to continue out of incompetence, uncertainty or cynicism is not clear. Foreign trade makes up a small proportion of the US gross national product. A steadily cheapening dollar affects the average man less in the United States than the sagging pound or lira does in Britain and Italy. It also has the happy side-effect of ruining foreign competitors like Swiss watchmakers and German car manufacturers. The risky side of the Eurodollar became more obvious, as national banks tried to dam the flood. The inevitable storms on the Eurodollar sea produced huge waves of currency sloshing about but mostly in one direction: out of the dollar. The first of these was the wave of speculation of late April—May 1971, when as much as $600 million of hot money was transferred to Switzerland in one day. The franc was revalued by 7% but in August of 1971 there was another currency panic. The Swiss reserves had to absorb $2,000 million. An international conference in December 1971 tried to stop the storms by revaluing all currencies, but another crisis followed in the summer of 1972. By now international currency uncertainties had begun to have profound effects on Swiss domestic price levels. Foreign money found its way not only into bank vaults but into villas, unbuilt parcels of land and investment funds. In order to have the necessary powers, the *Bundesrat* put before the voters in June of 1972 a bill which would enable it to intervene directly in the property market and in the credit and currency spheres. Three weeks later, they made use of the new powers. Foreigners were forbidden to invest in domestic mortgages, securities or property. No accounts opened by foreigners after the end of 1971 were to bear interest. The banks and the country, with the exception of poorer cantons doing a thriving business in selling scenic beauty to wealthy aliens, accepted the new measures with relief. Clearly Switzerland alone could not cope with what by December 1972 was a wholesale collapse of the system of fixed parities among the world's currencies. On 4 December 1972 the *Bundesrat* introduced another group of measures to combat inflation, including the establishment of a prices commission, restriction on hire purchase and other forms of credit, a freeze on building in various categories and lowering of the limits for depreciation. Parliament approved new taxes of SFr. 400 million and in January the National Bank raised the discount rate to $4\frac{1}{2}$%. Finally after a hectic week, on 23 January 1973, the National Bank threw in the towel and stopped supporting the dollar by official purchase as required under the international agreements. The Swiss franc was 'floating'.

The world of Swiss banking is dominated by the Big Three (the Union Bank of Switzerland, the Swiss Bank Corporation and the Swiss Credit Bank), and 'big' in this case is no exaggeration. According to its 1974 annual report, the Union Bank had a balance sheet total of SFr. 40,710 million (about £6,800 million at present exchange rates), the Bank Corporation stood at SFr. 41,040 million and the Credit Bank at SFr. 32,130 million. There were no other banks even remotely in their class. The Volksbank with a balance sheet total of SFr. 9,790 million and Bank Leu at SFr. 2,120 million were mere pygmies and, as a point of reference, the largest Zürich private bank, Julius Bär & Co., with its head office of over 300 employees and great international prestige, has a balance sheet sum about SFr. 1,000 million. The Big Three banks have balance sheet totals which are almost as large as the gross national product of Switzerland (in 1974 estimated at SFr. 139,490 million). They made more net profit collectively (over SFr. 300 million) than the total tax revenues of the three original cantons, Uri, Schwyz and Unterwalden, put together. One could go on multiplying examples; even the Basel chemical companies look small by comparison.

Clearly institutions so out of proportion to the size of the environment must have great influence, but in Switzerland it is not necessary

to wield it crudely. Partly this is because relations between government and the big banks are mediated by a central bank, which, as in the
British case, frequently puts the government's case to the banking
community and vice versa. Of course, there are rows behind the
scenes which occasionally burst into the open. The big banks de-
nounced the central bank's interest rate policies during 1974 at press
conferences called for the purpose, and in 1975 the finance ministry
and the central bank apparently let it be understood that they would
welcome an end to 'numbered accounts', those legendary accounts on
which only an identifying number appears. The banks hotly defended
the numbered accounts 'on general economic grounds'. The row was
more symbolic than real for under the Bank Secrecy Act of 1934 numbered accounts are no more protected against disclosure than named
ones, and in any case the directors of a bank know the names behind
the numbers. Numbers do prevent chance exposure or a calculated leak
by a junior employee. It is easy to imagine the sensation which would
greet the news that there was an account in Switzerland in General
Amin's name or that Himmler's account still existed in a private
bank in Zürich. Abolition of numbered accounts would hit the small
evaders, individuals escaping their country's exchange controls, while
the big evaders, Mafia bosses, oil sheikhs, international gamblers and
the like, could afford to shelter behind the brassplate companies which
make up so prominent a feature of Lugano's economic enterprises.
The numbered account is a symbol of the best and worst of Swiss
banking. Recently, the French finance minister dropped a hint that
Swiss attempts to return to the European currency 'snake' would
be more favourably received if the number system disappeared, and
central bank executives would find it convenient if they knew at least
the scale of such holdings and the actual total of such accounts.

The structure of the Swiss National Bank has a lot to do with the
absence of conflict between the government and its 'over-mighty
subjects' on the Bahnhofstrasse. The working executive of the National
Bank is the directorate. There are three members: a president, the main
spokesman who deals with political matters, a director who runs the
Bern office which handles the bank notes, volume of gold and currency
in circulation and bank investments, and a director in the Zürich office
in charge of the money market and foreign exchange sides of the bank's
work, a field generally left to a foreign exchange expert. There is a board
or *Bankausschuss*, composed of ten members, mostly influential
Zürich banking figures, who meet the directors monthly to talk policy.

The directors, since they are appointed directly by the state, consult but need not follow the views of the *Bankausschuss*. The *Ausschuss* in turn reports to the *Bankrat* or bank council of forty, twenty-five of whose members are appointed by the government. It would be naive to imagine that the big banks cannot make their weight felt through such a system but it would be even more naive, as some critics suggest, to believe that the big banks dominate the central bank. The system works smoothly because it is structurally an extension of the Swiss practice in other walks of life. The National Bank, which incidentally also has private shareholders, is not unlike the *Dorfzwing* in Malters. One might see it as a financial *Gemeinde* where citizenship devolves on the managers of companies whose balance sheets are larger than SFr. 500 million.

The image of the National Bank as a gigantic village commune is certainly overdrawn, but it points to an interesting problem. Most people have semi-conscious ideas about how things ought to be done. Ask a typical Englishman to chair a meeting and he will call up a garbled version of House of Commons procedures. He gets confused if the participants start using amendments and points of order but in a roughish way he can follow widely understood rules. The Swiss are no different. It would be hard to run the discussions in the *Bankausschuss* on lines other than those of the local *Gemeinde*, especially if the members use *Schwyzerdütsch* at any time. The language naturally evokes the spirit of the *Gemeinde*, the home and hearth. Swiss banks are not just banks chartered in Switzerland; the atmosphere is different. There is a Swiss way of life, a Swiss way of business, a Swiss style of office hours (start early and work late).

The way of life is housed in a political structure. There is a modern state called Switzerland, so there must be an economy to go with it complete with currency, taxation, legal system and customs barriers, in short, what you would expect to find in any contemporary state. However fashionable it may be to forget it, the national state by its mesh of laws erects an invisible outer shell around the economic activities within its frontiers. There is a Swiss economy, just as there is a Danish or Dutch one. There are also characteristic products of that economy: watches, chocolate, cheeses, numbered bank accounts, Victorian hotels in the Alps and a railway that runs to time. On the other hand, the majority of products produced in Switzerland today are not so closely identified with their country of origin. A piece of anodised aluminium tubing or a kilo of urea-formaldehyde condensate could be produced anywhere. The structure of enterprise in Switzerland is much like the structure elsewhere. There are large, medium-sized and small firms operating in the manufacturing sector. Swiss large firms, as we have seen, are larger in relation to their economic base than any other. A Swiss multi-national company dwarfs its surroundings. Nestlé's turnover is larger than the federal budget. The Netherlands and Sweden spring to mind as parallels, but the Dutch economy is half as large again as the Swiss. Unilever and Philips are giants but on a broader pedestal. The big Swedish companies are not as big as the Swiss. Few Swedish companies can claim to be the largest producer of anything in the way that several Swiss firms can, but in the end there is only a difference in degree and not kind. An international company is just that. In the process, the company loses its distinctive national character or, at least, some of it. There is a Swiss economy but it grows more like other European economies every day. Even watchmaking has been regrouped into huge holding companies like those of their Japanese competitors.

The disappearance of a distinctively Swiss economic structure may be very important and worth reflecting on for a moment. In *Das Kapital* Marx used an image from one of Horace's odes to describe the organisation of a typical Swiss industry at the time he was writing: 'etiam disjecti membra poetae' ('even dismembered the limbs of a poet'). The watchmaking industry (and ribbon-making in Basel, cotton textiles in Zürich and embroidery in St Gallen) was literally just that, *disjecti membra*. The capitalist was a severed head controlling the dismembered organs by an external stream of money. The basic unit of internationally known enterprises was an individual peasant cottage or the tiny firm. Capitalism flourished. Enormous profits were made but the traditional framework of Swiss life remained. A cellular economy grew up around the tiny urban cantons which at the same time preserved the rural ones. Peasant democracies survived because the peasants had become half-bourgeois half-proletariat, while still on the land. The post-war boom has swept all that away. The Swiss economy today is more like the economies around it than at any time since the Middle Ages. The *disjecti membra* have been conjured back together. The distinctive presence of the small-holding free peasantry is gone. Swiss agriculture today occupies a tiny part of the population. The sturdy Alpine peasant has become a type of landscape gardener living off state subsidies. The trading patterns of Switzerland reflect the growth of the Common Market which supplies two-thirds of all

Swiss imports and takes about two-fifths of all exports. The country is full of foreign workers who will not go home, and the economy runs on oil, not 'white coal'. In short, the Swiss economy is like any other in its basic structural characteristics. The special chapter in Swiss economic history is over.

The political structure reflects the old Switzerland, not the new. Its parts are still *disjecti membra*. There are still some sovereign bodies called cantons; there are still self-governing *Gemeinden*. The elaborate machinery to register every twitch of the popular will continues to spin smoothly, like a sewing machine made in the 1880s, but the popular will finds it harder to see itself reflected in the output of the machinery. Tiny communes cannot stop big chemical companies from polluting the water or prevent consortia from erecting atomic power plants. The changes wrought by the modern multi-national Swiss economy are not easily solved within the antique framework nor by using the historic levers and pulleys of political action. The federal government itself looks more and more like a façade. A gap has appeared between the institutions of political and social life and the structures of the economy. The old Switzerland dissolves like the grin on the Cheshire Cat, and many Swiss have become very excited about the fact. The flapping of ravens' wings can be heard in editorial offices. But there have always been gaps between economic and political structures. Institutions are sticky. They live on into ages for which they were not designed. Medieval guilds outlived the Middle Ages and forced new economic activities to grow up outside their jurisdiction, such as ribbon-making in Basel outside the city walls. Monarchies survive in north-western Europe and *Landsgemeinden* still meet in Switzerland. The old shell can fill up with new content. The opulent livery companies of the City of London play at being guilds but are frequently business and scientific associations. The Salters' Company support research in chemical engineering. Other examples are easy to find. There is no obvious relationship between structure and function at any given time in the history of a community.

Must there be any relationship at all? Why have I assumed that there must be a Swiss economic framework which fits the peculiarities of the Swiss historical, political and linguistic structures? Partly there is the dumb instinct of all historians that everything at a given historical stage belongs to that age. Historians easily slip into thinking of time as an objective fluid, bearing us all along. This is, of course, an illusion inherent in the metaphor. The times of development differ according to the rate of change of the phenomena studied. As Perry Anderson shrewdly observes, 'their dates are the same: their times are separate'.[37] It is equally natural to assume that everything is related to everything else around it. After all, the line between economic and other categories is man-made. Each of us is an actor in an immensely complex matrix of forces. Take anarchism in the 1870s, as a typical case. How else do you explain the fact that only Protestant French-speaking Jura watchmakers joined the Fédération, when their equally exploited and equally numerous, Catholic workmates did not?[38] I reach for my trusty 'factors' to show how the *historical* (the old territory of the bishopric of Basel), the *political* (Canton Neuchâtel and Canton Bern), the *religious* (Protestant v. Catholic) and the *economic* (the decentralised structure of the watchmaking industry and the depression of the 1870s) fuse to produce an *ideology* (anarchism). It looks neat and may be right, but it is a description, not an explanation. It rests on what Hans-Ulrich Wehler has called the 'interdependence theorem': everything depends on everything else. The theorem is popular because it covers everything, including the historian's flanks. After all, he rightly points out, 'who wants to be accused of not looking at things in all their complexity?'[39] Something more precise is needed here. I am not saying that everything depends on everything else but that a given structure of economic enterprise fitted a given political structure. The relationship between the cellular economy and the cellular state made Switzerland different from all other developed European economies until well into the twentieth century. Since the cellular economy has disappeared, the next question must be: can Switzerland maintain a distinctive political, linguistic, religious and cultural character when the economic framework has utterly changed? Is there a necessary relationship between structure in economic activity and structure in the others?

Marx was the first, as he was not slow to point out, to see what the question meant. He began his greatest work, *Das Kapital*, by looking at the 'elementary form of capitalism', *die Ware* or commodity. Commodities look objective, but in reality they embody 'sachliche Verhältnisse der Personen und gesellschaftliche Verhältnisse der Sachen' (objective relations of persons and social relations of things) and, as soon as we see that, 'all the mysticism of the world of commodities, all its spells and spirits' are dispersed.[40] Marx saw that every commodity embodies physically a bit of the social organisation, material forms of production, design criteria (hence values) of the community and the economy which produced it. Marx believed that once those social relations could be made reasonable, the commodities and their mode of exchange would be reasonable: 'The form of the social process of life, that is, the process of material production will only drop its veil of mist, when it stands as a product of freely socialised human beings under conscious, planned control . . . through daily, transparent rational relations to one another . . .'[41] The abolition of private property in the means of production was, Marx believed, inherently reasonable. Socialism was the necessary physical expression of rational relationships among human beings. There is, therefore a structure of the social order which fits a given arrangement of the economy. Thorstein Veblen took the argument in a slightly different direction in a brilliant book published just before the First World War. Veblen believed that the inherent rationality of modern industrial development must ultimately smash inherited traditional ones. He used the case of the Kaiser's Germany, which in his view 'is necessarily inimical to modern science and technology, as well as to the modern scheme of free or popular institutions, inasmuch as it is incompatible with the mechanistic animus that underlies these habits of thought'.[42]

The trouble with both these great analyses is not that they are wrong but that they have become unhinged from contemporary realities. Marx thought he knew what a commodity was. *Das Kapital* uses examples such as a roll of linen cloth, a piece of glass, an article of clothing. Veblen thought he understood the character of machines and factory production. It is far from clear that we understand either of these things today. Let us take a contemporary commodity, one of the most characteristic of our times: a computer software program. Professor Frederick P. Brooks Jr, the 'father of the IBM Operating System/360 project', defines it on one level as simply a 'message from man to machine', but it is also a shelf six feet long of operating manuals and flow charts as well as being 'only slightly removed from pure thought-stuff . . . castles in the air . . . concepts and very flexible representations thereof'.[43] It is also a syntax and a language, sets of algorithms (that is elaborate patterns of instructions linked in questions) and tens of thousands of individual instructions, all of which must be perfect or red lights go on. Marx's assumption that 'value is defined in exchange, that is, in a social process' undoubtedly still applies to the software program but at so general a level as to be hard to use. The user of the commodity takes part in the production process and the relationship between supply and demand in computer software bears almost no likeness to the sale of goods in the market. Market is hardly even a relevant metaphor. Nor is there anything mechanistic about a thousand highly skilled technicians organised in loose groups, working on several different sites, possibly in different countries, trying to put thought-stuffs into formal notations. Writing a program is more like the designers in Keller's cotton print factory, drawing stars and tendrils to their hearts' content. The product is a huge, objectified idea, made up of millions of little ideas, like a giant, disembodied coral. Software programs are so new that even the experts are uncertain about how they ought to be made. Strange, very unmechanistic things happen. It turns out that at a certain level of scale the more people you employ to produce the commodity the worse the result. Professor Brooks sums it up in 'Brooks's Law': 'adding manpower to a late software project makes it later'. The paradox occurs, apparently, because software engineering is a form of communication. The programs written by each sub-group must fit into every other; all must harmonise and all must operate perfectly.

If each part of the task must be separately co-ordinated with each other part, the effort increases as $n(n - 1)/2$. Three workers require three times as much pairwise intercommunication as two; four require six times as much as two. If, moreover, there need to be conferences among three, four, etc. to resolve things jointly, matters get worse yet.[44]

There is an interesting parallel between Professor Brooks' description of the logic of production in software and Marx's analysis of watchmaking. In the nineteenth-century example, Marx could see easily how the logic of production determined a corresponding social arrangement. I defy anyone to do that for the software manufacturing process. There is no agreed way to organise the production of large programs. The system builders constantly run up against invisible limits, possibly inherent in human beings, which make the production of very large software programs difficult. 'Debugging', that is, correcting mistakes, is the most important, expensive and time-consuming element of the enterprise. There would appear to be a limit here too. After a while, a program has been 'debugged' so often that further repair produces more 'bugs' than it eliminates. In the nineteenth century, products were products and machines just machines. Large assertions rested on the transparency of the relations of production and the objectivity of the things produced. The production of 'thought-stuffs' has introduced entirely new categories of human enterprise, most of which the common or garden historian like me has never heard of.

If there is any necessary relationship between the organisation of modern industrial production and the socio-political arrangements of contemporary society, I do not know what it is. My instinct tells me that in a period in which technological change is on an exponentially rising curve (software technology is just one of the countless staggering scientific and technical changes of the last thirty years) the chances of any grand syntheses as compelling as those of Marx or Veblen recede, rather as the earth's surface seems to blur as the rocket's trajectory rises. No one man can repeat Marx's achievement. Teams of men who try will run into Brooks's Law. What remains is a deepening identity crisis, as the rate of change whips us away from the stable truths of the past. The answer to the question about the relation between economic structures and socio-political ones cannot be given. Things are changing too fast for us to keep up with them.

The Swiss suffer from the same historical vertigo as all the rest of us, but because their economic order was so unusual, its disappearance in a mere thirty years is much more unsettling. Continuity is lost and with it the landmarks by which identity is judged. As the gap between the old political forms and the new economic ones yawns, the Swiss seem to feel their national identity crumbling, and it is to that crisis that I now want to turn.

6. Identity

In February 1972 thirty-two priests and ministers of both confessions announced that in future they would refuse to do their compulsory military service. In September of the same year nearly 50% of those voting said Yes to an initiative to forbid Swiss firms to export arms. In February 1973 Colonel Corps-Commander P. Hirschy, chief instructor officer of the Swiss army, was to lecture at Bern University in a series entitled 'The Meaning and Significance of our National Defence'. A student Action Committee Against Militarism organised a demonstration, occupied the large lecture hall and, to cries of *Kein Heer im Haus — Hirschy Raus'* (a complex pun on the slogan of an army education programme) and *'Hirschy nein — Giap ja'*, prevented the lecturer from speaking. The Dean and the Rector of the University were shouted down and chased from the platform. At the annual party congress of the Social Democratic Party of Switzerland in Luzern in July 1974, the delegates adopted an eighteen-point programme demanding among other things the abolition of military justice, the introduction of participatory democracy in the army, the establishment of an alternative civilian form of national service and the end of all subsidies for military organisations, public relations and propaganda activity. In 1974, Max Frisch's *Dienstbüchlein*, a series of reflections on his army days during the Second World War, was published. In it Frisch calls the Swiss army 'an army of the Fatherland-owners'.[1] In January 1975, Dr Ernst Morgeli, press officer of the Federal Military Department, attacked a children's bedtime programme on television because 'it agitated in an unsympathetic way against the army'. Thirty thousand people signed a petition in May 1975 against harsh sentences on conscientious objectors and demanded a general amnesty.

I can add a revealing experience of my own to this montage of public conflict. In 1973 I gave a talk to the Rotary Club of Entlebuch in Canton Luzern, hardly the home of radical dissent. The audience was mainly middle-aged, largely drawn from local business, with a scattering of professional people. Virtually without exception the men present had been 'in service'. I raised the question of public attacks on the army during the discussion after my talk, but instead of the unanimous condemnation of pacifism laced with anti-communism which I had expected, a fierce argument broke out. A minority seriously doubted that Switzerland needed an army at all; another minority defended the army passionately. The majority in the middle agreed that the army, while necessary, needed reform. Faces grew flushed, voices were raised and fists were pounded on the table. I heard later that older members had been deeply ashamed that such a discussion had taken place in front of a foreigner. Everybody agreed that five years earlier the dispute would not have happened. Even the soldiers themselves admit openly that the army has become *verunsichert* (uncertain) under the onslaught of public hostility. Colonel Max Kummer, writing in the semi-official monthly of the Swiss Officers' Association, put it very bluntly: 'Our historical images are used up, however we may regret it. Youth senses that, distrusts the images and sees in them empty pathos . . . This is the real calamity for our army, as loyalty declines more and more into disgust at having anything to do with the army at all.'[2]

The phenomena I have cited are not unique to Switzerland, but the Swiss army is. It is a militia based on universal service and as such unlike any other army except that of Israel, which adopted the Swiss model. To attack the Swiss army is to attack the Swiss state and the image of the armed free citizen on which it rests. To attack the army is to attack the *status quo*, for a militia stretches like a tight garment around the shape of the existing social order. To attack the army is to assail the very identity and self-image of the Swiss people. The old folk song puts it well:

> Was brucht e rachte Schwyzerma
> 'n-es subers Gewehrli a der Wand,
> 'n-es heiters Lied fürs Vaterland.
> (What does a true Swiss man need?
> A clean little gun on the wall
> And a cheerful song for the Fatherland)

The Swiss have always been a nation in arms. Switzerland was created in battle, reached its present dimensions by conquest and defended its existence by armed neutrality thereafter. During the great age of Swiss expansion contemporaries saw clearly that the armed free peasant made a formidable fighting machine. The free man fought as no slave could, for only the free could be safely armed. Machiavelli wrote: 'gli Svizzeri sono armatissimi e liberissimi' (the Swiss are most armed and most free). For him and for generations of foreign observers afterwards the connection remained the key to Swiss survival. The

Swiss agreed, and even today the free man goes armed to the *Lands-gemeinde* in token of his status. The connection between freedom and the gun is even enshrined in the American Bill of Rights. Article 2 states: 'A well regulated militia being necessary to the security of a free state, the right of the people to keep and bear arms shall not be infringed.'

The true Swiss is armed. Popular culture has been saturated with military activities, with rifle competitions, with gun lore, with a certain Alpine bellicosity, with the wrestling, the drinking and the ponderous camaraderie. As Frisch says in *Dienstbüchlein*, if you do not know what a true Swiss is (and, interestingly enough, he uses the same term of art as the folksong, the *rechter Schweizer*) you learn about it in the army: 'To feel yourself a true Swiss, you don't have to be a peasant or the son of a peasant but a certain rustic (not rude, of course) manner goes with being a true Swiss, whether you are a lawyer or a dentist or a clerk, at least when you are talking man to man among other true Swiss.'[3] The modern Swiss army still has a vestigial atmosphere which goes back to the unruly crowd of armed, free peasants who slaughtered the flower of Burgundian chivalry by flailing at them with five-foot pikes.

It is easy to see how the army and the state became synonymous. In a federal union, in a state divided by linguistic, religious, geographical, economic and social distinctions, the army alone united all citizens. It was (and is) the only institution which really transcends the cellular structures of Swiss life. For many young men, the only time they ever meet their co-nationals of a different language, region or creed is in the army. Unity and the universal militia stand and fall together, at least, many Swiss think that. There is therefore some justification for beginning a chapter called 'Identity' with a discussion of the crisis in the army. The dilemmas of the Swiss military establishment have much in common with those in most NATO countries, but they have, as always, features unique to Switzerland. Because Switzerland is like no other European country, its army is like no other European army.

The Swiss constitution lays an obligation on every Swiss male to do military service. If a man is physically unfit or abroad, he may commute his service by paying a compensatory tax; the tax is a symbol of his obligation. The obligation to serve lasts for thirty years for enlisted men and thirty-five for officers. Swiss conscription sounds worse than Tsarist Russian, which only amounted to twenty-five years of servitude, but the Swiss conscript is not under arms the whole time. In practice service falls into three categoriës. Men between the ages of twenty and thirty-two are in 'active service'; those between thirty-two and forty-two serve in the *Landwehr* (rather like the Territorial Army in Britain or the National Guard in the United States), and those between the ages of forty-three and fifty serve in the *Landsturm*, a second-line reserve. Most officers are also citizen-soldiers. Regimental commanding officers and the majority of the General Staff are militia-men, going from their desks or laboratories to serve at regular intervals and returning to their work. There is almost no standing army. It is an army 'in being', always there to be mobilised. Only a tiny skeleton staff remains in service all the time: the commanders of the four army corps, the divisional commanders, and the very senior air staff. There are also permanent men in the fortifications squadrons and one or two other auxiliary services, but for the rest it remains an army of civilians. The key to operational efficiency in the Swiss army is the training scheme, which falls into two basic types — an initial lengthy period (seventeen weeks of basic training for all recruits, courses for non-commissioned officers, officers' training schools, staff college and the like) and the refresher or *Wiederholungskurs* which every Swiss soldier, regardless of rank or technical speciality, has to attend at certain regular intervals during his active service. The Military Department reported that in 1974 there were 31,354 men in recruit status, 27,153 in advanced training and 286,734 in *Wiederholungskursen*. The young Swiss of twenty may expect to serve in small doses for a long period. If he remains a private, his minimum obligation will amount to:

1 recruit period of basic training	118 days
8 refresher courses	160 days
3 supplementary courses	40 days
2 courses for the *Landsturm* (the over 43s to 50)	13 days
Total	331 days

The activity is more intense in the period of the first eight years when the young soldier will have to attend eight refresher courses of three weeks each. He will do his basic training in one year and spend three weeks of his next eight summers in training within the framework of an actual combat unit. As Colonel H. R. Kurz emphasises, the essential pecularity of the Swiss training system is that there is no 'training-in-one-piece' as in most armies but instead a system of numerous, short periods of service in their own units. He sums it up this way: 'Because of our structure of military training the citizen is never decisively alienated from civil life. On the other hand, training in peace-time confers on all age-groups of the army the advantage of somehow remaining in constant defence practice.'[4]

For those who enjoy the activity and challenge, Colonel Kurz's analysis is fair. They go to the extra courses to become officers or radar technicians, enjoy the three-week refresher courses and go happily to regular shooting practice in their home towns. Officers' training school involves eighteen months of schooling, admittedly spread out over several years, and the staff college is even worse. One General Staff officer, the managing director of a successful medium-sized firm, told me that he had never been through anything more gruelling in his life than staff college and that he had several times been on the point of throwing in the sponge.

Every soldier in the Swiss army keeps his equipment at home. This includes uniform, weapon, live ammunition and other supplies. Since he keeps his weapon at home he is legally and financially responsible for its maintenance. The same regulations would apply to a military bicycle and used to apply to the cavalryman's horse. It may even extend to a military vehicle. The Military Department has no objection if the soldier uses his equipment or means of transportation in his peace-time occupation as long as it is ready when it is needed. This arrangement extends to the maintenance of specified amounts of food reserves by the supermarkets. It saves a great deal of money. The individual or the firm bears a cost which would otherwise fall on the state. Paper work by officers, when they are not on active duty, must be done by the officer in his private capacity. Large firms which may have a great many high-ranking officers among their senior personnel not uncommonly provide at the company's expense a military secretary whose job it is to do the correspondence of all the officers in the building.

Because the Swiss army reaches so deeply into civil society, it is paradoxically more vulnerable to unrest than a professional army would be. Every citizen serves and forms his own ideas about how good or bad the army is. As social values change, they collide with the army's traditions. The demand for more democracy in society at large catches the Swiss army in an awkward position. In theory, it is perfectly democratic. The professor may be a private and the bricklayer a captain. The social structure of the army is supposed to give men a chance to succeed in one field who have been less successful in others. In practice no such thing occurs. The general structure of society is faithfully reflected in the class divisions of the army. Officers and NCOs tend to come from the right backgrounds for their ranks. The system ensures that. The *National-Zeitung* recently published a list of the civilian employment of the entire officer corps of Border Division 2 which had been stolen by some members of an underground soldiers' group. Among the officers in the division were forty-seven directors and managing directors of small and medium-sized firms, thirty-nine senior employees of large Swiss industrial companies, twenty-nine self-employed, twenty lawyers and accountants, twelve heads and agents of insurance company branches, twelve doctors and chemists, eight senior executives of foreign companies, five directors of employers and trade associations, four senior police officers, four clerks, and three students. There were, of course, no workers. The firms represented were a *Who's Who* of Swiss business and include: CIBA—Geigy, Esso, Bulova, Lonza, Ebauches, Dubied, Swissair, Swissboring, Nestlé, Landis and Gyr, Holderbank, Hoffmann—La Roche, First National City Bank, the Union Bank, the Swiss Bank Corporation, the Swiss Credit Bank, Volksbank, von Roll, IBM, Honeywell, etc. The authors of the pamphlet conclude simply: 'The bosses in civilian life are the bosses in the army. We are still in the same boat: some row, others steer.'

The first seventeen weeks of recruit school are the periods in which the social selection takes place. Cadre NCOs and training officers are always on the look-out for the right sort of chap, and inevitably class and other biases creep in at this point. To be an officer involves a lot of time. A man has to have a long-suffering employer or private means to be able to afford the absences from work. Administrative and technical skills are more likely to be found in recruits from middle-class backgrounds than among working-class conscripts. The problem for the training personnel is to convince likely recruits that the extra time and effort is worth it. A man can be ordered to accept higher rank, but no commander would try such methods. A much more common device is to point out the practical advantages in civil life which will accrue to those who become officers. Most Swiss know in general terms what the *National-Zeitung* revealed in detail. Swiss officers and Swiss senior executives tend to be the same men. If two equally qualified men apply for a job, and one is and one is not an officer, most Swiss accept that the officer will get it. The argument runs that since Swiss companies know what goes into the making of an officer they tend to prefer someone who has survived that to someone who has not. This is a touchy field of inquiry and evidence of the kind drawn from Border Division 2 is very rare. Disaffected middle-aged men frequently tell you that they would be at head office, not branch managers, if they had become officers. I know a man who has been litigating with a federal department for years, who is convinced that, had he been an officer, he would have been able to settle the case ages ago.

None of this is surprising but it does shake some myths. The army is not now and never has been perfectly democratic, because Switzerland never was either. We saw in Chapter 2 that even the armed free peasants of William Tell's day recognised the local gentry as their natural leaders. In modern times distinctions between officers and men were rigidly maintained. During the First World War, both the government and the army leadership ignored the severe hardships which long periods of mobilisation imposed on the working classes. During the Second World War the army was much less rigid and more egalitarian in temper. Efforts through the operation *Heer im Haus* (the army in the home) were made to enlist the full psychological as well as physical support of the home front. Soldiers who lost wages during military service got better compensation. The people saw the need for defence and the *réduit* mentality included everyone. Class distinctions were not obliterated even in the Second World War. Frisch recalls that his fellow soldiers could not understand how *ein Studierter* was not an officer. His working-class comrades felt his presence in the ranks as slightly improper. Their attitudes to officers, he recalls, were similar. No worker dreamt of becoming an officer. What would he say to them in the evening in the mess? 'From the workers' point of view officers were genuinely educated or at least well off, hence entitled to lead troops and sleep in beds. They knew how to use foreign words. What they might be worth under fire had nothing to do with it.'[5]

Distinctions of class merged with assumptions about style. The Swiss army, more than any other area of Swiss German life, accepted the primacy of Prussian models during the great days of Imperial Germany. The Swiss German officers borrowed the code of honour and personal style of the aristocratic Junkers and in a fascinating fusion of images the Swiss officer sought to combine the deep respect which the Swiss accord to earned rank, to the *Herr Doktor* and *Herr Direktor*, with the Prussian respect for inherited rank, *Exzellenz von und zu X*. Since both models were profoundly authoritarian, the Swiss officer corps absorbed a double dose of values essentially inappropriate to the serene management of a little militia in a bourgeois democracy. The collapse of the Prussian model and the erosion of traditional Swiss deference has stripped the officer corps of its code of behaviour at the moment when it needs one most. A perplexed unit commander quite rightly put his finger on the trouble when he wrote: 'The crisis of the army is a crisis of the officers and not of the men. The officer, who does not represent the army off duty, harms it more than any long-haired soldier could.'[6] But how can he 'represent' an army which has lost its own, inherited style? A possible alternative to the Germanic models of the past might be the Israeli citizen-soldier of the present. After all, the Israelis consciously adopted Swiss methods and especially mobilisation procedures. The Israeli officer shuttling between desert command and the lecture room comes closer to the Swiss ideal than any other contemporary officer. The Swiss undoubtedly admire and feel close to the Israelis in many ways and are on balance more pro-Israel than any other European country. Still they hesitate to emulate, if that were possible, the turbulent, noisy, shirt-sleeved egalitarian style of the Israel Defence Force. The spectacle of generals shouting at one another in public forums and being bawled at by hysterical crowds of pushing citizens is not the Swiss way.

Since the Israeli model cannot be transplanted, the Swiss officer corps faces the turbulence of the young dissidents with very little inner confidence. The historic language of command has lost its purchase. The values embedded in words like *Ehre* (honour), *Pflicht* (duty) or *Zucht* (breeding) have evaporated so completely that contemporary young people can hardly make sense of the terms at all. There are no words to use which are common to both sides of the generation gap or which transcend the division in styles of life. The social foundation of the Swiss army has also shifted, as economic change transforms the old Switzerland into an urban, flat-dwelling, modern, consumer, society. The armed, free peasant has gone as surely as the heroic Switzerland of the Rütli Oath, General Guisan and the *réduit*.

The alienation of the young has led to a new problem. Attacks on the undemocratic character of the army carry over to more general attacks on the society as a whole. The citizen may well be 'alienated' from civilian society even before he joins the colours. In that moment, the very pervasiveness of the militia system becomes its undoing. With a professional army remote from the populace a government can do what it likes and commit all sorts of blunders. A citizen army is more vulnerable. It operates, as does the democratic state, on consent. Here the parallel so often praised really does apply. If the citizen withdraws his consent from the democratic machinery or no longer accepts the rules of its operations, democracy disintegrates. If the citizen no longer consents to universal military service, the militia system disintegrates.

The first crack in the unity of the army and society ran along the issue of conscientious objection. During the 1960s a pacifist movement began which questioned the need for an army and the morality on which it rested. Others, politically more radical, attacked the society which they saw reflected through the military hierarchy. For both groups, the law was pitiless. Until very recently no alternative was even considered to actual service in a military unit. During the past few years, an initiative drafted by the so-called Münchenstein Committee has been hotly argued. Under its terms a citizen could opt to do his national service in some worthy civilian activity, such as social work or hospital service. The federal Military Department conceded the point at a press conference in 1973, when Federal Councillor Gnägi announced his department's willingness to consider proposals of that kind. The Military Department intends in due course to draft a constitutional amendment which must go to the voters in a referendum but before it does so, its experts must collect opinions and try to reconcile the very real differences on the issue. Walter Biel, writing in *Die Tat*, sums up the arguments in favour of the Münchenstein Initiative very well:

The strength of a country does not rest on force but on the awareness of its citizens and on their willingness to serve the community. The inner strength of a society shows itself also in the way in which it respects and protects the rights of minorities — and conscientious objectors will remain such a minority.

The difficulty for the military authorities arises from the fact that the credibility of Swiss defence depends on the militia. As the late Colonel Alfred Ernst put it:

If the choice between military and civil service were made a free one, we should have to reckon with a rapid fall in the number of troops, especially in view of the strong propaganda now being launched at the army. Our militia-system could not bear that. The fighting potential of our army lies in its numerical strength. This compensates for weaknesses in equipment and in training but only up to a certain point. The actual numbers of the army, were they to be reduced, would be insufficient for the maintenance of our defence posture... The dissolution of a single division would make a defence of the circumference in the form of 'Area Defence' impossible... Given the short training and service periods, we could never train our forces to the point at which they were equal to a 'Mobile Defence'.[7]

Colonel Ernst goes on to examine the alternatives to universal military service: the acquisition of the means of mass destruction (chemical, biological and atomic weapons); a 'Mobile Defence' using small, highly efficient, flexible units; the replacement by civil defence of much of the army's present activities; and the adoption of guerrilla warfare. Colonel Ernst shows, in my view convincingly, why the present strategy and militia system end up providing the cheapest, most efficient and most favourable options for a defensive strategy. The dilemma tightens. If the army cannot operate without its present arrangements and the young make the further working of the present arrangements impossible, what happens to the army?

Have young Swiss men rejected the army to that extent? Colonel (General Staff) Pierre Wenger actually tried to find out. In April of 1972 he went to several Zürich and Winterthur grammar schools to find out what schoolboys thought. He also used the same questionnaire in several teacher training colleges. Altogether 605 young men participated. Here is an abbreviated table, with some excerpts from the questionnaire and the replies:[8]

Question:
   Do you think there is a threat to the independence of the central and western European countries which could become dangerous in the next ten to twenty years?

Answers:	*Yes*	*No*
All replies	43.3%	32.5%
Schoolboys	41.6%	32.5%
College students	55.7%	32.8%

Question:
   Do you think we should stick to the policy of armed neutrality?

Answers:		
All replies	54%	27.4%
Schoolboys	53%	28.6%
College students	61.4%	18.5%

Question:
   Do you consider the political institutions of Switzerland to be worth defending?

Answers:		
All replies	60%	11.5%
Schoolboys	57%	12.3%
College students	82.8%	5.7%

Question:
   Should Switzerland do more, the same, or less to defend itself?

Answers:	More	Same	Less
All replies	9.9%	40.6%	35.8%
Schoolboys	8%	39.4%	36.2%
College students	17%	50%	32.8%

Question:
  (a) Are you looking forward to military service?
  (b) Do you enjoy your military service (for the college students)?

Answers:	Yes	No
(a) Schoolboys	15%	62.2%
(b) College students	10%	78.5%

Question:
Are you in favour of the 'Münchenstein Initiative' (i.e. to introduce an alternative civil service in place of military)?

Answers:	Yes
All replies	63.8%
Schoolboys	62.2%
College students	75.7%

Question:
If you had had the choice, would you have opted for the civil service instead of the military service?

Answers:	Yes	No
All replies	51.2%	32.2%
Schoolboys	50.4%	31.5%
College students	57%	37%

It would be hard to imagine more dramatic confirmation of the problem facing the Swiss military authorities. While it is some consolation to see that the majority of pupils believe Switzerland worth defending (an overwhelming majority in the case of the college students), their rejection of military service is equally clear. Worse, the response of those who have begun it, the college students, is more unfavourable than of those, the schoolboys, who have yet to try. The strong support for the Münchenstein Initiative and the preponderance of those who would choose civilian service, if they could, reinforces the dilemma. The young are not anti-Swiss but they are anti-army. If, therefore, the army is the model and expression of Swiss society as it is, then they may be said to reject that society. A crisis about military service is, therefore, a crisis of Swiss identity.

The rest of Colonel Wenger's article consists of a finely spun analysis of the deeper causes of the changes he sees expressed in his statistics. He cites several important social psychological, sociological, economic and political trends of the past thirty years: decline of parental authority, the disappearance of the agrarian population, transformation of the concept of 'manly' and 'male', the new versions of egalitarian ideology, and the excrescences of modern capitalism. The diagnosis is as shrewd and subtle as any I have read anywhere, but the remedy is feeble. Colonel Wenger knows what is wrong but not what to do about it. Like Max Lerner's typical liberal he plants his feet firmly in mid-air. On the one hand, he rejects the main accusation of the dissidents: 'the assertion of the young left-wing extremists, our army is an instrument of the so-called "ruling class for the maintenance of the existing capitalist structure" cannot stand a sober confrontation with reality ... It can only be met if higher officers from regimental to corps commanders *systematically seek* contact and exchange ideas with young people and thus slowly dismantle the projections . . .' But he has to confess that 'in the last few years there has been a certain tendency in selecting men for higher commands to choose those persons who have already achieved leading positions in politics or business . . . I have to point out that such a tendency will be misunderstood by the young who will see in it an intention to fortify the existing order through an accumulation of posts of power...'[9] Unfortunately this will not do. The army *does* operate to defend bourgeois capitalism. That happens to be the economic system of the country. The army *does* provide a good avenue into the upper reaches of the elite. Men will naturally want to improve their political and economic position by achieving military rank and vice versa. Ultimately there is no 'sober confrontation with reality'. If the rebellious private does not like the *status quo* no amount of avuncular talk with *Oberst-Divisionär* over a bottle of *Schnapps* will alter that. He may learn to see his colonel as a human being and not a cardboard cut-out, but he will not suddenly stop worrying and learn to love the *Rekrutenschule*.

The unwillingness to serve, if it is carried into overt resistance, will rapidly put an end to the Swiss militia and with it, by a chain reaction, to a whole chapter of Swiss history. Armed neutrality could come tumbling down. Switzerland's special position in international affairs would end, and she might find herself facing the sort of unpalatable choices which confront states of comparable size. The Danish politician who would like his country's defence establishment reduced to a tape-recording with the following text: 'This is Copenhagen. We capitulate!' may find an export market for his 'early warning system' in Bern.

Another enemy of the army is inflation. While the *Bundesrat* hesitated during the past decade about re-equipping the Swiss air force, the price of modern jet planes became astronomical. In 1972, the *Bundesrat* narrowed its choice to an American and a French model only to find both too expensive. In great embarrassment, it bought thirty second-hand Hawker Hunters instead. This pleased Hawker Siddeley, but it made the Swiss government and the Swiss defence establishment look ridiculous. To save face, the Military Department appointed a new Chief Procurement Officer, Herr Charles Grossenbacher, and asked him to go back to square one. Since 1972, tests have been carried out on the Hawker Harrier (vertical take-off), the Swedish Viggen and the French Mirage F. The latest, most advanced American planes were all too expensive, and in the end the Swiss government could only afford to buy seventy-two of the Northrop Tiger II F-5 E, which is a stripped down, off-the-peg jet for the poorer Afro-Asian air forces and even those will cost SFr. 1,170 million (£236 million). Similar problems face the military planners who have to choose a new tank. Here a Swiss-designed model, the Panzer 68, stands in competition with the British Centurion and the German Leopard. Decisions involving huge sums have to be made now if there are to be advanced tanks ready by the middle of the 1980s. For about SFr. 400 million, the Military Department hope to order 110 advanced and improved Panzer 68s. The Arab–Israeli war threw further spanners into the armourers' works by pointing to the importance of one- and two-man guided missile launchers, such as the Russian SAMs. Since the expenditure of SFr. 1,170 million only bought seventy-two Tiger II F-5s, the anti-aircraft men argue that computer-steered, guided missile radar defences would be cheaper and more effective. There is a Swiss 'Skyguard' system, which has its advocates. In the midst of all this technology, the friends of the recently abolished cavalry mounted a noisy initiative to reverse the decision to phase out mounted units. As Herr Ulrich Kägi wrote bitterly, 'the army is becoming a museum'.

The economic crisis of the Military Department is clear from the figures in the accompanying tables. None of the European states in Table 6.1 spend less of their gross national product on defence than the Swiss. In Table 6.2 money expenditure and real expenditure are compared. In real terms the amount of money being spent on defence is declining. National defence has also declined as a percentage of the federal budget from 39% in 1959 to just over 21% in 1974.

In spite of the cost–price squeeze, the Swiss military establishment looks formidable, on paper at least. The Federal Republic of Germany, for example, has ten times the population of Switzerland. It has

TABLE 6.1   Military expenditure of several European states in percentage of gross national product

	1966	1967	1968	1969	1970	1971	1972
Czechoslovakia	5.7	5.7	5.7	3.7	3.6	3.8	4.1
East Germany	3.3	3.7	5.7	5.0	5.1	5.2	5.3
Poland	5.3	5.4	4.8	3.9	4.1	4.1	4.0
Belgium	2.9	2.9	2.9	2.8	2.6	2.1	2.0
Great Britain	5.6	5.7	5.4	5.0	4.9	4.5	4.6
West Germany	4.2	4.4	3.6	3.5	3.3	2.9	2.9
Norway	3.6	3.5	3.6	3.8	3.3	3.3	3.2
Netherlands	3.7	3.9	3.6	3.8	3.5	3.5	3.5
Sweden	4.2	3.9	3.9	3.8	3.4	3.4	3.6
Switzerland	2.5	2.4	2.1	2.2	2.1	1.9	1.8

Source: *ASMZ*, No. 12, December 1974, p. 624.

twelve divisions composed of thirty-three brigades, of which twenty-five are mechanised. Switzerland can mobilise an army of twelve divisions, made up of seventeen brigades, just under half the German strength. Switzerland's nominal military manpower, 600,000 under full mobilisation, compares favourably with NATO's 580,000 troops and the Warsaw Pact's 1,000,000. Switzerland has 500 tanks compared to Italy's 1,000 and East Germany's 2,000, and has 300 military aircraft compared to 500 for France, 500 for Czechoslovakia and 215 for Spain. These are respectable figures, but they too pose difficulties. The cost of standing still rises with inflation, and hence the army is caught in a pincer. As the costs of keeping the army at its present level rise,

TABLE 6.2   Total military expenditure 1965–72 in money and real terms (SFr. million)

	Money	Real (1965 prices)
1965	1,532	631
1966	1,653	688
1967	1,657	648
1968	1,598	557
1969	1,761	619
1970	1,876	592
1971	2,050	591
1972	2,206	507

Source: *ASMZ*, No. 12, December 1974, p. 624.

there is less money for new weapons whose costs rise even faster. The balance between new equipment and maintenance is completely askew, as Fig. 3 shows. Divisional-Colonel Hans Rapold, chief of the planning section, says: 'Fairly soon the army will only have enough money to maintain its present position.'

All this is extremely sour sauce for a nation which prides itself on its 'perfectionism'. The idea rankles that Swiss airmen and sappers should have to make do with secondhand or outmoded equipment. Yet it is hard to see what else lies ahead. The medium-sized European powers, Great Britain and France, are rapidly finding the defence game too expensive for them too. The Royal Navy's nuclear submarines have not been equipped with the latest Poseidon missiles but continue to use 'cheaper' Polarises instead. The new missiles are simply too expensive for the British to contemplate. If British and French defence ministers cannot afford the latest weapons with GNPs seven or eight times as large as that of Switzerland, what hope has the poor Swiss? If new weapons are not purchased, can the Swiss army look plausible? The question ceases to be 'can Switzerland afford a modern army?' and becomes 'does Switzerland need an army at all?' Roman Brodmann has recently published a little fantasy entitled *Switzerland without Weapons!*[10] In it a group of left-wing radicals and liberal sympathisers

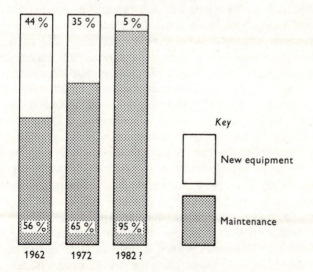

Fig. 3   Maintenance v. new equipment in military expenditure

have organised an initiative based on the 'Biel Manifesto' calling for the total abolition of the army. They get the 50,000 signatures required and a vote is arranged for the eventful Sunday which the book describes. Nobody expects the initiative to be passed, but it is – by a small majority. The army is to be abolished. As the news is broadcast by Swiss radio and TV, crowds begin to pour into the streets. The *Bundesrat* goes into emergency session that Sunday evening, and in Zürich a group of officers begin to prepare for a putsch. The federal president appears on TV with a typically Swiss, lukewarm speech and announces that the Federal Assembly will meet in extraordinary session on Monday morning. Meanwhile, a signals officer reveals the putsch plans, and the troops who were already taking up positions march docilely back to barracks. The following day the Federal Assembly meets, discusses the initiative and has no option but to approve it. The people remain pretty calm throughout. The army has been abolished. It makes headlines in the foreign papers. The great powers agree that Switzerland has set a fine example. Nothing happens. The world forgets about Switzerland after a day or two and life goes on as usual. Brodmann's sketch of the mentality of the Swiss is not far off the mark. A very large number of people I have talked to agree with him. Nothing would happen if the army were abolished. Or would it?

Defenders of the army put it this way. We had no army to speak of in 1798 and look what happened to us. We had a fine army in 1914 and 1940 and look what did not happen to us. It is impossible to prove that the army actually deterred either the Kaiser or Hitler. Even if it had that effect then, whom does it deter now? The Russians? The Americans? NATO? The French? The answers seem more absurd than the question. The Military Department sticks to traditional doctrines. In its strategic review of 1973 it came up with a new word, 'dissuasion', for the old strategic defence: 'that strategic posture which will cause a potential opponent to decide against unleashing an armed attack. He must be brought to see that a disproportion exists between the gains which he seeks and the risks which he runs.' Thirty secondhand Hunters are not likely to dissuade any serious aggressor. Besides, the likeliest threat of war is a clash in Germany between NATO and the Warsaw Pact. What are the Swiss supposed to do militarily if such a war begins? Armed neutrality against all comers must mean that a Swiss government will prevent by force, if necessary, the use of their air space and rail links by those states, the NATO powers, whose defeat must mean defeat for Switzerland too. The idea of a neutral, capitalist

Switzerland surviving on its own in a Bolshevik Europe is too silly to think about. The letter of the law says that Switzerland is neutral; the spirit puts her firmly in the Western camp. The next logical step leads to the abandonment of armed neutrality in its historic form, then to neutrality in any form, and then, to what? Could Switzerland continue to be what it has been, if it joined NATO, the UN and so on?

The Swiss no longer have a credible defence and everybody knows it. The difficulties begin when they try to think of what to do. For reasons we have already seen, the army is very closely, uniquely closely, identified with the domestic *status quo*. Yet it remains an instrument of foreign relations. If it loses its credibility abroad, it loses its credibility at home. The erosion of neutrality in turn reduces the credibility of the army. Take the case of the Common Market. Since 1973, Switzerland has been well and truly integrated into the EEC in all but name. The free-trade treaties with the EEC are just the beginning of a long-run historical process about which nobody in the federal Political Department has any real illusions. Within a few years, many Swiss will see that they are in the worst of both worlds. They belong to the Common Market economically but cannot share in its decisions. The pressure to join will mount. To join would mean to limit the powers of the sovereign people in their referenda and initiatives. Not to join will limit them just as much. In this thicket of dilemmas how does the doughty Swiss militia find a strategy?

The collapse of support for the army is, I believe, just a symptom of that vast transformation of Swiss life which is going on in the economy, in technology, in social attitudes, in urbanisation and living styles. It is no good demanding, as Colonel Wenger does, 'reform of our old Switzerland, not just little revisions or retouching of surfaces but reform from the bottom up . . .'[11] The bottom has already been so transformed that the old Switzerland is in danger of becoming an irrelevant façade. In this sense, the crisis about the army reflects the deeper 'Helvetic *malaise*'.

One element of that *malaise* is worldwide, and that is the general crisis of inherited authority. I have in front of me a Swiss example of that crisis. It is taken from *Note 1*, a little mimeographed magazine published by students in two grammar schools near Bern. They ask the following questions: 'In school hours many orders are given which frequently cannot be justified and can only be carried out by using authoritarian measures. Why are such orders given? Why does a teacher have to demonstrate his position of power to his pupils down to the last detail?' The first answer is not rational but it comes to mind: 'Because that's the way it always has been!' The pupils reply that it ought not to continue. The thoughtful teacher pauses. Should it continue? Is the relationship between teacher and taught one of authority—submission or is it cooperative? Two extreme models occur to me: the school is a hierarchical structure where a fixed body of right learning and truth is implanted in foolish, ignorant and vile young people. That is the conception of the nineteenth-century *Gymnasium* or workhouse. Sinful human beings should be coerced to be virtuous and punished for vice. The opposite model shimmers hazily through the lines of *Note 1*. School is a democratic *polis* in which teacher and pupil share equally, in which all have duties and all have rights. Equality before the law is not enough. There must be equality of substance. Decisions must be rational. The governed must consent to them. There is no truth, only a method for approaching it. Values are relative and not enforceable. These two models collide head-on in Swiss schools, in Swiss families and in the Swiss army.

The application of the political idea of democracy to all aspects of society is one part of the 'Helvetic *malaise*' and not the least of it either. The Swiss necessarily find this more difficult to comprehend precisely because they have been so much more democratic in the purely political sense for so much longer than anyone else. How dare the young, they seem to say, accuse us, of all people, of being undemocratic? But the young are right too. Swiss society has certainly been democratic but it has also been sluggish, conservative and very self-satisfied. 'Switzerland is innocence itself' Max Frisch once wrote, and in Swiss eyes it could not be undemocratic. Its schools, its homes, its shops and offices, its large companies, its churches and army battalions were frequently dark with the shadow of authoritarianism but, until this generation, only the rebel or crank noticed it. The habits of the people, the deference shown to wealth and rank, the extensive use of titles, the slavish use of High German, all reflected a deeply authoritarian strain. Change came more slowly in Switzerland than elsewhere because two wars, a depression and violent anti-communism kept Switzerland isolated in its *réduit* for nearly fifty years. The 'lucky threat' from outside the frontier has now disappeared, and the young ask a whole series of questions to which there is no longer an obvious, immediate and unquestioning answer. Both sides use the same words but mean entirely different things.

There are certain other reasons why the Swiss find these problems unusually hard to face. They confront the demands of the post-war generation crippled by their unique strengths and blinded by their own peculiar vision. One element of this, as Karl Schmid points out, is the immense importance of physical space, of locality and, above all, of borders. In his famous essay, 'Swiss Self-awareness Today', he observed: 'Much more than most of us realise, our generation was deeply informed by the awareness of political boundaries. It goes deep down within us, just as deep as the feeling that from outside our borders danger threatens. We have to be watchful and on guard against anything from outside . . .'[12] This watchfulness and hostility to outside influence is perfectly understandable. Imagine being a Jew in Schaffhausen or a Social Democrat in Basel in 1941, looking across the slender strip of darkened frontier into the insanity and depravity of Nazi Germany. Imagine being a journalist in one of those towns, going to bed each night and wondering whether the knock at 6 a.m. would this time not be the milkman. All other characteristics of Swiss life combined in this hedgehog posture. Seven centuries of foreigners marching across the Swiss passes left their mark. A secretiveness and wariness toward the stranger lurk behind the formal politeness of the hotelier and railway conductor. As Peter Bichsel writes, 'For the Swiss there are two worlds: home and abroad. If I go abroad, my mother says, "watch out that nothing gets stolen. Don't let your bags out of your hand." Swiss carry their money abroad in purses under their shirts or sewed into their underwear. For us the word "abroad" always has the ring of wretchedness.'[13] Being shut away during the wars from 'abroad' and being flooded by 'abroad' after them has reinforced the suspiciousness of foreign influences. The worldwide Communist conspiracy probably has a higher proportion of believers in small Swiss cities than in Dallas, Texas, or Los Angeles, California. Trouble in paradise is a contradiction in terms. Hence whatever unrest there is must come from abroad.

Today's itinerant young have recaptured a carelessness in these matters which Europe has not enjoyed since the time of Erasmus. They seem to feel less pull of nationality or place. Regardless of politics or class or religion or national origin, they wander across Europe and Asia with rucksacks and guitars. The mobility of this entire generation runs into the rootedness of the previous one and there are sparks. How much more is this the case in a society as rooted and embedded as is the Swiss? There is no country in Europe where place matters more. Your voice, your identity, your accent, your politics will vary if you come from Schwändi or Sarnen, separated by all of 3 kilometres. Much of 'Swissness' is awareness of the steep, rock-ribbed compartments into which the human community 'naturally' falls. The medieval 'Tell Song' described the cradle of Swiss liberty, Canton Uri:

> Das Land ist wol beschlossen yn,
> dann Gott ist selbst der murer gsin.
> (The land is well enclosed therein,
> for God himself has walled it in.)

The traditional Swiss 'self-awareness' was an affair of steep slopes, walled towns, self-sufficiency and occasional isolation. A people so constituted by geography and language and history as the Swiss find it unusually hard to cope with the drifting habits of today.

Rootedness has preserved in Switzerland the awareness of the land and the inheritance of the peasant. In some parts of the country, *Schwyzerdütsch* is called *Buredütsch*, 'peasant German', and it is a term of honour. Karl Schmid puts it this way: 'It is not entirely absurd to argue that our spiritual structures are still essentially of a peasant type. In the foreground there is for us this small plot of earth we call "Fatherland" which we have to till as best we can . . .' This structure of the soul creates its own habits. Schmid sees in it the deep sources of Swiss resistance to change, the preference for conceptions of place instead of those of time. 'The spirit of our nation dislikes "time" as something open, uncertain, renovating. It tends to see in the future only attacks on the existing order. The little state which never expects anything good from the great winds of "world history outside" tends to understand its politics as a defence against the force of time itself.' Here too the facts of modern life must make the Swiss uneasy. The peasants disappear. The mountains depopulate and the urban centres swell. Above all, the young tend to think more easily of time and of the future, less naturally of place and of the past. Their language and mentality has less and less of the country man's homely rootedness and more and more of the international patois.

One reaction has been brilliantly described in a piece of almost photographic journalism by Niklaus Meienberg. In his *Reportagen aus der Schweiz* he describes a caravan site not far from Stein am Rhein, where the citizens, mostly middle-aged or older, have built a perfect, stable model Switzerland. The site is ruled by the owner, Herr Näf, a benevolent dictator whose word is law. The citizens have arrived at nearly perfect equality. Each has his 'mobile home' discreetly set in a postage stamp of lawn, dotted with garden gnomes and edged with geraniums. The residents assemble every weekend to live orderly, communal, quiet lives in their little bungalows.

'Get out of the mess' is the refrain, out of the dirty city, out of the isolation, into the solidarity of building little walls, mowing lawns, neatening up. On Saturday life begins and Monday morning it stops . . . Once upon a time, one took one's caravan along the roads, changed places, but in today's traffic most of them have given that up. They have become sedentary. The horizon is closed. Not much new will happen. A 'Prosit', a 'Prosit' of togetherness.[14]

This agreeable weekend world of the middle-aged workman or policeman or insurance salesman is a death mask of a Switzerland now gone.

There is a good deal of conviviality on the caravan site. It is a faint echo of that organised conviviality of the old *Gemeinde*. Traditional Swiss life swarmed with organisations. The village community spawned *Vereine* for every purpose. There was the *Musikgesellschaft*, the Catholic Young Men's league, the Jodel Club, the *Turnverein*, the Protestant Women's Social Circle or the Workingmen's Club and on and on. The key word was *Kameradschaft*, comradeliness, a certain amiable, often beery, chumminess. There was the inn where one sat at the *Stammtisch*, the 'regular table', and met the *Stammgäste*, played *Jass*, the national card game, drank beer, told stories or did a little business. On festive occasions there would be singing into the wee hours. 'If you put a canvas top over all of Switzerland, you would have one big *Fest*' (untranslatable; — certainly not the pale English 'party'), as the popular saying has it. This social life of the group is exactly the opposite of the inward-looking, self-preoccupied sensibility of much of the generation born since 1945. Their private inner world of the senses, sharpened often by marijuana and encased by electronic sound, is intrinsically opposed to the cheerful communal world of the inn. If one joins a group, it is not for *Kameradschaft* but for *Aktion*, to get something done, to fight militarism or keep the air clean.

Traditional patriotism is waning as rapidly as traditional *Kameradschaft*. Switzerland is in the embarrassing position of not having a proper national anthem. As the Swiss humorist Hans Gmür put it in his column in honour of the Swiss National Day, nobody knows what to sing beside the traditional bonfire:

'Rufst Du mein Vaterland', which was once so well known and of which we even knew the words of the first stanza, has been taken out of circulation because of its shocking blood-thirstiness. 'Trittst ·im Morgenrot daher' — only provisionally declared the national anthem — has proved to be pretty unpopular. The new 'Swiss Anthem' which was recently launched by an ad agency as the musical-patriotic egg of Columbus did not — as it must be put in the jargon of the trade — 'take'. So what are we going to sing tonight?

The 'traditional' bonfire and the 'traditional' bell-ringing (dating from the late nineteenth century) go on, but the 'traditional' 1st of August speech on a patriotic theme has given place to a plaintive lament about the passing of true values or alternatively in progressive communes to a blissful silence. Fewer Swiss seem to care about these things, and fewer bother to vote, which was the problem that first moved Max Imboden to coin the phrase 'Helvetic *malaise*'.

As distressing as the death of the old is the birth of the new. The protest against the construction of an atomic power plant at Kaiseraugst near Basel is an interesting example. For a small country the Swiss atomic energy programme had been very ambitious. The first two large plants, generating about 350 MW each went into operation in 1969 and 1971 without opposition. The third at Muhleberg near Bern began generating electricity in 1972, but from 1971, as the environmental impact of the great surge of nuclear energy building began to become clear, the protests mounted. When the federal authorities forbade the construction companies to use the waters of the Aare and Rhine for cooling, on ecological grounds, the consortia had to redesign their plants to include large cooling towers. As a result they had to go back to the communes for additional planning permission and this gave opponents of the projects new leverage. Kaiseraugst was finally cleared for construction in 1974, to go into service in 1980, in spite of a long, complicated costly blocking attempt by concerned citizens.

On Easter Monday 1975, some 15,000 people occupied the construction site of the Kaiseraugst nuclear power station, the biggest and most dramatic 'sit-in' in Swiss history. A general assembly rather like a *Landsgemeinde* assumed the sovereign power and turned itself into the Gewaltfreie Aktion Kaiseraugst (the Non-violent Kaiseraugst Action). Support came from underground movements from every part of the country and sometimes from abroad. Television brought pictures of long hair and other manifestations of the modern counter-culture into Swiss homes. But support came from respectable quarters too. The Grand Council of Basel voted nearly unanimously for a resolution to call a halt to further work on Kaiseraugst. The GAK organised a demonstration in Bern at the end of April in which several thousand demonstrators marched through the city to the federal buildings. The

Federal Council took a high line, refusing to negotiate until the site had been cleared. The assembly of the GAK refused to evacuate the site until their demands had been met and so there was deadlock. Tempers began to wear thin as May turned into June. The authorities in Canton Aargau announced that they intended to force an evacuation and the consortium of companies building the plant took out civil complaint proceedings against named individuals. The assembly of the GAK refused to leave the site unless and until they had been given written confirmation of a month-long moratorium, a programme of negotiation and a promise not to fence the building site. Finally on 11 June 1975, the assembly received written acceptance from the consortium, Kraftwerk Kaiseraugst AG, of agreement to all the demands. The victory was theirs, and they left the site voluntarily.

At the end of the month, the federal parliament debated the issues raised by the atomic energy programme and by Kaiseraugst. Reactions were unusually varied. The left-wing socialist and Basel lawyer Andreas Gerwig, who had represented the GAK in negotiations with federal and cantonal authorities, argued that parliament had grown so remote that 'we can no longer hear the language of the people'. Others charged the government with failure to plan properly, with failure to implement internationally recognised ecological norms, with failure to introduce a modernised legal framework for atomic energy and with gross insensitivity. The Nationale Aktion joined the critics and Valentin Oehen demanded resignations all around. For some deputies, the whole thing had been staged by 'extremists'.

The ultimate outcome of Kaiseraugst and other projects is not the issue here. What Kaiseraugst revealed was the exhaustion of traditional Swiss democracy. None of the legal methods had worked. None of the relevant political bodies which opposed Kaiseraugst on communal or cantonal level had been able to fight the consortium. The courts had failed. Direct action was the only way to force a halt, and it worked. It is too early to assess the full significance of the occupation. To conservatives of every hue, it confirms their worst fears and makes them more determined than ever to defend the one bulwark against extremists they know: the army. While most military spokesmen cite the threat from abroad, they and their listeners know that the Russians are not likely to invade Switzerland in the near future. They really fear a threat from within. Some think of it as a threat of armed conspiracy. They believe that revolution or at least urban violence can occur at any moment and that unidentified communist agents direct a vast plot to that end. Others, and I include here a great many very thoughtful officers, fear something much less concrete. My reading of their anxieties would go something like this: like most foreigners, the Swiss do not believe that their country is 'natural'. They can well understand the Pays de Vaud or Schaffhausen as real, natural communities, but the federal union seems to them an abstraction and rather a bloodless one at that. Federal patriotism used to be fired by doctrinal liberalism and radicalism. The state was the heroic guardian of liberty against the obscurantists in the cantons. Then the state was the guardian of liberty against outside threats, especially of nazism, fascism and communism. Now the ideological colour seems to have drained from the central state and only the army remains as the national sinew, the physical bond which holds the country together. Relax that sinew and Switzerland will lose its shape. The army must continue to act as the 'school of the nation', where every Swiss male renews his commitment to being Swiss as opposed to being a Luzerner or a Ticinese.

The view is plausible and may be right. It rests on an idea of nationality which I discussed in an earlier chapter, the romantic fusion of people, language and state. My own feeling is rather different. Switzerland is no less 'natural' than any other European state, for naturalness is a matter of habit and conditioning. The Swiss have lived for centuries under a variety of complicated political, social and economic institutions and have operated them under invisible restraints which are etched in the consciousness of all Swiss, young and old. Even the members of the Progressive Marxist League will use the Swiss German dialect and in so doing absorb those intangible, yet profound cultural substances which create a certain kind of inner world recognisably Swiss. I do not believe that Switzerland is a community of the will, which requires the active assent of its citizens to survive. It will do fine with their passive consent. 'Es ist ja auch wurst' (somewhere between 'What the hell' and 'I'm all right, Jack') is not a sign of crumbling civic dignity but of sensible disengagement. The Swiss vote when it matters. 'Swissness' is a complex creation of history and can survive the end of the militia system or low polls at referenda.

Switzerland has only one really serious social problem: the future of the foreign workers. It has one quite important political issue: establishment of an autonomous authority for the Catholic Jura. For the rest, it is a happy, prosperous, attractive country. Its institutions may not function perfectly but they function. It may not do well in protecting the environment or coping with rebellious young people, but it does not do much worse than comparable societies. It may be very bourgeois or middle class and it is certainly very capitalist. Yet it would be hard to beat bourgeois capitalism in its Swiss variant as a system for making more people healthier, happier and longer lived than at any time or place in human history. The system of power is, I confess, not very transparent, and the country is certainly not run against the wishes of the big chemical companies and the banks. Yet they run it quite well and have no cause to feel uneasy when they are charged with running it. If the leaders of industry dropped their absurd penchant for secrecy and allowed the press, the radio and the financial writers to see what was really going on, the Swiss public would, I think, be amiably surprised to see how much like the local *Gemeinderat* or *Turnverein* the rooms at the top were. The corridors of power in Switzerland are, after all, filled with Swiss people.

Switzerland will change rapidly over the coming ten years, and change does not come easily to a densely integrated, extremely conservative, stubborn, suspicious and democratic people. The grinding and gnashing of teeth will be as audible as the tinkle of cow bells in the Alps. The old army will go. The old neutrality will have to go, as Switzerland grows closer to the European Economic Community. Switzerland will probably join the United Nations. The cantons will be reduced to something much more like the English county authority than the American state. There will be severe social tension as the children of the foreign workers born in the 1950s begin to assert their political and economic rights. There will be more strikes and there will be Swiss unemployment (not just export of *Fremdarbeiter*) as the structural changes in the economy fuse with the long-term effects of the sharp revaluation of the franc and the energy crisis. Dialects will decline in richness and variety under the impact of television from abroad and large-scale internal migration at home. The Swiss are going to loathe these changes, and predict the imminent demise of the Confederation. It will not happen. The essential Swissness will remain. The mysterious vitality which seems to be inherent in European culture and which works to preserve even the tiniest cultural entities will see to that.

7. Why Switzerland matters

The reader who has followed me this far will not need to be convinced that Switzerland is unusual. He may even have begun to find Switzerland interesting. I now want to suggest that what happens in Switzerland matters. Switzerland is not simply another, rich, small state in the heart of Europe. It is the living expression of a set of ideas, which may be summed up:

> Although the will of the majority makes law and constitutes the only true sovereign authority, the minorities, however small, have inalienable rights. The dilemma of majority will and minority rights can be overcome by the ingenuity of men.

There is nothing startling or very new about these ideas, but it is striking how little they are observed. The Swiss believe that there will always be a political compromise or bit of constitutional machinery which will get round a given difficulty, whether it is the rights of the Jurassiens or conscientious objectors. That the Jurassiens have rights seems to them so obvious that they hardly need to emphasise it. They also believe that no machinery is sacred. The constitution of 1848 underwent total revision in 1874, and there is in Bundesrat Furgler's department at this moment a committee at work on the 'total revision' of the present structures. When something does not work, the Swiss tinker with it for a while, sometimes even for decades, and, if it cannot be got working, they scrap it.

The United States pays a heavy price for neglecting the need for constitutional change. The constitution of 1787 has been turned into a sacred piece of parchment, above politics and beyond the reach of men. Jefferson who had doubts about the document wanted something less remote. He refused to be alarmed in the 1780s by the turbulence of the mob. 'A little rebellion now and then is a good thing, and as necessary in the political world as storms in the physical', he wrote. In his *Notes on the State of Virginia* of 1784 he argued that since the people were the only legitimate fountain of power, government should return to it whenever necessary to remodel the pieces of the constitutional apparatus. Unfortunately, his friend Madison, and many other advocates of the new constitution, had no such optimism. Madison put the opposite view in *The Federalist Papers*, No. 49: 'It may be considered as an objection inherent in the principle that as every appeal to the people would carry an implication of some defect in the government, frequent appeals would, in great measure, deprive the government of that veneration which time bestows on everything and without which perhaps the wisest and freest governments would not possess the requisite stability.'

Against Madison, the Swiss in their lumpish, practical way assert the defectiveness of all government at all times, and they are right to do so. Government must always be defective by precisely that gap in time which separates the date of the creation of a given set of institutions from the present moment. The United States now struggles to operate within the dusty mechanisms of an antique. Checks and balances, wheels and pulleys, designed to mesh for an agrarian, decentralised and thinly settled federation seize up under the pressure of an industrial, cosmopolitan, world empire. The prospect for the future is unpleasant. Madison was certainly not wrong about the other issue: the creation of stability. Time does bestow a lustre on institutions which helps to make them permanent, but real stability is the cause of that lustre, not the other way round. If the foundations are stable, the constitutions will last. Real stability comes from below.

The English reader may feel that these lessons, however relevant to their ill-advised American cousins foolish enough to write things down, need have no application in Great Britain. I think they would be wrong. Take the hallowed House of Commons. Is it today more than an empty debating chamber in which a very large number of restless men play at political games, while real decisions are made elsewhere? The only function which parliament now performs is to select the people who will eventually be ministers and to ratify the decisions of those who already are. The nominating function is an important one. The selection of leadership within the parliamentary party provides a useful and flexible device for ensuring that those selected can govern with the full support of the rank and file. By rewarding loyalty with promotion and punishing independence with banishment to the darker back benches, it ensures that the majority rarely crumbles and that decisions once taken are suitably rubber-stamped. The average citizen (or his MP for that matter) has very little chance to find out what is going on and practically no chance to alter it. In this country, the people get not the government they deserve but what the senior civil service and front bench of the governing party think they ought to have. Imagine what would happen, for a minute, if the Swiss initiative and referendum were regularly used in the United Kingdom, and not just to evade divisions within the Labour Party. Would capital punishment have been abolished? Would there have been a second BBC channel? Would the Home Office have admitted the Ugandan Asians? Would Britain have joined the Common Market initially? Suppose the answer to all these questions had been No, as it well might have been. Would you, my English reader, be very unhappy? I suspect that you shudder with relief that there is a sane, civilised system in Britain which prevents the people from getting what they want. The truth is that the United Kingdom is no democracy and the majority of intelligent Englishmen from left to right do not want it to be. They share, in secret, Alexander Hamilton's belief that 'your people, Sir, are a great beast'.

The Swiss have always operated on a different premise. The people, they think, are themselves. The ancient Fundamental Law of Canton Schwyz recognised: 'that the May *Landsgemeinde* is the greatest power and prince of the land and may without condition do and undo, and whoever denies this and asserts that the *Landsgemeinde* be not the greatest power nor the prince of the land and that it may not do and undo without condition is proscribed. Let a price of one hundred ducats be set on his head.'[1]

The man who denies the sovereignty of the community is no member of it. He is proscribed, outlawed and subject to a severe penalty. Harsh certainly but utterly democratic. The community makes and unmakes laws, and there is no law outside it. The Swiss cannot imagine that the people should not have a say on virtually everything. The results are often tiresome, obstructive or even reactionary, but not always. The city of Basel may serve as an example. The sovereign people voted to spend a very large sum of money to acquire two extremely expensive Picassos for its museum. We have seen other examples both of stubborn truculence and enlightened good sense. The people turn down one set of tax proposals but vote for the revised packet later. The recent referendum on the Common Market in the United Kingdom is eloquent testimony that we, the people, are perfectly capable of thinking for ourselves in spite of what politicians may think.

I am not so foolish as to set one society up to be imitated by another. The reasons why the Swiss trust the people and the British do not go deep into the very different histories of the two societies. The US constitution has ossified because the USA has developed in its own special way. The illusions of the eighteenth-century *illuminati* that one could write a constitution for one state which would do quite well in another have long since been shattered. Yet the study of Switzerland has its uses. Because the Swiss are so different, they serve as a mirror in which we see our own assumptions more clearly. For example, Switzerland reminds us of the reality of frontiers and the national state. The Swiss nation state is very present and its influence can be seen in the astonishing 'Swissness' of every part of the country, regardless of language, religion, geography or economic features. Where a political frontier has existed for any length of time, culture develops differently on either side of it. What was once an imperceptible grading of one region into another becomes an absolutely basic difference of kind. I can illustrate this by an example of a frontier in Switzerland. One Sunday in 1972 I took the little local train from Lugano to Ponte Tresa on the Italian–Swiss border. The train rattled along the sun-drenched, manicured Val d'Agno through silent, deserted villages. The streets of the Swiss Ponte Tresa were also absolutely empty, save for the steady stream of traffic pouring across the frontier. The heavily barred windows of the banks and jewellery shops glittered respectably in the hot Italian sun. I walked the bridge crossing the Tresa, and found myself in the cacophony of Ponte Tresa (Italy). The streets were jammed with noisy, jostling people. I bought a newspaper and sat for half an hour in an overcrowded sidewalk café gulping down great draughts of bad news: strikes, scandals, murders, kidnappings, governmental and financial collapse, speculation against the lira, the usual disastrous record of daily life in the Republic of Italy. I browsed in a bookshop and thumbed through self-serving accounts by fascist field officers of their role in the Africa Campaign and paperback histories of the battles of the First World War. The books were awful but alive, the newspapers shocking but engrossing. By contrast the *Corriere del Ticino* or the *Giornale del Popolo*, the two main Italian Swiss papers on sale on the other bank of the river, had no news in them: a fire in Mendrisio, an exhibition of modern painting in Bellinzona, the problems of the new cantonal library in Lugano. There was no scrap of evidence in any Italian shop of the presence of that Switzerland three hundred yards away. The *New York Herald Tribune* was on sale at the kiosks, but not Swiss papers.

As I crossed back into Switzerland where the plumbing works and the trains run to time, I began to reflect on the mystery of frontiers. The little railway stations with their *Jugendstil* ornaments in wrought iron could have been anywhere in the Germanic world. The Ticinese railwaymen belong to the same stock as the men of the Varesotto on the other bank, but they look different, trimmer, more reserved. Swiss Italians do not behave in public like Italians. On a hot, starry southern evening I went to watch F.C. Lugano play La Chaux-de-Fonds in the Swiss First Division, a very tense game in a beautiful, tropical stadium. The crowd were as docile and quiet as they used to be at Wimbledon. There is more passion, Latin temperament and violence at Stockport County v. Doncaster Rovers than there was in that apparently 'Italian' stadium.

The Swiss Italian and French are Swiss because they live on one side of a frontier, not because they belong to a different people or even, on one level, to a different culture from the people on the other side. Over time, the political institutions, laws, economic arrangements, educational processes, social structures on one side have transformed the inhabitants. They become, as Denis de Rougemont noticed about the Swiss French, part of a Germanic community by a kind of osmosis. The smallest artifacts of daily life, doors, window frames, coins, pencils, street signs, price tags in shops began to 'look' Swiss, as the invisible walls of tariffs and customs barriers gradually created a national market. Swiss towns look Swiss because for so many years all architects were either trained at, or influenced by, the Eidgenössische Technische Hochschule in Zurich. A small regulation, such as the one which required Swiss architects to train in Switzerland if they wished to practise, created the uniformity of townscape which makes its own subtle but very real contribution to the national community. As long as the effective frontier is that which divides members of the Common Market from each other, there will be no united European state. As that frontier gradually disappears, as it did in Swiss history, an imperceptible European atmosphere will emerge.

The Swiss by their differences from the European norm remind us unintentionally of the limits of our certainties. The words we use are terrible oversimplifications. What is a language? What is a state? What is a people? What is a national economy? Sometimes we incline to the view that we know the answers. When that happens, we ought to think about Switzerland for a moment, for the survival of the Swiss Confederation from the high Middle Ages to the present day is a mysterious process. As Dr Johnson warns us: 'We must consider how very little history there is; I mean real authentick history. That certain Kings reigned, and certain battles were fought, we can depend upon as true; but all the colouring, all the philosophy, of history is conjecture.'

APPENDIX: How to vote for parliament (*Nationalrat*) in Switzerland

The information and examples given in this Appendix are based on the official guide to voting, *Die Politischen Rechte der Schweizerin und des Schweizers* (Bundeskanzlei, Bern, 1971). I am grateful to the Federal Chancellor for permission to reproduce the examples.

Every canton and half canton makes up a constituency for the elections to the *Nationalrat*. Registered voters have as many members to elect as their canton or half canton is entitled to in proportion to the population. Some cantons have only one member because of the size of their populations while others may have several. Single member cantons (Uri, Obwalden, Nidwalden, Glarus and Appenzell I.Rh.) elect members by simple majority. In multi-member cantons the election is based on proportional representation based on the procedures described in Chapter 3 (pp. 55–6). After the number of seats to which each party is entitled has been calculated, the members themselves are elected who had the highest number of votes on their party's list.

Each party which wishes to take part in an election submits a list of candidates to each voter, the so-called 'party list', which contains a number of candidates equal to the number of members for that canton. The electoral authorities also provide voters with a blank list as well, which contains as many spaces as there are members to elect. The voter can use the prepared party list or the blank list. Below are some examples of the possibilities open to a voter in a canton with seven *Nationalrat* members.

PARTEI A	PARTEI B	PARTEI C	LISTE:___
Hans B.	Arnold A.	Rudolf B.	1.____
Trudi D.	Emil F.	Erwin G.	2.____
Fritz E.	Marie H.	Eva H.	3.____
Rolf J.	François K.	Andreas L.	4.____
Peter M.	Karl M.		5.____
Urs M.	Therese P.		6.____
Thomas S.	Walter S.		7.____

Parties A and B have made full use of the lists by nominating seven candidates while Party C has chosen to nominate four only. A voter is free to fill out the remaining spaces on that list or not, as he chooses.

If you use a party list

You have a variety of possibilities open to you: You can put a straight party list into the ballot box.

PARTEI A
Hans B.
Trudi D.
Fritz E.
Rolf J.
Peter M.
Urs M.
Thomas S.

If a voter puts Party A's list into the box, Party A gets *seven party votes* and each individual candidate gets *one candidate vote*.

You can strike out the name of any candidate you do not want to vote for on Party A's list.

PARTEI A
Hans B.
Trudi D.
~~Fritz E.~~
Rolf J.
Peter M.
Urs M.
Thomas S.

The candidate omitted (Fritz E.) gets *no candidate votes*, while the others get one each.

The Party still gets *seven party votes*, even though you have crossed out one name, because you have used a party ballot.

You can cross out several names on the list.

Party A still gets *seven party votes*, but only those candidates whose names appear get a *candidate vote*. Warning: Only names which appear on a list can be written in, and, to be valid, a list must show at least one name on it.

Cumulation

If you want to give a particular candidate more chance of being elected, you can cumulate, that is, put him down *twice*. A name which is already on the list will be repeated.

PARTEI A
Hans B.
Trudi D.
Fritz E.
Rolf J.
~~Peter M.~~ *Rolf J.*
Urs M.
Thomas S.

The candidate whom the voter has so preferred is *cumulated*. He gets *two candidate votes* (i.e. Rolf J. in the example).

The candidate whom the voter does not want to see elected is crossed out and gets *no candidate votes* (i.e. Peter M.).

Party A gets *seven party votes*.

No name may be written three times. If it is, the third vote will not be counted.

If empty spaces exist on the list, you can cumulate without crossing out anybody, as in the case of Party C.

Panachage

You can also vote for candidates of other parties by altering your party list to include them, as in the examples below. This process is called *panachage*. The altered party list will only yield as many party votes as there are candidates of that party, still on the list. Your votes for candidates transferred from other lists will be added to the number of party votes of the parties to which they belong. There are several options:

PARTEI B	PARTEI A	PARTEI C
Arnold A.	~~Trudi D.~~ Arnold.A	Rudolf B.
Emil F.	Fritz E.	Erwin G.
Marie H.	Rolf J.	Eva H.
François K.	~~Peter M.~~ Eva H.	Andreas L.
Karl M.	Urs M.	
Therese P.	Thomas S.	
Walter S.		

(a) Take one or more candidates from another party's list and put them on the list of your own party by crossing out some of the printed names. In the example given, Party A gets *five party votes* and surrenders one to each of the other parties. All seven names on the Party A list get *candidate votes*.

(b) Take candidates from other lists and *cumulate* them, as in the example below:

PARTEI B	PARTEI A	PARTEI C
Arnold A.	~~Hans B.~~ Emil F.	Rudolf B.
Emil F.	~~Trudi D.~~ Emil F.	Erwin G.
Marie H.	Fritz E.	Eva H.
François K.	~~Rolf J.~~ Andreas L	Andreas L.
Therese P.	Peter M.	
Walter S.	~~Urs M.~~ Andreas L.	
	Thomas S.	

In this example, Party A only gets *three party votes*, losing two each to Party B and Party C; Emil F. and Andreas C. get *two candidate votes* each, while Fritz E., Peter M. and Thomas S. get one.

If you use a blank list

You will find that there are as many spaces as there are vacant seats to be filled and that there is also a space for the party label. You need not place anything in the place for the party's name. If you do not, no party gets credit for any blank spaces you choose to leave, as in the case below:

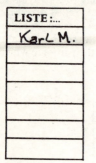

In this case Karl M. gets *one candidate vote* and his party *one party vote*. The other six spaces do not count.

You can put several candidates down who are taken from different lists (A and C):

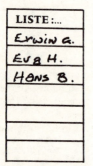

In this case each of the candidates written in gets *one candidate vote* and brings the party to which he or she belongs a *party vote* as well. Party C gets two votes (Erwin G. and Eva H.) while Party A gets one vote (Hans B.) The four blank spaces do not count.

You can write in the names of candidates you take from other lists once or twice (i.e. you can *cumulate* them). Below you will find an example:

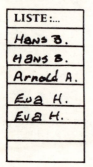

Candidate Hans B. (from List A) and Eva H. (from List C) get *two candidate votes* each, while Arnold A. (from List B) gets one. Parties A and C get *two party votes* each and Party B one. Two blank spaces do not count.

You may, of course, use all the spaces in this way and thus lose no chance to vote for a person or party.

If you choose to fill in the blank space at the top, you guarantee that any blank spaces not given to candidates will count toward the total number of party votes of the party of your choice. You still have the same possibilities of writing in the names of candidates from other lists as if you had not designated a particular party. You may write in the names of candidates you choose to cumulate as well. In the example below, you designate your ballot as a party list but take names from other parties:

LISTE:
Partei B.
Arnold A.
Emil F.
Trudi D.
Rudolf B.
Rudolf B.

Here you write the names of two candidates from Party B, two candidates from other parties, one of whom you cumulate. The reckoning works out as follows: Arnold A., Emil F., and Trudi D., get *one candidate vote* each, and Rudolf B. gets two.

For the parties the result is:
Party A: 1 party vote (Trudi D.)
Party C: 2 party votes (Rudolf B.)
Party B: 4 party votes of which
    1 is from Arnold A.
    1 is from Emil F.
    2 are from 2 blank spaces.

Who may vote?

1. Every Swiss citizen, male or female, who has reached his twentieth birthday and according to the laws of the canton in which he or she resides has not been deprived of his civil rights may vote.

2. To vote a registration card is required. In some cantons this may be issued for a long period of time; in others it will be issued before each election.

3. The right to vote is exercised where one lives regardless of the place where one is specifically enrolled as a citizen (*Ortsbürger*).

4. In contrast to the regulations in some cantonal elections, no deputy may cast your vote in a federal election.

Notes

1. Why Switzerland?

1 Boswell's *Life of Johnson*, ed. R. W. Chapman (Oxford, 1970), p. 113.
2 *Statistisches Jahrbuch der Schweiz* (Bern, 1973), 'Arbeitstreitigkeiten', p. 319; *Die Volkswirtschaft* (Bern, February 1975), p. 64.
3 F. R. Allemann, *25 mal die Schweiz* (Munich, 1965), p. 547.
4 Urs Altermatt, *Der Weg der Schweizer Katholiken ins Ghetto* (Zürich/Einsiedeln, 1972), p. 21.
5 Quoted in Edgar Bonjour, *Geschichte der schweizerischen Neutralität*, 6 vols. (Basel, 1965—71), Vol. 1, p. 133.
6 Edgar Bonjour, *Die Gründung des schweizerischen Bundesstaates* (Basel, 1948), Part II, Doc. 8, pp. 206—7.
7 Boswell's *Life*, p. 112.

2. History

1 Georg Thürer, *St Galler Geschichte. Il Aufklärung bis Gegenwart* (St Gallen, 1972), Vol. 2, p. 107.
2 F. R. Allemann, *25 mal die Schweiz*, pp. 572—3.
3 Francesco Quirici, *Lineamenti di storia ticinese e svizzera* (Bellinzona/Lugano, 1969), pp. 117—19.
4 Cited in Hans Kohn, *Nationalism and Liberty: The Swiss Example* (London, 1956), pp. 81—2.
5 Giovanni Bonalumi, *La giovane Àdula (1912—1920)*. Collana, 'Scrittori della Svizzera Italiana', 13 (Chiasso, 1970), pp. 202–3.
6 Kurt Spillmann, 'Zwingli und die zürcherische Politik gegenüber der Abtei St Gallen', *Mitteilungen zur vaterländischen Geschichte des Kantons St Gallen*, xliv, 1965, p. 16, n. 30.
7 Perry Anderson, *Passages from Antiquity to Feudalism* (London, 1974), p. 203, n. 15.
8 Hans Conrad Peyer, 'Frühes und Hohes Mittelalter. Die Entstehung der Eidgenossenschaft', *Handbuch der Schweizer Geschichte* (Zürich, 1972), Vol. 1, pp. 169—70.
9 Adolf Gasser, *Geschichte der Volksfreiheit*, 2nd ed. (Aarau, 1947), pp. 104—6.
10 Walter Müller, 'Die Offnungen der Fürstabtei St Gallen', *Mitteilungen zur vaterländischen Geschichte*, xliii, 1964, p. 50.
11 Perry Anderson, *Passages*, p. 191.
12 Hans Conrad Peyer, 'Frühes Mittelalter', pp. 202—3.
13 Perry Anderson, *Passages*, p. 202.
14 Leonhardt von Muralt, 'Renaissance und Reformation', *Handbuch*, p. 395.

15 Hans Conrad Peyer, 'Frühes Mittelalter', p. 201.
16 Perry Anderson, *Passages*, p. 153.
17 Text in the translation of G. Bohnenblust, in *Schweizer Brevier* (Bern, 1972) p. 89.
18 Walter Ullmann, 'Zur Entwicklung des Souveränitätsbegriff im Spätmittelalter', *Festschrift Nikolaus Grass*, 2 vols. (Innsbruck, 1974/75), Vol. 1, p. 22.
19 Christopher Hughes, *Switzerland* (London, 1975), p. 21.
20 Peter Bichsel, *Des Schweizers Schweiz* (Zürich, 1969), p. 16.
21 Benjamin Barber, *The Death of Communal Liberty. A History of Freedom in a Swiss Mountain Canton* (Princeton, N.J., 1973), p. 92.
22 Walter Schaufelberger, *Der Wettkampf in der alten Eidgenossenschaft. Zur Kulturgeschichte des Sports vom 13. bis ins 18. Jahrhundert* (Bern, 1972), pp. 62—3 and p. 154.
23 Perry Anderson, *Passages*, pp. 197—205 for a brilliant marxist analysis of the elements of the 'general crisis' of the fourteenth century.
24 Georg Thürer, *St Galler Geschichte*, p. 27.
25 Benjamin Barber, *The Death of Communal Liberty*, pp. 34—6.
26 Hans Conrad Peyer, 'Frühes Mittelalter', p. 222.
27 Jean-François Bergier, *Naissance et croissance de la Suisse industrielle* (Bern, 1974) pp. 28—9.
28 Georg Thürer, *St Galler Geschichte*, p. 26.
29 Leonhardt von Muralt, 'Renaissance und Reformation', *Handbuch*, p. 398.
30 Walter Schaufelberger, *Der Wettkampf*, p. 92.
31 Leonhardt von Muralt, 'Renaissance und Reformation', *Handbuch*, p. 408.
32 Max Frisch, *Wilhelm Tell für die Schule* (Frankfurt/Main, 1971).
33 Kurt Spillmann, 'Zwingli', pp. 77—8.
34 Cited in Edgar Bonjour, *Geschichte der schweizerischen Neutralität*, 6 vols. (Basel, 1965—71), Vol. 1, p. 25.
35 Cited in H. Nabholz *et al.*, *Geschichte der Schweiz* (Zürich, 1932), Vol. 2, p. 6.
36 William L. Shirer, *Berlin Diary* (New York, 1941), p. 234.
37 Carl Spitteler, *Unser Schweizer Standpunkt* (Zürich, 1915), p. 21.
38 Perry Anderson, *Lineages of the Absolutist State* (London, 1974), p. 20.
39 *Ibid.*, p. 425. See also A. Gramsci, *I Risorgimento* (Rome, 1971), pp. 21, 32—3.
40 Abraham Stanyan, *An Account of Switzerland* (London, 1714), p. 144.
41 Georg Thürer, *St Galler Geschichte*, p. 212.
42 R. R. Palmer, *The Age of the Democratic Revolution*, 2 vols. (Princeton, N. J., 1959 and 1964), Vol. 1, p. 128.
43 Edgar Bonjour, *Die Gründung des schweizerischen Bundesstaates* (Basel, 1948), Part II, Doc. 4, p. 196.
44 *Ibid.*, Doc. 20, p. 246.
45 J. H. Plumb, *The Growth of Political Stability in England, 1675—1725* (London, 1967), pp. xvi—xvii.
46 David Lasserre, *Étapes du fédéralisme* (Germ. ed. trans. by Adolf Gasser) (Zürich, 1963), p. 106.

47   A. Lawrence Lowell, *Governments and Parties in Continental Europe*, 2 vols. (Cambridge, Mass., 1896), Vol. 2, p. 241.

48   Georg Thürer, *Free and Swiss. The Story of Switzerland* (London, 1970), p. 114.

49   Prussian Minister to the Vatican to Frederick William IV, 16 January 1857, in E. Bonjour, *Neutralität*, Vol. 1, p. 354, n. 17.

50   Carlo Cattaneo, *Tutte le opere*, ed. Luigi Ambrosoli (Milan, 1967–), Vol. 4, p. 738, 19 June 1849.

51   Cavour to G. Durando, 6 June 1860, in Dennis Mack Smith, *Cavour and Garibaldi* (Cambridge, 1954), p. 29.

52   André Allaz, *L'helvétisme: péril national* (Fribourg, 1914), p. 5.

53   Carl Spitteler, *Kritische Schriften*, ed. Werner Stauffacher (Zürich, 1965), p. 179.

54   Carlo Salvioni, 'Le condizioni della coltura italiana nel cantone Ticino', 25 April 1914, in G. Bonalumi, *L'Àdula*, p. 211.

55   Romberg to Bethmann Hollweg in E. Bonjour, *Neutralität*, Vol. 2, p. 590.

56   Bundesrat Karl Scheurer, *Tagebücher 1914—1929*, ed. Hermann Böschenstein (Bern, 1971), p. 50.

57   *Ibid.*, p. 150.

58   Paul Stauffer, 'Die Affäre Hoffmann/Grimm', *Schweizer Monatshefte*, Sonderbeilage zu Heft 1 des Jg. 1973/74, p. 22. See also E. Bonjour, *Neutralität*, Vol. 2, pp. 613 ff.

59   Willi Gautschi, *Der Landesstreik 1918* (Zurich/Einsiedeln, 1968), p. 32.

60   Erich Gruner, *Die Parteien in der Schweiz* (Bern, 1969), p. 183 and Table 10, pp. 184—5.

61   Willi Gautschi, *Landesstreik*, p. 108.

62   Edgar Bonjour, *Neutralität*, Vol. 5, p. 440.

63   Guido Calgari, 'L'Umanità di Giuseppe Motta — Commemorazione alla Radio svizzera', 24 January 1940, reprinted in *Schweizer Rundschau*, Vol. 70, November/December 1971, pp. 394—5.

64   Edgar Bonjour, *Neutralität*, Vol. 4, p. 53.

65   William Shirer, *Berlin Diary*, p. 235.

66   Edgar Bonjour, *Neutralität*, Vol. 5, p. 437.

67   *Ibid.*, p. 154.

68   Alfred Ernst, *Die Konzeption der schweizerischen Landesverteidigung 1815—1966* (Frauenfeld, 1971), p. 204.

69   Edmund Wehrli, 'Wehrlose Schweiz — eine Insel des Friedens?' *Allgemeine Schweizerische Militärzeitschrift*, No. 9, September 1973, pp. 10—14.

70   A curious manifestation of this questioning is Max Frisch's *Dienstbüchlein* (Frankfurt/Main 1974), in which he rewrites not only the years of his own active service as a gunner but an earlier patriotic work of his own *Blätter aus dem Brotsack*, published in 1940. It is an odd, ambiguous book, the motto of which is the passage on p. 44: 'When I recall today how things were then, naturally I see them the way I think of things now. I am amazed how much one could experience without seeing it.'

3. Politics

1   Perry Anderson, *Lineages of the Absolutist State* (London, 1974), p. 11.
2   Christopher Hughes, *The Parliament of Switzerland* (London, 1962), p. 39.
3   Jean Meynaud, *La Démocratie Semi-Direct en Suisse* (Dissertation, privately published, 1970), p. 3.
4   *Annuario Statistico del Cantone Ticino 1971* (Bellinzona, 1972), pp. 22 and 76.
5   *Ibid.*, p. 215.
6   A. Lawrence Lowell, *Governments and Parties in Continental Europe*, 2 vols. (Cambridge, Mass, 1896), Vol. 2, p. 185.
7   Christopher Hughes, *The Federal Constitution of Switzerland* (Oxford, 1954), p. 5.
8   Adolf Gasser, *Der Jura im Kanton Bern* (Basel, n.d.), p. 7.
9   *Ibid.*, p. 31.
10 Benjamin Barber, *The Death of Communal Liberty*, pp. 173—4.
11 *Ibid.*, p. 176.
12 A. L. Lowell, *Governments and Parties*, pp. 291—2.
13 Denis de Rougemont, *La Suisse ou l'Histoire d'un peuple heureux* (Paris, 1965), p. 125.
14 Jean Meynaud, *La Démocratie*, p. 14.
15 Max Imboden, *Helvetisches Malaise* (Zürich, 1964), p. 7.
16 Jürg Steiner, Erwin Bucher, Daniel Frei and Leo Schürmann, *Das politische System der Schweiz* (Munich, 1971), pp. 146—7.
17 Erich Gruner, *Die Parteien in der Schweiz* (Bern, 1969), p. 29.
18 François Masnata, *Le parti socialiste et la tradition démocratique en Suisse* (Neuchâtel, 1963), p. 244.
19 Bundesrat Karl Scheurer, *Tagebücher*, p. 42.
20 Christopher Hughes, *The Parliament*, p. 98.
21 Max Frisch, *Mein Name sei Gantenbein* (Frankfurt, 1964), p. 36.
22 Christopher Hughes, *The Parliament*, p. 80.
23 Celio's speeches have been published and make interesting trilingual reading — Nello Celio, *Demokratie im Wandel-Démocratie en marche-Democrazia Dinamica*, (Frauenfeld, 1972).
24 Giovanni Orelli, *La Festa del Ringraziamento* (Milan, 1972), p. 62.
25 *Die Volkswirtschaft*, Eidgenössisches Volkswirtschaftsdepartement, 48. Jg., H. 1, Bern, January 1975, p. 16, and November 1974, pp. 688—91.
26 *Ibid.*, March 1975, pp. 120—32.
27 Pierre A. Tschumi, 'Umweltskrise und Bevölkerungspolitik in der Schweiz', *Schweizer Monatshefte*, Vol. 53, No. 1, April 1973, p. 10.
28 Peter Gilg, 'Der Erfolg der Rechtsgruppen in den Nationalratswahlen von 1971', *Schweizerische Zeitschrift für Volkswirtschaft und Statistik*, 4, 1972, p. 591.

4. Language

1   Tullio de Mauro, *Storia linguistica dell'Italia unita*, (Bari, 1972) p. 43.

2 Perry Anderson, *Passages*, p. 127.
3 For a useful, if technical, introduction to these matters, cf. R. E. Keller, *German Dialects* (Manchester, 1961).
4 *Ibid.*, pp. 6—7.
5 Ludwig Fischer, *Luzerndeutsche Grammatik* (Zürich, 1960), p. 32.
6 J. A. Cremona, 'The Romance Languages' in *Literature and Western Civilisation*, ed. David Daiches and Anthony Thorlby, Vol. 2: *The Medieval World* (London, 1973), p. 62.
7 Olga Neversilova, 'Schweizerdeutsch: Abenteuer der Sprache', *National-Zeitung*, Basel, 29 July 1972.
8 Peter Bichsel, *Des Schweizers Schweiz*, pp. 43—4.
9 Cited in Hermann Burger, 'Schreiben in der Ich-Form', *Schweizer Monatshefte*, Vol. 53, No. 1, April 1973, p. 50.
10 *Ibid.*, p. 51.
11 Peter Ruedi, 'Geflickt, aber suuber', *Die Weltwoche*, No. 9, 5 March 1975.
12 Dieter Fringeli, *Dichter im Abseits. Schweizer Autoren von Glauser bis Hohl* (Zürich, 1974), p. 8.
13 T. de Mauro, *Storia*, pp. 129—35.
14 Gottfried Keller, *Der grüne Heinrich*, complete works, Vol. 1 (Basel, no date), p. 10.
15 For those who want to sample some recent Swiss writing, try Adolf Muschg, *Liebesgeschichten* (Frankfurt/Main, 1972) a brilliant, moving collection of stories; Peter Bichsel, *Eigentlich möchte Frau Blum den Milchmann kennenlernen* (Olten & Freiburg, 1964); Elisabeth Meylan, *Räume, unmöbiliert* (Zürich, 1972); Hermann Burger, *Bork* (Zürich, 1970); E. Y. Meyer, *Ein Reisender in Sachen Umsturz* (Frankfurt/Main, 1972); Urs Widmer, *Die Forschungsreise* (Zürich, 1974).
16 J. A. Cremona, 'The Romance Languages', p. 59.
17 I am grateful to Dr Spiess for allowing me to quote an unpublished lecture. See also F. Spiess, 'Lingua e Dialetti nella Svizzera italiana', *Dal dialetto alla lingua*, Atti del IX Convegno per gli Studi Dialettali Italiani (Pisa, 1974).
18 F. Spiess, 'Lingua', pp. 360—1. Dr Cremona drew my attention to the French parallel.
19 *Annuario Statistico del Cantone Ticino* (1971), p. 84.
20 Ursula Zenger, 'Die Vier Sprachgruppen in der Bundesverwaltung', *Die Weltwoche*, 22 August 1973.
21 Dott. Flavio Zanetti, 'Il Ticino all'inizio degli anni settanta', *Jahrbuch der eidgenössischen Behörden* (Bern, 1971), p. 192.
22 Andri Peer and Jon Pult, *Die Raetoromanische Sprache* (Pro Helvetia Press Service, II, 1972), p. 11.
23 Denis de Rougement, *La Suisse*, p. 173.
24 *Ibid.*, pp. 189—90.
25 Pierre Cordey, 'La Presse et l'Information', *Die Schweiz seit 1945*, p. 239.
26 J. A. Cremona, 'The Romance Languages', p. 61.
27 J. W. von Goethe, *Dichtung und Wahrheit* (Goldmann Ausgabe) (Munich, 1961), Part I. p. 246.

5. Wealth

1   Leonhardt von Muralt, 'Renaissance' in *Handbuch*, p. 398; Hektor Ammann, 'Die Diesbach—Watt Gesellschaft. Ein Beitrag zur Handelsgeschichte des 15. Jahrhundert', *Mitteilungen zur vaterländischen Geschichte St Gallens*, xxxvi, 1928, p. 157.

2   Hektor Ammann, *Schaffhauser Wirtschaft im Mittelalter* (Thayngen (SH), 1950), pp. 256—8; Hajo Holborn, *A History of Modern Germany*, Vol. 1. The Reformation (London, 1965), p. 79 and pp. 72—6.

3   What constitutes intolerable inequality? For a fascinating foray into this difficult terrain by an economist, see J. E. Meade, *Efficiency, Equality and the Ownership of Property* (London, 1964), especially pp. 27—33.

4   Georg Thürer, *St Galler Geschichte*, p. 92.

5   *Ibid.*, pp. 212—14.

6   *Ibid.*, p. 229.

7   Karl Marx, *Das Kapital*, Vol. 23 *Marx Engels Werke* (Berlin, 1962), Book I, IV. Section, Ch. 12, p. 365.

8   *Ibid.*, pp. 362—3.

9   R. A. G. Miller, *The Watchmakers of the Swiss Jura, 1848—1900* (unpublished, D.Phil. dissertation, Oxford, 1974), pp. 10—18.

10   *Ibid.*, p. 355.

11   *Ibid.*, p. 212.

12   P. A. Kropotkin, *Memoirs of a Revolutionary* (New York, 1966), p. 281.

13   *Ibid.*, pp. 285—6.

14   David Landes, *The Unbound Prometheus. Technological Change and Industrial Development in Western Europe from 1750 to the Present* (Cambridge, 1969), pp. 168—9.

15   Georg Thürer, *St Galler Geschichte*, pp. 460—5.

16   *Ibid.*, p. 462.

17   R. A. G. Miller, *The Watchmakers*, p. 12.

18   J.-F. Bergier, *Naissance et croissance de la Suisse industrielle* (Bern, 1974), p. 128.

19   K. Marx, *Das Kapital*, p. 363, n. 32.

20   *Schweizer Brevier*, p. 45; J. Früh, *Géographie de la Suisse*, T. II. *Géographie Humaine* (Lausanne, 1939), pp. 91—2.

21   Ammann, 'Diesbach—Watt', p. 8.

22   G. Thürer, *St Galler Geschichte*, p. 205.

23   Gottfried Keller, *Grüne Heinrich*, Vol. 1, p. 203.

24   David Landes, *Unbound Prometheus*, p. 276.

25   On printing see Rudolf Wackernagel, *Geschichte der Stadt Basel* (Basel, 1924), Vol. II, pp. 166—77. See also Paul Burckhardt, *Geschichte der Stadt Basel* (Basel, 1942), p. 4, pp. 81—2, 202, 217. *The Story of the Chemical Industry in Basle: 75th Anniversary of CIBA* (Basel, 1959).

26   Jakob Burckhardt, *Briefe an Gottfried und Johanna Kinkel*, ed. Rudolf Meyer-Kraemer (Basel, 1921), no. 15, 24 November 1843, p. 63.

27   David Landes, *Prometheus*, p. 275.

28   'Die schweizerische Konjunktur im Jahre 1974 und ihre Aussichten für 1975', Mitteilung No. 231, *Kommission für Konjunkturfragen*, January 1975.

29 *Ibid.,* p. 5.
30 Georg Thürer, *St Galler Geschichte,* p. 463.
31 *Ibid.,* pp. 470—2; J. Früh, *Géographie,* p. 260.
32 Peter G. Rogge, 'Die Zukunft der mittleren Industriebetriebe in der Schweiz', *Schweizer Monatshefte,* Vol. 52, No. 10, January 1973, pp. 711—21.
33 These statistics are drawn from Wilhelm Bickel, 'Wachstum und Strukturwandel der Wirtschaft', *Die Schweiz seit 1945: Statistical Data on Switzerland 1973,* Federal Bureau of Statistics, Bern; *Die Volkswirtschaft,* April 1975, p. 205.
34 Nello Celio, *Demokratie,* pp. 128—9.
35 'Die Wirtschaftslage', Mitteilung No. 232, *Kommission für Konjunkturfragen,* March 1975, p. 10.
36 *Die Volkswirtschaft,* August 1974, p. 499, and April 1975, p. 165.
37 Perry Anderson, *Lineages,* p. 8.
38 R. A. G. Miller, *The Watchmakers,* pp. 195—6.
39 Hans-Ulrich Wehler, *Modernisierungstheorie und Geschichte* (Göttingen, 1975), pp. 25—6.
40 K. Marx, *Das Kapital,* Vol. 1, pp. 86 and 90.
41 *Ibid.,* p. 94.
42 Thorstein Veblen, *Imperial Germany and the Industrial Revolution* (New York, 1954), p. 270. First published 1914.
43 Frederick P. Brooks Jr, *The Mythical Man-Month. Essays on Software Engineering* (Reading, Mass., 1975), pp. 164, 7 and 15.
44 *Ibid.,* pp. 25 and 18.

6. Identity

1 Max Frisch, *Dienstbüchlein* (Frankfurt/Main, 1974), p. 156.
2 Oberst Max Kummer, 'Die Motivation in der Armee', *Allgemeine Schweizerische Militärzeitschrift* (abbreviated below as *ASMZ*), No. 6, June 1975, p. 218.
3 Max Frisch, *Dienstbüchlein,* p. 47.
4 Colonel (General Staff) Dr Hans Rudolf Kurz, *Analysis of the Swiss Military Establishment* (Pro Helvetia Press Service, 1971), p. 10.
5 Max Frisch, *Dienstbüchlein,* p. 34.
6 *ASMZ,* No. 9, September 1974, p. 438.
7 Oberstkorpskommandant Alfred Ernst, *Die Konzeption der schweizerischen Landesverteidigung, 1815—1966,* p. 420.
8 Colonel Pierre Wenger, 'Unsere Jugend und die Landesverteidigung', *ASMZ,* No. 10, October 1972, pp. 530—9.
9 *Ibid.,* p. 539.
10 Roman Brodmann, *Die Schweiz ohne Waffen* (Bern, 1973).
11 Pierre Wenger, 'Unsere Jugend', p. 537—9.
12 Karl Schmid, 'Schweizerisches Selbstverständnis heute', *Neue Zürcher Zeitung,* 9 April 1972.
13 Peter Bichsel, *Des Schweizers Schweiz,* p. 9.
14 N. Meienberg, *Reportagen aus der Schweiz* (Darmstadt, 1974), pp. 38—40.

7. Why Switzerland matters

1 F. R. Allemann, *25 mal die Schweiz,* p. 40.

Index

(Note: Swiss towns have their cantonal location in brackets)